The Human Tradition in America

CHARLES W. CALHOUN
Series Editor
Department of History, East Carolina University

The nineteenth-century English author Thomas Carlyle once remarked that "the history of the world is but the biography of great men." This approach to the study of the human past had existed for centuries before Carlyle wrote, and it continued to hold sway among many scholars well into the twentieth century. In more recent times, however, historians have recognized and examined the impact of large, seemingly impersonal forces in the evolution of human history—social and economic developments such as industrialization and urbanization as well as political movements such as nationalism, militarism, and socialism. Yet even as modern scholars seek to explain these wider currents, they have come more and more to realize that such phenomena represent the composite result of countless actions and decisions by untold numbers of individual actors. On another occasion, Carlyle said that "history is the essence of innumerable biographies." In this conception of the past, Carlyle came closer to modern notions that see the lives of all kinds of people, high and low, powerful and weak, known and unknown, as part of the mosaic of human history, each contributing in a large or small way to the unfolding of the human tradition.

This latter idea forms the foundation for this series of books on the human tradition in America. Each volume is devoted to a particular period or topic in American history and each consists of minibiographies of persons whose lives shed light on that period or topic. Well-known figures are not altogether absent, but more often the chapters explore a variety of individuals who may be less conspicuous but whose stories, nonetheless, offer us a window on some aspect of the nation's past.

By bringing the study of history down to the level of the individual, these sketches reveal not only the diversity of the American people and the complexity of their interaction but also some of the commonalities of sentiment and experience that Americans have shared in the evolution of their culture. Our hope is that these explorations of the lives of "real people" will give readers a deeper understanding of the human tradition in America.

Volumes in the Human Tradition in America series:

Ian K. Steele and Nancy L. Rhoden, eds., *The Human Tradition in Colonial America* (1999). Cloth ISBN 0-8420-2697-5 Paper ISBN 0-8420-2700-9

Nancy L. Rhoden and Ian K. Steele, eds., *The Human Tradition in the American Revolution* (2000). Cloth ISBN 0-8420-2747-5 Paper ISBN 0-8420-2748-3

Ballard C. Campbell, ed., *The Human Tradition in the Gilded Age and Progressive Era* (2000). Cloth ISBN 0-8420-2734-3 Paper ISBN 0-8420-2735-1

Steven E. Woodworth, ed., *The Human Tradition in the Civil War and Reconstruction* (2000). Cloth ISBN 0-8420-2726-2 Paper ISBN 0-8420-2727-0

David L. Anderson, ed., *The Human Tradition in the Vietnam Era* (2000). Cloth ISBN 0-8420-2762-9   Paper ISBN 0-8420-2763-7

Kriste Lindenmeyer, ed., *Ordinary Women, Extraordinary Lives: Women in American History* (2000). Cloth ISBN 0-8420-2752-1 Paper ISBN 0-8420-2754-8

Michael A. Morrison, ed., *The Human Tradition in Antebellum America* (2000). Cloth ISBN 0-8420-2834-X Paper ISBN 0-8420-2835-8

Malcolm Muir Jr., ed., *The Human Tradition in the World War II Era* (2001). Cloth ISBN 0-8420-2785-8   Paper ISBN 0-8420-2786-6

THE HUMAN TRADITION IN
ANTEBELLUM AMERICA

The Human Tradition in
ANTEBELLUM AMERICA

No. 7
Human Tradition in America

Edited by
Michael A. Morrison

A Scholarly Resources Inc. Imprint
Wilmington, Delaware

Scholarly Resources Inc.
104 Greenhill Avenue
Wilmington, DE 19805-1897
www.scholarly.com

Library of Congress Cataloging-in-Publication Data

The human tradition in antebellum America / edited by
   Michael A. Morrison.
        p. cm. — (The human tradition in America ; no. 7)
     Includes bibliographical references and index.
     ISBN 0-8420-2834-X (cloth : alk. paper) — ISBN 0-8420-2835-8
(paper : alk. paper)
     1. United States—History—1783–1865—Biography. I. Morrison,
Michael A., 1948–   . II. Series.

E339.H9   2000
973'.09'9—dc21
[B]   00-027911

⊚ The paper used in this publication meets the minimum requirements
of the American National Standard for permanence of paper for printed
library materials, Z39.48, 1984.

For two special children,
Natty and Katie,
whose extraordinary lives have taught me
more than I could ever teach them

About the Editor

MICHAEL A. MORRISON, whose Ph.D. is from the University of Michigan, Ann Arbor, teaches antebellum and U.S. political history at Purdue University. He is also coeditor of the *Journal of the Early Republic*. Michael Morrison is the author of *Slavery and the American West: The Eclipse of Manifest Destiny and the Coming of the Civil War* (1997) and the coeditor with Ralph D. Gray of *New Perspectives on the Early Republic: Essays from the* Journal of the Early Republic, *1981–1991* (1994). In 1998 he was named Indiana Professor of the Year by the Carnegie Foundation for the Advancement of Teaching.

I believe in aristocracy, though—if that is the right word, and if a democrat may use it. Not an aristocracy of power, based upon rank and influence, but an aristocracy of the sensitive, the considerate and the plucky. Its members are to be found in all nations and classes, and all through the ages, and there is a secret understanding between them when they meet. They represent the true human tradition, the one permanent victory of our queer race over cruelty and chaos. Thousands of them perish in obscurity, a few are great names. They are sensitive for others as well as for themselves, they are considerate without being fussy, their pluck is not swankiness but the power to endure, and they can take a joke.

—E. M. Forster, *Two Cheers for Democracy* (1951)

Contents

Introduction—Shuttles of a New Nation
The Private Lives and Public Actions of Ordinary Americans

Michael A. Morrison

In his diary of an eighteen-month sojourn in America, English novel-ist Frederick Marryat observed in 1839 that in the New World all was energy and enterprise; everything was in a state of transition. " 'Go ahead' is the real motto of the country," Marryat wrote, "and everyman does push on, to gain in advance of his neighbor." Amid an environ-ment endowed with unparalleled advantages and with a form of gov-ernment admirably suited to the pursuit of the main chance, Americans, their energies unshackled, directed their careers to any goal they pleased, and in the race the best won. Yet, Marryat cautioned, ambition and drive played out in a fluid economic and political environment resulted in vice as much as virtue, in inegalitarianism as much as equality. Only a small number of Americans could raise themselves by talent. Wealth, however, was attainable by all. Because Americans had no aristocracy, honors, or distinctions to which to look forward, the acquisition of wealth had become "the only means of raising himself above his fellows left to the American."[1]

If equalitarianism produced avarice and ostentation in private life, in the public sphere it ushered in a democracy ruled not "by the col-lected wisdom of the people, but by the majority who are [as] often wrong as right." Under President George Washington, Marryat claimed, America had been a "pure and . . . virtuous republic," but by Martin Van Buren's presidency, it had sunk to a lowly democracy. As Americans multiplied and grew wealthy, Marryat asserted, so, too, did they degen-erate. The more vicious they became, the more vicious became their institutions. "Upon one point I have made up my mind," he sniffed; "with all its imperfections, democracy is the form of government best suited to the present condition of America, insofar as it is the one under which the country has made, and will continue to make, the most rapid advances."[2]

Although Jacksonian mobs threatened to whale Marryat mightily in order to soften his arrogance and cleanse him of such infamous ideas, one suspects that more sober-minded historians might conclude that he was not far off the mark. In a richly nuanced, insightful, and often brilliant study, Lewis Perry has situated the origin of modern American culture in the early republic. Much the same as Marryat, Perry portrays an emerging modernist culture emerging from a protean world constantly in motion and continually in the process of evolution and self-definition. A highly mobile lot traveling widely at home and abroad, Americans in the early republic "were shuttles weaving a new civilization." In their diaries, travelogues, and memoirs, antebellum Americans embraced a collective outlook that was at once doggedly optimistic about persistent improvement and anxiously adrift "in a sea of uncertainty." They recorded, reflected, and pondered the tensions noted by Europeans such as Marryat, Alexis de Tocqueville, and Fedrika Bremer between a leveling democracy and the uncertain potential of a fluid society riven by slavery.[3]

The individual biographies of the ordinary individuals contained in this collection both confirm and extend these observations. Theirs are the voices that until recently have been silent in historical texts and monographs—African Americans, women, ethnic groups, and workers. The subtheme that runs throughout these essays is the recurring question of what it meant to be an "American" in the early republic. As these biographies clearly indicate, there was no single "American experience." Moving beyond the older, outdated historical narratives of political institutions and the great men who shaped them, they offer revealing insights on gender issues, working-class experiences, race, and local economic change and its effect on society and politics. Raising new questions from fresh perspectives, these biographies contribute to a broader understanding of the dynamic forces that shaped the political, economic, social, and institutional changes that characterized the formative years of the nation.

However diverse these individual lives may be, certain broad themes emerge from them. Most notable in the early republic are the democratization of politics and society and the corresponding decline of the politics of republican meritocracy. The American Revolution fashioned a political and economic climate that undermined the world of deference that had characterized the colonial era. During the war traditional political elites in the now sovereign states widely advocated the sovereignty of the people and drafted state constitutions based on a broader suffrage. Nevertheless, these elites assumed that a hierarchy of gentlemen would control postrevolutionary governments; they miscalculated badly. Postwar politics prove plainly that working- and middle-class voters had no intention of throwing over a British aristocracy only to have it replaced by an American one. As historian Alan Taylor has pointed out, the revolution created unprecedented opportunities for aspiring men to compete with the gentry for electoral office, to supply armies, and to compete for economic advantage.[4]

Much has been made—rightly so—of the election of Thomas Jefferson to the presidency and, as he later put it, the "Revolution" of 1800. Yet the historical analysis of events surrounding these political developments generally focuses on national figures and federal policy making. Stephen Grossbart's study of Abraham Bishop's political career shows how those national events were connected to the lives of the ordinary citizens of Connecticut. By demonstrating the vitality and activism of a local politician such as Bishop, Grossbart challenges the traditional top-down approach to politics in the early national period. Grossbart's study of Bishop's life makes a clear-cut case for the decline of deferential politics and opens a new perspective on the enthusiasm and dynamism that local voters and their agents experienced in this newly emerging democratic political culture.

Ruth Alden Doan's essay on the life of John Wesley Young indicates that ordinary Americans were challenging elites in other areas besides politics. Doan argues that at the time of the revolution, Methodism was poised to take advantage of the new social context of religious freedom and democratic culture. Methodism, which first emerged as a reform movement within the Church of England, challenged regular church attendance as a measure of true religiosity by emphasizing conversion, frequent weekday preaching, and larger gatherings known as camp meetings. Moreover, itinerant circuit riders such as Young, who lacked formal theological training, competed with and tended to subvert the authority of the minister as the true spiritual leader. Relying on the camp meeting to energize their audiences into a religious frenzy, itinerants such as Young promoted Methodism and, more broadly, the growth of different sects and denominations that both democratized Protestantism and promoted a sense of popular acceptance of diverse faiths.

The democratization of politics and society constitutes one important theme of the early republic. Equally notable and arguably more significant was widespread economic transformation and growth of a market economy. The early republic, Paul Gilje contends, "was *a* crucial, if not *the* crucial, period in the development of that trademark characteristic of American society and economy, modern capitalism."[5] Merchant capitalism, the spread of wage labor, and an immigrant working class emerged during the first quarter of the nineteenth century. Tensions between the older colonial republicanism, which emphasized a common good, and an emergent liberal capitalism, which embraced the ethos of self-interest advocated by the philosopher John Locke, affected politics, the economy, and social relations within towns and villages, East and West.

Craig Thompson Friend's study of the business activities of Trotter & Sons reveals the economic opportunities that developed on the western frontier and the concurrent social challenges that commerce posed to the community. Although Thomas Jefferson, James Madison, and other like-minded Republicans (and historians) believed that the West would be home to, and ensure the preeminence of, an agrarian republic, S.&G. Trotter was but one of many family enterprises that brought capitalism to the frontier and thereby helped transform the new nation in the early republic. The success of the Trotters' business enterprises, however, depended as much on the family's ability to demonstrate a sense of moral obligation and responsibility to their neighbors and customers as it did on providing them with a wide array of attractive goods. The story of these local merchants indicates how rapidly the market revolution penetrated the western frontier, and it also suggests that older, more traditional notions of a moral economy and a commonweal did not automatically or quickly disappear.

Hiram Hill was another self-made man. Whereas the experiences of Trotter and his sons bring to light the social tensions that issued from a market economy, the story of Hill's life uncovers the private dilemmas that acquired wealth and prestige engendered. Gary Kornblith's essay illustrates clearly how individuals born into modest circumstances could become economically independent and socially prominent through their own efforts in this emerging market economy. Kornblith also shows that success came at an emotional price. Born in Rhode Island two years before George and Samuel Trotter opened their first store in Kentucky, Hill, too, became a successful entrepreneur. Apprenticed as a carpenter, he abandoned his craft for commercial enterprise. A wealthy lumber merchant, happily married, and a staunch defender of the established order in Rhode Island, Hill was plagued by ambivalence about his pursuit of material gain. If he, along with the Trotters, embraced the opportunities of economic modernization, Hill privately brooded about the social priorities of this new world.

The meteoric rise and fall of Senator John Smith of Ohio evinces no similar uncertainties about pursuit of the main chance. Andrew Cayton's study traces the overlapping and mutually reinforcing impulses of economic and political self-interest. Like John Wesley Young, Smith achieved prominence as a preacher; unlike Young, though, his real interests were purely secular. The fluid and open political system of the Northwest Territory provided the context for his political success. Yet, as Cayton notes, he made his fortune in the marketplace. The commercial revolution, which had come to the Ohio frontier just as it had to Kentucky, placed Smith at the center of a community of profit and contacts. The U.S. Army, which was to protect and extend that frontier, was his customer. The blurred line between public and private interests allowed Smith to acquire fortune then fame. He crossed it once too often, however, and he became entangled in the alleged Aaron Burr conspiracy to separate the Southwest from the United States and establish an independent western empire. Personal profit and professional politics led to success and, not without irony, to his undoing.

The intricately bound relationships among personal gain, professional politics, and the military are further traced in the lives of Arsène Lacarrière Latour and Thomas Sidney Jesup. As Gene Smith argues, Latour was characteristic of the adventurers who were attracted to the Southwest frontier in the early national period. His aristocratic world destroyed by the French Revolution, Latour traveled first to Haiti then to Louisiana as an advance agent for Napoleon's new empire in the Western Hemisphere. Reminiscent of Hiram Hill, Latour parlayed occupational skills—architecture and engineering—into personal success. He served as General Andrew Jackson's principal architect for the defensive works around New Orleans during the War of 1812. Although he had become an American citizen, after the war, Latour found another lucrative career as an operative of the Spanish government in the American Southwest. His changing loyalties echo the problematic nature of personal attachment to an expansive republic so clearly evinced in the life of John Smith. Like James Trotter, Latour's experiences as architect, engineer, and historian illustrate the openness of the frontier and the many opportunities for personal advancement and economic gain that could be found there.

For Jesup, the army was his career and the path by which he made his way to success. Samuel Watson's study of this little-known figure offers a variety of perspectives on the emerging modernization of the U.S. Army. Jesup served during the War of 1812, rising quickly to the rank of major. After the war, he was able to employ his political connections to secure the new post of quartermaster general. He spent the next eighteen years improving the army's administrative procedures and bringing systemization and regularity to the army's method of supplying its troops and the means of accounting for those transactions. Although as a modern, professional soldier, Jesup diligently tried to avoid political entanglements, he could not. He became embroiled in an endless number of personal and professional conflicts while helping General Winfield Scott remove the Creek Indians from Alabama and Georgia and then the Seminoles from Florida. Jesup's personal and professional relationships suggest the intersection of public and private elites so evident throughout the career of John Smith.

Removing Indian tribes from their territory and coming to terms with racial differences proved troublesome to this genteel white army officer. These issues infused and gave shape to another less attractive aspect of the early republic. Concomitant with the growth of commerce was the expansion of the nation into the trans-Appalachian West. The extension of the frontier, in turn, engendered federal-state and party disagreements over the removal of Native Americans. Conflict between Native Americans and whites was coeval with the establishment of British North America. If, however, many whites in the eighteenth century viewed the Indians as "noble savages," by the 1830s Jacksonian Americans considered them simply "savages" incapable of civilization. Racism, fear of interminable conflict and violence on the frontier, and, most of all, an unquenchable desire for the valuable territories possessed by eastern tribes provided the rationale of, and force behind, the demand for removal. The weakness and collusion of the national government made it possible, if not inevitable.

The politics of Indian removal are well known. So, too, is President Andrew Jackson's complicity with state actions that effected it. The lives of John Ross and Peter P. Pitchlynn, both of mixed heritage, add a new and illuminating inside-out dimension to this national tragedy. At one time the conventional view of the Age of Jackson presupposed the triumph of egalitarianism and democracy. The personal experiences of these two men, however, suggest inequality and oppression that contradict that historical paradigm.

If whites were certain that Indians were incapable of civilization, John Ross begged to differ. As Mary Young notes, Ross, a Cherokee, be-lieved race to be irrelevant to intelligence and accomplishment. Indeed, the Cherokees in Georgia were closely tied to the land and had developed a sophisticated culture with a written language and a formal constitution. They were particularly adept at resisting white encroachment. As Principal Chief of his tribe, Ross consistently worked to force the United States to fulfill its treaty obligations and to protect the Cherokee Nation from additional loss of land. The U.S. Supreme Court and lesser Georgia courts upheld his position on Cherokee rights. Young demonstrates that federal hostility toward Ross and Georgia's aggression against the Cherokees (abetted in large measure by the spread of the states' rights doctrine) successfully undermined these legal protections. Political rivalries within the nation, encouraged and fostered by the national government, further eroded Ross's authority and critically undermined the unity of the nation. External pressures and internal divisions placed the Cherokees on the "The Trail Where They Cried," or Trail of Tears, that long, forced journey from the Southeast United States to Indian Territory that later became Oklahoma. Neither Ross nor the Cherokees shared in the glory and promise of Jacksonian America.

Peter Pitchlynn also occupied a unique position in American society. Euro-Americans considered him nonwhite and hence inferior. But Donna Akers contends that as an individual of mixed heritage neither was he fully Choctaw. Pitchlynn spoke English, moved easily through the halls of Congress, was a man of considerable wealth, and held slaves. Along with Ross, he opposed removal and supported tribal unity. Also, Pitchlynn's opposition to white encroachment, like that of Ross, was undercut by intratribal divisions. Yet, Ross's life reflects the conflicts among traditional full bloods, moderates such as the Principal Chief, and younger educated mixed-bloods who favored removal, while Pitchlynn's syncretic identity continually placed him at the crossroads of white-Indian cultural conflict. His experiences reveal how Native Americans of mixed heritage negotiated and contested racial boundaries. His life opens up new, if troubling, vistas on the behavior and motives of the oppressed and their oppressors.

As the lives of Ross and Pitchlynn indicate, race was central to the early republic and to nation building. In the revolutionary era a defense of individual liberty and equality coexisted with a growing commitment to, and investment in, African slavery. In the Age of Jackson the spread of universal white manhood suffrage occurred simultaneously with the suppression of the rights of free African Americans. Efforts to abolish slavery had been made before the American Revolution. Slavery, which had existed in all thirteen colonies, had been abolished in the North by the early nineteenth century. However, in the early 1830s what limited antislavery sentiment there was in the South had vanished, and in the North the movement was rapidly losing strength. Moreover, during this same decade, there was a sharp rise in racist sentiment and racial violence in the free states.[6]

Against this backdrop of racism and violence, George Price sketches the life of the neglected black abolitionist Hosea Easton. Price maintains that antislavery and antiracist activism among African Americans preceded and existed independent from the Garrisonian movement that began in 1831 and demanded the immediate emancipation of slaves. In fact, Easton's father, James, mounted his own "revolution" in 1800 in a Massachusetts church. Hosea, a black clergyman and member of the African American elite, labored his entire adult life to improve and uplift his community. When mobs destroyed his community, his church, and his hopes, however, they also demolished Hosea's belief in African American self-improvement. At this point, he fashioned a critical account of slavery and race relations in the United States.

Besides rescuing Easton from historical oblivion, Price uses his life to great advantage as a vehicle to examine early radical African American thought that has long been ignored by, and lost to, students of the antebellum abolition movement. Anticipating similar arguments made by W. E. B. Du Bois in the early twentieth century, Easton analyzes the environmental effects of slavery and the psychological damage it inflicted on African Americans. Although his activism heralded the radicalism of William Lloyd Garrison, Easton's reputation was overshadowed and then eclipsed by more noted black abolitionists such as Frederick Douglass. But, as Price establishes, Easton made important contributions to abolitionist thought and the struggle against racism.

Black abolitionists such as Easton demanded that white Americans live up to the premise and promise of the revolutionary heritage of liberty and equality. So, too, did an increasing number of women throughout the 1830s and 1840s. The American Revolution loosened the bonds of hierarchy and deference for women as well as men. The revolutionary era gave shape to a new consciousness of women's political worth and capacities that made their official exclusion from the public sphere increasingly awkward. Enlightenment and republican thinking also shifted perspectives on family authority from a patriarchal view linking father, king, and God to a republican emphasis on contract, duty, and consent. This new emphasis reinforced the home as a center of sociability, sentiment, and virtue and prompted a new understanding of marriage that underscored emotion, companionship, and mutuality, if not egalitarianism.

The transformation in gender roles and relations, however, was not wholly positive for women. They had more freedom of choice in marriage partners and enjoyed a newly elevated status as mothers and wives, but they still remained dependent on men. And not everyone accepted the revised view of women's intellectual and political abilities. In the early national period the boundaries between work and home remained permeable, and ideas about gender were neither fixed nor static. The tensions and opportunities to which this era gave rise are evident in the lives of the three women profiled in this book.

Laura Wirt Randall's life demonstrates both the range of possibilities for vivacious, intelligent women and the outer limits of those options. Anya Jabour's examination of Randall's tragic life limns the contradictory expectations that her parents and, by extension, society had for women in the antebellum era. Urged by her father to excel in academics, Randall enjoyed her studies and pursued a wide range of intellectual pursuits. Suited by temperament and intellect to a life of "single blessedness," she evinced little interest in either homemaking or marriage. But if Randall was ready to challenge and break free from the idea of a "woman's proper sphere," her parents were not. They pressured her into a respectable though emotionless marriage. Her husband, even less tolerant of any deviation from traditional assumptions about a woman's role in society, took her to Florida, where she died after giving birth to their fourth child in six years of marriage. She was only thirty at the time of her death. In her short life, Randall felt both the exhilarating new sense of possibility that women were gaining in antebellum America and the stifling restrictions that still hedged them in.

If contradiction was the primary characteristic of Randall's life, controversy attached itself to Rebecca Reed. Daniel Cohen's study of Reed reaffirms the significance of separate spheres and the limited options for women in the public sector. Her involvement in the bitter public controversy surrounding the burning of the Ursuline Convent in Charlestown, Massachusetts, in 1834 proves that the line between public and private spheres was important as a gender ideal. But Cohen also suggests that it was by no means an impassable barrier for respectable women. He centers his biography of Reed in the mutually reinforcing contexts of nativism and sectarian conflict so prevalent in northern port cities in the antebellum era. He shows how women of low or ambiguous social status, such as Rebecca Reed, occasionally could seize upon religious affiliation as an instrument of personal fulfillment and upward mobility. Like thousands of men of her generation in pursuit of the main chance, the obscure Reed paid a price. They went bankrupt; she saw her reputation publicly assailed.

The uncertain status of women in the early republic produced a personal tragedy for Randall and shaped a public controversy that swirled around and brought down Reed. When Margaret Eaton challenged those conventional assumptions, she produced a national political crisis. Though better known and more socially prominent than Randall and Reed, Peggy Eaton experienced the same conflicting expectations and stifling limitations. As John Marszalek describes her struggle to maintain her independence and her dignity, Eaton's story echoes the same frustrations and ambiguities that resonate throughout the lives of her contemporaries. Her experience and that of official Washington in the battle over her reputation reflect the highly contested nature of gender boundaries and the complexion of democratic politics in the Age of the Common Man.

The final two biographies in this collection bring together trends that marked the evolution of American society from the Jeffersonian era to the Age of Jackson. They also foreshadow the issues that would culminate in and be resolved by the American Civil War. Benjamin Tappan's life makes the point neatly. Born three years before the revolution, Tappan died three years before Lincoln's election and South Carolina's secession from the Union. Daniel Feller convincingly portrays Tappan as a man of his time who began his career as a Jeffersonian, became a Jacksonian Democrat, and died a Republican. He melded political, scientific, and social aspirations into a successful if stormy career. Ever the religious skeptic (he would have set John Wesley Young's teeth on edge), his pursuit of human improvement through secular means puts him squarely amid the romantic reform movement of the antebellum era. Tappan, Feller asserts, also embraced one of the era's contradictions. A virulent opponent of slavery, Tappan denounced abolitionism and sometimes opposed the antislavery efforts of his brothers Arthur and Lewis.

Tappan's life reflected the possibilities and parameters of life in the free states, whereas George Washington Harris proved to be both a product and critic of southern culture. Like most of his generation—North and South—he was deeply religious, restless, and extraordinarily ambitious. He worked hard in a variety of occupations but never quite made it to the gentry. He devoutly supported states' rights, secession, and the Confederacy. Harris's racism was matched only by his hatred of Lincoln, the Republican Party, and Reconstruction policies. Yet, John Mayfield's insightful and revelatory essay demonstrates that Harris was also a shrewd, caustic critic of antebellum southern society. Mayfield argues that Harris's creation, Sut Lovingood, could only have originated in the South: the dry business culture of the North could not have sustained him. Hiram Hill would have neither understood Sut nor thought him funny. Harris, speaking through Sut, ridicules the pretensions of the slaveholding class and thereby offers an overlooked vantage on southern life behind the plantation facade. Sut, not men like Tappan, would have the final comment on the demise of the Old South.

Separately and together these lives provide a window on a world that we have lost. They remind us of the importance of those ordinary Americans whose collective experience shaped and gave meaning to the national character as it evolved in the early republic. These men and women reflect the optimism, the possibilities, and the boundlessness so characteristic of these years. Yet, they also reveal the contradictions and tensions between the ideological premises of that political culture and the real experiences of individuals who were ignored, marginalized, or oppressed by the majority. The lives portrayed in this collection show us the centrality of uncertainty, hope, ambition, frustration, determination, and resignation to the human condition. The issues that concerned them—economic security, religion, race and gender relations, national security, and political ambition—remain central to the American experience. Carefully listening to the voices of these little-known Americans brings their world alive and makes us part of it.

Notes

1. Captain Frederick Marryat, *Diary in America*, ed. Jules Zanger (Bloomington, IN, 1960), 42–43.

2. Ibid., 44, 47, 48.

3. Lewis Perry, *Boats against the Current: American Culture between Revolution and Modernity, 1820–1860* (New York, 1993), 129, 215.

4. Alan Taylor, "From Fathers to Friends of the People: Political Personas in the Early Republic," *Journal of the Early Republic* 11 (Winter 1991): 466.

5. Paul A. Gilje, "The Rise of Capitalism in the Early Republic," in Paul A. Gilje, ed., *Wages of Independence: Capitalism in the Early American Republic* (Madison, WI, 1997), 1.

6. James Brewer Stewart, "The Emergence of Racial Modernity and the Rise of the White North, 1790–1840," *Journal of the Early Republic* 18 (1998): 181–236. See also the special winter issue, "Racial Consciousness and Nation-Building in the Early Republic," ibid. 19 (1999).

1

Abraham Bishop

Teacher, Lawyer, Orator, and Politician

Stephen R. Grossbart

Abraham Bishop's career as an orator and politician challenged not only the Federalist gentry's assumption of authority and its presumption to govern but also our tendency to view politics from the top down and from the center of government out to the periphery of the nation. Bishop, who came of age in the era of the American Revolution, was both a °Ütness to that democratic upheaval and a beneficiary of it. As society, politics, and the economy became more open and fluid in the post-revolutionary war era, men such as Bishop competed with the prewar ruling class for prominence and power. As an important though not well-known participant in the formation of the nation's first party system, he provided a critical link between the leaders of Thomas Jefferson's Republican Party and its rank-and-file constituency in Connecticut. Bishop was a forceful critic of Alexander Hamilton's Federalist Party, its program of commercialization, and, above all, the deferential politics that had been characteristic of the colonial era. As such, Abraham Bishop participated in another rebellion: the election of Thomas Jefferson and his "Revolution" of 1800. The effect of this bloodless political upheaval was just as influential on the nation's polity and society as the uprising of 1776.

Stephen R. Grossbart is an independent scholar in Salt Lake City, Utah. He is coauthor, with David Waldstreicher, of "Abraham Bishop's Vocation; or, The Mediation of Jeffersonian Politics," which was selected as the Ralph D. Gray Prize for the best article published in the *Journal of the Early Republic* in 1998.

On September 8, 1800, Abraham Bishop (1763–1844) stepped out before an audience of fifteen hundred curious spectators, including many ladies and eight clergymen. They gathered in New Haven's White Haven meeting house, where Bishop delivered what was to have been the annual Phi Beta Kappa lecture at Yale's commencement. He was supposed to have spoken at the nearby First Church meetinghouse, but earlier, after receiving an advance copy of the oration, Bishop's fellow society members had withdrawn their invitation.[1] The address,

Connecticut Republicanism: An Oration on the Extent and Power of Political Delusion, announced Bishop's intention to attack Connecticut's "Standing Order" of Federalist politicians and Congregational clergyman just one week before the fall election.

The oration proved to be the most controversial in Bishop's controversial career as a teacher, lawyer, orator, and politician. Abraham Bishop, who had already participated in many of the major political debates of the day, had attacked the core of Connecticut's political and religious establishment. *Connecticut Republicanism* was a frontal assault on the state's aristocracy. This, the first of many attacks, was "the most vicious and devastating of any made in the entire period of the early Republic."[2] The oration and the campaign techniques introduced by Bishop and the Republicans in 1800 transformed politics in Connecticut and placed the state on the road to becoming a modern democratic society.

In *Connecticut Republicanism*, Bishop attacked the Hamiltonian commercial system and the quasi-war with France that it provoked. Federalist war policy depended on "the great, wise and rich men [who] well understand the art of inflaming the public mind" into "*the delusive bubble of national glory.*" Federalist war fever was "calculated to destroy a condition of equal rights, and to sacrifice . . . social happiness on the altar of national greatness." The Federalists' objectives were "to crush the [political] opposition" and create "an energetic, aristocratic, monarchic government, which can move without controul."[3]

Bishop asked his listeners, "How is it possible that our greatest and most pious men should betray us? I answer, because you have every thing to lose, and they every thing to gain." The "agents" of delusion included the "the *best informed* men in society." They dominated public discourse on political topics and through "well directed and eloquently enforced" arguments led the populace "astray on questions of mere right and wrong." These men used the "elastic" language of the Constitution to justify their actions. They dominated political festivities, Fourth of July celebrations, the press, and the pulpits in most churches to carry that message to the people. The nation's Federalists "know well the force and power of every word: the east, west, north and south of every semicolon; and can extract power from every dash or asterism." Bishop finally attacked the notion that the Federalists were disinterested men most fit for ruling. Instead, they were the "most proud, avaricious, and tyrannical," in sum, an aristocracy. "For my own part," he lectured, "I am willing to be governed by men greater, wiser and richer than myself" but not ones "so great that their altitude must be taken by a quadrant, and their width by a four-rod chain."[4]

Connecticut Republicanism provoked a dramatic outcry from Federalists, first in Connecticut then throughout the nation.[5] While Federalists agonized over Bishop's words, Republicans across the country quickly embraced him as a spokesman during the heated election of 1800. The oration went through seven editions, with printers in New Haven, Philadelphia, Bennington, New Jersey, and Albany producing copies. Excerpts appeared in as many as seven newspapers from Vermont to North Carolina. *Connecticut Republicanism* so pleased Thomas McKean, the Republican governor of Pennsylvania, that he invited Bishop to deliver the speech again before that state's legislature. The following month, Aaron Burr, the Republican candidate for vice president, recommended the "justly celebrated" Bishop in a letter to a fellow Republican, noting that "his talents, his principles and his zeal entitle him to entire Respect and Confidence." In Washington, DC, Republican presidential candidate, Thomas Jefferson, awaited the pamphlet's arrival at the local bookseller. Jefferson reported that the pamphlet was "making wonderful progress, and is said to be the best anti-republican eye-water which has ever yet appeared."[6] While Federalists cried, Bishop's reputation as a Republican spokesman soared. Bishop's oratory and the controversy surrounding *Connecticut Republicanism* established him as an essential political point man for Connecticut's Republican Party and garnered him the nickname "the Connecticut Orator." Bishop was one of many political activists in the early nineteenth century who would mediate between state and national political leaders and the common folk whose votes were sought. But he was also one of the most innovative political middlemen of his time. As a political organizer, Bishop, his enemies claimed, "revolutionized" Connecticut and helped democratize the state.[7]

Who was this man who brought joy to Republicans and whose words, if we are to believe Jefferson, brought Federalists to tears? Abraham Bishop was born into a respectable New Haven family, the son of Samuel Bishop and Mehetabel Bassett. His father was a deacon in the White Haven Church and held a variety of local offices, including deputy in the Connecticut House of Representatives, town clerk, justice of the peace, chief judge of the County Court of Common Pleas, and judge of the probate court. In 1793 the people of New Haven elected him mayor, a post he retained until his death in 1803. In 1801, Thomas Jefferson appointed the senior Bishop collector of the port of New Haven, outraging the Federalist gentry, who interpreted the move as a political reward for his son Abraham.

The path to political respectability was far less smooth for Samuel Bishop's son. Abraham graduated from Yale in 1778 at age fifteen. His classmates included Joel Barlow, Noah Webster, Zephaniah Swift, and Oliver Wolcott Jr. After his graduation, Bishop briefly held a clerkship in Philadelphia then studied law. He returned to New Haven and joined the bar on April 6, 1785. Bishop was unable to establish a viable practice, and in early 1787, like many respectable young men, he traveled to Europe. He returned the following year "full of Improvm[en]t & Vanity," according to Yale president Ezra Stiles. Bishop was especially struck by what he saw in London. In March 1787, he wrote to his friend David Daggett about his access to great libraries and his attendance at the debating sessions at the Coachmaker's Hall. "There are so many of these [debating] societies," he wrote, "I can attend one or the other every evening."[8]

Bishop's enthusiasm for public debate was apparent when he returned to New Haven in late 1788. He quickly established himself as an articulate and controversial public speaker. One of Bishop's first speeches, delivered on October 16, 1788, criticized the new Constitution. The following week, Bishop took to the "Stage in the Brick Meet[in]g House" and lectured "On the Evidences of the Christian Religion." Yale president Ezra Stiles disapproved of Bishop's anticlerical topic and seemed especially disturbed by the audience's reception of the talk. "A great Concourse—clapped him."[9]

It was Bishop's antifederalist views, however, that gained him notoriety. During a special session of the General Assembly in January 1789, a prominent young New Haven lawyer, William Hillhouse Jr., attacked Bishop's antifederalist notions. Bishop was not one to stand by quietly. Just three days after Hillhouse's attack, Bishop replied with a "political Lecture against the new Constitution." The newspapers provided extensive coverage of this debate, and Hillhouse published his oration the following week.[10]

Hillhouse's oratory was no match for Bishop's. "Leonidas," an anonymous federalist writer, was disappointed in Hillhouse's federalist critique. Hillhouse's "weak and flimsy" argument persuaded few in the audience. This poor oratory stood in sharp contrast to Bishop's, which presented "a chain of logical argumentation [that] . . . incontestibly proved that the new constitution would destroy our liberties." What impressed this critic most was Bishop's ability to win over his audience: "Many doubting federalists were confirmed in antifederalism, and many firm friends to the new government entirely converted." Mr. Bishop's oratory "gently leads you along the smooth way." His arguments resemble "a still, gentle yet swift river, which silently undermining its sides, at length removes every obstacle." Leonidas also charged that Bishop intended his oration to bolster the damaged political career of "a professed antifederalist," James Wadsworth. A recent scandal had forced the resignation of Connecticut's state treasurer. Antifederalists, who had a strong minority in the lower house, attempted to appoint Wadsworth to fill the vacancy. Bishop used his lecture to defend the political stand that Wadsworth took during the ratification debate in 1788. As Leonidas noted, "Such is the powerful operation of genuine oratory, oratory which . . . despite [its] deep rooted prejudices insensibly carries us into all the feelings of the orator." On the following day the lower house voted to appoint Wadsworth treasurer only to have his appointment blocked in the upper house.[11]

Bishop's antifederalism long antagonized New Haven's political leadership. David Daggett, a friend in 1789 who would later become one of Bishop's most persistent critics, stated in 1800 that Bishop "wrote, published, and preached wherever you could get hearers, against the new constitution." In a dramatic reinterpretation of the 1789 Bishop-Hillhouse debate, Daggett claimed that Hillhouse "administered to you a public chastisement, which, I fancy, you yet feel." Despite the scorn, Bishop was an unrepentant antifederalist, at least until 1798, when he became clerk of the superior court and quieted down. Before then, according to Daggett, he "was constantly whining and murmuring against government in all its departments."[12]

Though recognized as one of the most talented public speakers in New Haven, Bishop still had no career. This situation changed in February 1789, when he became director of the American Academy in New Haven. The directorship gave Bishop another forum for public speaking. In the spring of 1789, Bishop gave a series of public lectures on his European travels and even entertained his audience with a song. The academy charged nine pence for the pit and six pence for the gallery, but scholars were "entitled" to free tickets.[13] Bishop's academy was popular but controversial. When it opened, a series of essays appeared in the *Connecticut Journal* discouraging parents from sending their children to the school. One essay attacked the academy and Bishop's theatrics, insinuating that the school had turned "into a place of public exhibitions, and . . . will doubtless change its name from ACADEMY to THEATRE."[14]

Despite the controversy, Bishop had established himself as an influential spokesman for educational reform. He initiated a drive to consolidate the city's four grammar schools, encourage wider attendance, expand curriculum, and provide educational opportunities for girls. The town's leading ministers, officials, merchants, and lawyers endorsed Bishop's proposal. To bolster public support, Bishop again took to the stage at the Brick meeting house to give a lecture on "School Education." He followed this lecture with a four-part series on education in the local paper. Bishop was named headmaster of the Hopkins grammar school, launched his consolidation plan, and soon advertised the newly renamed Orleans Academy, of which he was the director, as "an association of Schools" where "the youth of both Sexes shall be instructed." He remained in this position for about six months, when either frustration or ambition for a different career led him to resign in late 1790.[15]

Teaching was not the career for which Bishop strove. Consequently, he left New Haven for Boston in 1791, where he attempted to launch a literary career. Bishop planned to write a three-book "Columbian Exercise" to establish his literary credentials. The first and thankfully only volume, *The Triumph of Truth: History and Visions of Clio* was published in Boston in 1791 under his pseudonym, "John Paul Martin."[16]

About the same time as his book appeared, Bishop became a frequent contributor to *The Argus*, a new Boston paper that often challenged the town's political establishment. Bishop composed essays on a remarkably wide range of topics. In the nine-week period between October 11 and December 6, 1791, he wrote at least thirty-one pieces using his pseudonym. Most of his essays focused on the need for educational reform, but he also penned essays on such diverse themes as his opposition to the theater, lotteries, and banks. He wrote an important piece on the necessity of female education and sparked more controversy with a series of essays that defended the slave revolt in St. Domingue.

In one significant series, Bishop advocated "Female Education." He complained that "even now, in some parts of United America, as well as among several other nations, who call themselves civil[ized]—Women are considered as little better than slaves to unfeeling parents, and to idle lordly husbands." Bishop argued that women had as much right to education as men did. "And happily, we do not limit merit, nor knowledge to either sex; both we consider as the natural growth of the human mind, and sure of flourishing, when moistened with the dew of wisdom, and warmed by the sun of knowledge." Female education would guarantee that "our daughters will shine as bright constellations, in the sphere where nature has placed them."[17]

His moderately advanced views on women were surpassed by the radical views on race that he penned in a series entitled the "Rights of Black Men." The essay defended the Haitian slave rebels and described them as true followers in the spirit of the American Revolution. "Let us be consistent Americans," Bishop wrote. "The blacks are entitled to freedom, for we did not say all *white* men are *free*, but *all men* are free." He challenged eighteenth-century racial ideology by asking, "If Freedom depends upon colour, we have only to seek for the whitest man in the world, that we may find the freest and for the blackest, that we may find the greatest slave." No less than the American Revolution, the Haitian's cause was just: "*The Universal Father seems now demonstrating that of one blood, he has created all nations of men.*"[18]

Bishop's prolific and controversial essays ultimately made him unwelcome during his stay in Boston. Dubbing him the "Connecticut Stranger" and "Jack Ranter," Bishop's critics were unusually harsh. One, "Old Wackum" (a reference to the rod that Bishop condemned in one of his essays on education), described Bishop as "an immense bladder of Vanity." He was criticized for his theatrics during his orations, which often included songs. A satirical poem mocked the theatrical Bishop for attacking the theatre: "I will write 'gainst all Plays/Altho' I'm a Player." Bishop's critics capitalized on his ego and vanity. One writer, falsely claiming to be John Paul Martin, wrote, "I . . . am a man of vast and immeasurable abilities. . . . I . . . consider MYself, from MY superior understanding and knowledge, to have *a right to direct*, not only the town of Boston, but the whole world."[19]

Perhaps as a result of such attacks, Bishop apparently left Boston at the end of 1791. He settled briefly in nearby Portsmouth, New Hampshire, where he might have taught school. But Bishop quickly became immersed in a new controversy in Portsmouth. The town's Congregational minister Samuel MacClintock criticized Portsmouth's Episcopalian priest, John C. Ogden. After the Episcopalian bishop, Samuel Seabury, voiced his support for Ogden, MacClintock unleashed an attack on Seabury. On December 21, 1791, Portsmouth's *New Hampshire Spy* announced that Bishop would present a public oration "in reply to

Mr. S. McClintock." Bishop, the son of a New Light Congregational deacon, stepped out on the stage—this time to defend an Episcopalian and to launch an anticlerical attack on a Congregationalist. The *Spy* published Bishop's lecture a few days later.[20]

While teaching in Portsmouth, Bishop met his future wife. He married Nancy Dexter, a sixteen-year-old boarding school student, on March 11, 1792, in Newburyport, over the objections of Nancy's father, the rich and eccentric "Lord" Timothy Dexter. Again finding himself without a steady career, Abraham and his new wife returned to New Haven. His marriage to this young woman was not a happy one, and it deteriorated rapidly. In an attack on Bishop published in 1802, Federalists charged that he had failed to establish a respectable household for Nancy. He was "often unkind, at times intoxicated at his own table, and always a mere animal." The portrait of Bishop as an abusive drunk may simply reflect the partisan motivation for this attack, but Bishop was clearly an unhappy and frustrated man after he returned to New Haven. A daughter was born in May 1793. Then in 1795, after the birth and death of a son, Nancy Dexter Bishop left her husband and returned to her father's home in Newburyport. Two years later, as Federalists reported, Bishop "completed his infidelity to her by obtaining a divorce for *wilful desertion.*"[21] In 1802, Federalists exploited the couple's unhappy marriage to portray Bishop as immoral. His former wife was their star witness until her own sobriety and mental stability came into question.[22]

After returning to New Haven, Bishop avoided the controversies that had been so central to his life since 1788. Between 1792 and 1797 Bishop's pen did not light on political or social topics. His voice did not address publicly an audience in an assembly hall or meetinghouse. Why Bishop fell silent is not clear. Evidence in the New Haven newspapers suggest he was busy and actively engaged in his legal practice. Maybe Bishop hoped to avoid antagonizing powerful political leaders. In 1794, he believed he would receive a legislative appointment as a New Haven County justice of the peace. When the position failed to materialize, Bishop placed blame on his then friend David Daggett, who was speaker of the Connecticut House of Representatives. Samuel Bishop helped his son obtain some political appointments. Bishop served as clerk of the New Haven County Court between 1795 and 1801 and clerk for the probate court between 1796 and 1801. In 1798, he received a post as clerk of the superior court; a position he held until 1800. Federalists purged Bishop (and other Republicans) from these appointive offices after partisan politics heated up in late 1800.

Bishop's political silence ended in late 1797, about the time his divorce from Nancy was finalized. It is hard not to make a connection between his marital problems and his political inactivity. Following his divorce, Bishop published *Georgia Speculation Unveiled*. This piece criticized the Yazoo Land Company and the state of Georgia for their role in the notorious fraud. Many speculators in New England, including Bishop, suffered when their investments went sour following the invalidation of the Yazoo claim. Bishop, using language that he would soon turn on his Federalist opponents, characterized the Yazoo land jobbers as

> Men who never added an iota to the wealth or morals of the world, . . . riding in their chariots—plotting the ruin of born and unborn millions—aiming with feathers to cut throats, and on parchments to seal destruction,—these are the robbers of modern days.—They bring desolation among our farmers—they spread distress in towns—they scorn the paltry plunder of pocket-books, and watches—they aim at houses and lands—strike at the foundation of many generations,—and would destroy families, root and branch.[23]

By the end of the 1790s, national political debate sharpened. The quasi-war with France, the Alien and Sedition Acts, and Federalist charges of the Bavarian Illuminati conspiracy led Republicans in Connecticut and throughout the nation to mobilize for the 1800 elections. Connecticut Republicans were buoyed by Gideon Granger's success in the spring nominating election for Congress. In Connecticut, voters elected eighteen nominees in April to stand for seven at-large congressional seats in the fall election. Federalists controlled both houses in Congress; every seat in the national legislature counted. Connecticut Republicans hoped to elect Granger during the September elections, and the party began an intense organizing campaign during the summer of 1800. This effort also offered Bishop an opportunity for a new career—party politician. Bishop emerged as a key point man that summer. He, and other Republicans, spent the summer canvassing support for Granger. In late August 1800 vice presidential candidate Aaron Burr met in New Haven with his uncle, Pierpont Edwards, as well as Granger and Bishop to plan the fall campaign. The meeting may have played a role in Bishop's selection of a topic for his Phi Beta Kappa lecture. Less than two weeks later, Bishop delivered *Connecticut Republicanism*.

After Bishop delivered his oration, politics became his primary career. Republicans, though they made a respectable showing in the fall 1800 elections, could not elect Granger, who captured only 32 percent of the vote. They were far from gaining control in Connecticut. As part of the minority, Bishop worked hard in the coming years to publish Republican essays, organize Republican rallies, distribute Republican newspapers, correspond with Republican leaders both within and outside of Connecticut, and develop strategies for advancing the Republican cause. In May 1801, Thomas Jefferson helped facilitate Bishop's new career by appointing his father collector of the port of New Haven. With the appointment of Samuel Bishop to the lucrative post, Abraham was able to step in and serve as his father's clerk.

The appointment was controversial. Jefferson removed Federalist Elizur Goodrich from the position. Goodrich, one of former President John Adams's "midnight appointments," had barely settled into his office before being tossed out by Jefferson. Party leaders, such as Gideon Granger, advised Jefferson that the Republican "cause requires the removal of Mr. Goodrich." Placing local Republicans into key federal offices was essential. Granger believed Federalists would seek revenge for their loss of the presidency: "The exertions of our Clergy and Aristocracy . . . have exceeded every thing before now" and they "design to make themselves terrible in the opposition." Pierpont Edwards, after consulting with other party leaders, recommended Samuel Bishop to the president. New Haven Federalists were furious that the seventy-seven-year-old Bishop was offered this office. They howled loudly that the post was really a reward for Abraham. The appointment became a cause célèbre for Federalists. Seventy-eight New Haven merchants sent a remonstrance to Mr. Jefferson complaining about Goodrich's removal. Other Federalists viciously attacked Abraham Bishop, "whom," Edwards claimed in a letter to Jefferson, "they hate above all men." One Federalist author described Abraham Bishop as "a flaming street orator, a bawling Lazaront, a monstrous [and] a most shocking patriot, a blazing meteor of republicanism, and a violent enemy of christianity." How could Jefferson, they asked, believe that Samuel Bishop "would be other than a *nominal* collector, while Abraham . . . should do the business and receive emoluments." In responding to the New Haven remonstrance, Jefferson seized on the opportunity to outline publicly his policies on federal appointments. Departing somewhat from the conciliatory tone of his March inaugural address, Jefferson made it clear to the New Haven merchants that he intended to remove Federalists from office on political grounds to ensure that his Republican supporters held key appointments.[24]

Following Samuel Bishop's death in 1803, Jefferson appointed Abraham as collector. Holding a lucrative federal post ensured that

Bishop had the time and resources needed to organize and manage Republicans in Federalist Connecticut. Bishop used his "emoluments" to support Republican pamphlets and newspapers. The office gave him time to compose political essays and organize political festivals and rallies. He, and other Republican office holders, used their salaries to subsidize political presses and to ensure that government printing contracts went to friendly Republican editors.

Even before the New Haven appointment was offered to Samuel Bishop, Connecticut Republicans had reason to rejoice. To celebrate Jefferson's inaugural in March 1801, Bishop organized the state's first Republican festival at Wallingford. Bishop joined the blacklisted Congregational minister Stanley Griswold in giving orations. Bishop began his speech by comparing the common folk of New England to southern slaves: "When a Southern slave breaks his fetters of bondage and declares for liberty, a hue and cry is raised, the daring culprit is apprehended and death is his portion. When a Northern slave declares for the emancipation of himself and his white brethren, all the masters are in an uproar, the pursuit is close, all means are fair and the daring wretch is doomed to all the vengeance of his oppressors."

Bishop argued that "THE SELF STILED FRIENDS OF ORDER" had created a "dreadful" and "invisible slavery" for white New Englanders. "Is it not a fact," Bishop asked, "that ecclesiastical and civil tyranny have formed a junction in New England, for the express purpose of enslaving the minds of men on religious and political subjects?" Bishop urged that "the white slaves [of New England] should rise in mass." If so, "they would be too much for their masters. It is high time that societies for the emancipation of white slaves were established in New England." Bishop's oration was a direct attack on the Connecticut religious establishment: "Church and state cannot be better served, than by keeping them distinct." Besides attacking the aristocratic tendencies of the Connecticut's Standing Order, Bishop's oration was a political appeal to religious dissenters, especially Baptists who "at this moment, [are] praying for the repeal of those laws, which abridge the rights of conscience." Attacking Congregational ministers for supporting Federalists, Bishop stated: "The clerical *politician* is an useless preacher; the *political* christian is a dangerous statesman."[25]

Bishop continued his assault on the religious establishment in his 1802 pamphlet *Proofs of a Conspiracy Against Christianity and the Government*. Bishop found a receptive audience for his writings among religious dissenters—Baptists, Methodists, and some Episcopalians—who despised the state-supported Congregational Church and its clergy. The established church served neither religion nor politics. Mocking the Federalist clergy's fear of the Bavarian Illuminatti, an imagined international conspiracy to destroy Christianity inspired by atheistic Jacobins, Bishop saw the true conspiracy in the Federalist church-state establishment. Bishop borrowed from leading Baptist proponents of religious liberty, such as John Leland, when he wrote, "If christianity needs the support of civil institutions, it has not come from God." Bishop, who most likely was a deist, wrote and spoke in a language that appealed to Connecticut's evangelical religious dissenters. They could only applaud when he concluded his analysis with these stern words: "The Political Clergy Are the Worst Enemies of the Church. The Federal Leaders Are the Worst Enemies of Our Revolution, and Both Are Enemies to the Common People."[26]

Bishop had a special talent for organizing political festivals, or rallies, like the one at Wallingford, which became a model for Republicans throughout the nation. Bishop had his hand in a series of festivals held in the early 1800s. The grandest one occurred in New Haven in March 1803. It promised "to celebrate our deliverance from aristocracy." The Republican press reported that 1,108 people marched in the procession. More heard speeches by U.S. District Attorney Pierpont Edwards and the well-known millennialist preacher David Austin. The festivities included a seventeen-gun salute that sounded twice during the day and toasts offered to the fourteen "Republican States." The audience even heard the famous radical Thomas Paine make a brief speech.[27]

By 1804, Republicans launched a drive for a constitutional convention. Bishop kicked off this campaign at the Republican festival in Hartford in May 1804. He condemned Connecticut's old colonial charter as a usurpation of the people's sovereignty. Through the maintenance of the old charter, argued Bishop, Federalists were able to subvert the republican sentiments of the people, particularly by enacting the "stand-up" law, which abolished the secret ballot. "On equal ground," he wrote, "the republicans of this state would long since have prevailed." He called for a convention to write a constitution that would prevent continued Federalist abuse.[28]

In the Hartford speech, Bishop touched on two closely related points: tax reform and universal suffrage. The latter would generate the former, and a new constitution would guarantee both. Both issues had long been championed by the state's mechanics, and the Republican position appealed to this constituency as well as to budding manufacturers. At the Hartford festival, Bishop called for reform of the tax system to provide "immense relief of the laboring classes of our people. . . . Every man, who pays money or renders public services common or military, should have a voice in the choosing of men, who are to gauge his pockets or estimate his strength, and there is no danger in suffering the poor man's vote to weight as much as the rich man's."[29]

The festivals that Bishop organized and often spoke at were more than mere forums for leading Republicans to announce the party's platform. They rallied Republicans on the eve of elections, encouraging men to apply for voting privileges and to invest their time in the day-long election day ritual. The festive rallies targeted key groups of Republican supporters, such as religious dissenters and mechanics. The celebrations, the newspaper articles leading up to these events, and the published orations that followed tied local issues and constituencies to national political discourse. Bishop helped forge a link between the common folk who voted and the more remote party leaders such as Granger and Edwards. Though he never held an elective office, Bishop the party manager and political middleman was key to creating these links and making the national Republican cause important to common people who voted in each election.

Despite the intense campaigns of the early 1800s, Bishop could not manage his party to victory before 1817. Nonetheless, Connecticut Republicans had built one of the most sophisticated political organizations in the new nation—a model for Republicans in other states and the envy of Federalists in his home state. Their accomplishments were impressive. In 1798, Republicans only won 18 percent of the vote in the April congressional nominations. Two years later, just as they began to put an organization into place, Gideon Granger received 32 percent of the vote in the fall congressional elections. By 1802, Republicans routinely attracted votes from nearly 40 percent of the freemen in gubernatorial, congressional, and council races. The party's most successful showing occurred in 1806, when they won 44 percent of the votes in the fall council races. More striking was the transformation of political behavior. In 1798 only 21 percent of the adult men voted for governor. By the early 1800s participation rates climbed to a high of 46 percent, an impressive showing given that nearly one-third of the men in the state could not vote because they lacked the property needed to qualify. The party's growth in the Connecticut House of Representatives was equally impressive. In May 1798, Republicans held twenty-six seats, or 14 percent of the total. By October 1800 that number had climbed to forty-two, 22 percent of the total. Their strength peaked at seventy-eight seats—40 percent of the total—in May 1804.

Although they gained ground, Republicans could not turn the corner and capture control of the government before unpopular Jeffersonian foreign policies—the embargo and then the war—dashed the party's hopes in Connecticut. Republicans continued to defend the national party, but they were in no position to break the Federalist stranglehold after 1807.[30] However, Federalists opposition to the war, their unwillingness to recognize the transformation of Connecticut's postwar economy, and their break with Episcopalians within the party caused a deep chasm in Connecticut's majority party in 1814 and 1815. At the instigation of Pierpont Edwards and with the support of Pierpont's loyal friend Abraham Bishop, Republicans quickly reached out to disaffected Federalists and launched an aggressive campaign for governor in 1816. The Republicans came within 1,216 votes (less than 1 percent of the total cast) of capturing the governor's office. The following year, Republicans won this prize and in the fall elections swept the nominations for council, ensuring control of the upper house following the April 1818 election. In July 1818, they enacted universal male suffrage and called a constitutional convention. Republicans quickly enacted many of the reforms that had been advocated by Bishop since the early 1800s.

Bishop, now one of the wealthiest men in New Haven, in part because of his lucrative post in the customs house, had become a respected and influential member of the community. In 1820, he contributed his extensive newspaper collection to Yale College. He served on school and cemetery committees and helped establish the new neighborhoods of Long Wharf and Wooster Square. He also actively supported internal improvements such as the Farmington Canal.[31] Even after church and state had been separated by Connecticut's new constitution, Bishop found occasion to voice his anticlerical views. In 1824, he penned a sharp criticism of Edward Dorr Griffin's call for increased foreign missions.[32] With some irony, Abraham Bishop lost his position as the New Haven collector in 1829 when the newly elected president, Andrew Jackson, replaced Bishop (who had supported John Quincy Adams), with a loyal supporter.

Bishop remained in New Haven until his death in 1844, a local man and a local politician. But Bishop was part of a national movement, the "Revolution" of 1800 that brought the Jeffersonians to power and changed the political direction of the new nation. His actions and his innovations forever transformed Connecticut politics and society. Bishop, as much as any person in the state, helped the people of Connecticut realize the democratic fruits that the American Revolution promised.

Notes

1. Abraham Bishop, "Appendix," *Oration delivered in Wallingford, on the 11th of March 1801, before the Republicans of the State of Connecticut, at their General Thanksgiving, for the election of Thomas Jefferson to the Presidency and of Aaron Burr to the Vice Presidency of the United States of America* (New Haven, CT, 1801), 102.

2. Gordon S. Wood, *The Radicalism of the American Revolution* (New York, 1992), 271.

3. Abraham Bishop, *Connecticut Republicanism: An Oration on the Extent And Power of Political Delusion Delivered in New-Haven, on the Evening preceding the Public Commencement, September, 1800* (1800; reprint ed., Albany, NY, 1801), 17, 21, 27–28. Emphasis in original.

4. Ibid., 30, 32–33, 35–36, 41. Emphasis in original.

5. [Noah Webster], *A Rod for the Fool's Back* ([New Haven], CT, 1800); [David Daggett], in *Three Letters to Abraham Bishop, Esquire, Containing Some Strictures on his Oration, Pronounced, in the White Meeting-House, on the Evening Preceding the Public Commencement, September 1800. By Connecticutensis* (Hartford, CT, 1800).

6. Aaron Burr to Tench Coxe, October 25, 1800, *Political Correspondence and Public Papers of Aaron Burr*, ed. Mary-Jo Kline, 2 vols. (Princeton, NJ, 1983), 1:452; Thomas Jefferson to Thomas Mann Randolph, November 30, 1800, *The Writings of Thomas Jefferson*, ed. Albert E. Bergh, 20 vols. (Washington, DC, 1907), 18:225.

7. Congressman John Cotton Smith wrote to fellow Federalist David Daggett about a Republican festival: "What was done at Wallingford 4th March? What is the prospect of being revolutionized?" Smith to Daggett, March 14, 1802, David Daggett Papers, Yale University Library, New Haven, CT.

8. Franklin Bowditch Dexter, ed., *The Literary Diary of Ezra Stiles*, 3 vols. (New York, 1901), 3:331; Abraham Bishop to David Daggett, March 10, 1787, Daggett Papers.

9. *Connecticut Journal* (New Haven), October 22, 1778; Dexter, ed., *The Literary Diary of Ezra Stiles*, 3:331.

10. *Connecticut Journal*, January 14, 1789; William Hillhouse Jr., *A Dissertation, In Answer to a Late Lecture on the Political State of America, Read in New-Haven, January 12th, 1789, During the Adjourned Sessions of the Honorable Legislature: To Which Is Added, a Short Poem Spoken at the Same Time* (New Haven, CT, 1789).

11. Leonidas, *Connecticut Journal*, January 21, 1789.

12. [Daggett], *Three Letters to Abraham Bishop*, 6.

13. *Connecticut Journal*, March 18, 1789.

14. Leonidas, *Connecticut Journal*, February 18, 1789.

15. *Connecticut Journal*, March 17, 1790.

16. John Paul Martin [Abraham Bishop], *The Triumph of Truth: History and Visions of Clio* (Boston, [1791]); "J.P. Martin to the Civil Spy," *The Argus* (Boston), November 8, 1791. An excerpt appeared in the *Columbian Centinel* (Boston), November 16, 1791.

17. John Paul Martin, "Address on Female Education," *The Argus*, November 18, 22, 1791.

18. John Paul Martin, "Rights of Black Men," *The Argus*, November 22, 25, December 2, 1791, reprinted in *Cumberland Gazette* (Falmouth, MA), December 5, 12, 1791; and *American Museum*, 13 (November 1792). Emphasis in original. This series is also reprinted in Tim Mattewson, "Abraham Bishop, 'The Rights of Black Men,' and the American Reaction to the Haitian Revolution," *Journal of Negro History* 67 (1982): 148–54.

19. *The Argus*, November 8, 1791; A.B. "Speech of Jack Ranter," ibid., December 2, 1791; "Another New Song, to Another Old Tune," *Columbian Centinel*, January 7, 1792; John Paul Martin, ibid., December 3, 1791.

20. *New Hampshire Spy* (Portsmouth), December 21, 24, 1791.

21. *Connecticut Courant* (Hartford), August 16, 1802.

22. In 1802, Bishop married Betsey Law and the couple had four daughters and a son who died in infancy. Following his second wife's death, Bishop married Elizabeth Nicoll in 1819.

23. Abraham Bishop, *Georgia Speculation Unveiled; in Two Numbers* (Hartford, CT, 1797), 38–39. Also see *Georgia Speculation Unveiled, Second Part. Containing the Third and Fourth Numbers; with a Conclusion, addressed to the Northern Purchasers* (Hartford, CT, 1798).

24. Gideon Granger to Thomas Jefferson, April 15, 1801, and Pierpont Edwards to Thomas Jefferson, May 12, 1801, in Gaillard Hunt, "Office-Seeking during Jefferson's Administration," *American Historical Review* 3 (1898): 272–78; Thomas Jefferson to Pierpont Edwards, July 21, 1801, *The Writings of Thomas Jefferson*, ed. Paul L. Ford, 10 vols. (New York, 1892–99), 8:74–75; Pierpont Edwards to Thomas Jefferson, June 10–18, 1801, quoted in Noble E. Cunningham Jr., *The Jeffersonian Republicans in Power: Party Operations, 1801–1809* (Chapel Hill, NC, 1965), 23; *Washington Federalist*, August 5, 1801. Bishop himself defended Jefferson and attacked the New Haven merchants in an article published in the *Sun of Liberty* (New Haven, CT), September 9, 1801, and republished as Tulius Americus [Abraham Bishop], *Strictures on a Pamphlet Entitled "An Examination of the President's reply to the New-haven Remonstrance," &c. . . . with an appendix* (Albany, NY, 1801).

25. Bishop, *Oration Delivered at Wallingford*, iii–v, 16, 41.

26. Abraham Bishop, *Proofs of a Conspiracy Against Christianity and the Government of the United States: Exhibited in Several Views of the Union of Church and State in New-England* (Hartford, CT, 1802), 108, 166.

27. *American Mercury* (Hartford, CT), February 10, March 3, 1803.

28. Abraham Bishop, *Oration, in Honor of the Election of President Jefferson, and the Peaceable Acquisition of Louisiana: Delivered at the National Festival, in Hartford, on the 11th of May, 1804* (New Haven, CT, 1804), 15.

29. Ibid., 22.

30. For Bishop's effort to defend Republican policy in these years see [Abraham Bishop], *Some Remarks and Extracts, in reply to Mr. Pickering's Letter, on the subject of the Embargo* (New Haven, CT, 1808?); and [Abraham Bishop], *New Haven Remonstrance. Together with an Exposition of the Remonstrants, Or a Curiosity for the Curious* (London, 1814) [New Haven, CT, 1814]. The essay's printed publication date, location, and the reference to the Federalist William Cobbett (Peter Porcupine) was de-

signed to ridicule the pro-British New Haven Federalists, especially Noah Webster. On page 24, Bishop humorously advertises "the works of a Custom-House officer," set against some "British" books: Webster's "[Rod for a] Fool's Back" and "Slave Trade Vindicated."

31. [Abraham Bishop], *Funeral Address*, in *Proceedings of the City of New-Haven, in the Removal of Monuments from its Ancient Burying-Ground, and in the Opening of a New Ground for Burial* (New Haven, CT, 1822); Abraham Bishop, *Farmington Canal: To the Citizens of New-Haven* (New Haven, CT, 1827).

32. [Abraham Bishop], *Remarks on Dr. Griffin's requisition for 700,000 ministers* (New Haven, CT, 1824).

Suggested Readings

Cunningham, Noble E., Jr. *The Jeffersonian Republicans: The Formation of Party Organization, 1789–1801*. Chapel Hill, NC, 1957.

———. *The Jeffersonian Republicans in Power: Party Operations, 1801–1809*. Chapel Hill, NC, 1965.

Dexter, Franklin Bowditch. "Abraham Bishop, of Connecticut, and His Writings." *Proceedings of the Massachusetts Historical Society*, 2d Ser., 19 (1905): 190–99.

Grasso, Christopher. *A Speaking Aristocracy: Transforming Public Discourse in Eighteenth-Century Connecticut*. Chapel Hill, NC, 1999.

Purcell, Richard J. *Connecticut in Transition: 1775–1818*. 1918. Reprint, Middletown, CT, 1962.

Schulz, Constance B. " 'Of Bigotry in Politics and Religion': Jefferson's Religion, the Federalist Press, and the Syllabus." *Virginia Magazine of History and Biography* 91 (1983): 73–91.

Waldstreicher, David. *In the Midst of Perpetual Fetes: The Making of American Nationalism, 1776–1820*. Chapel Hill, NC, 1997.

Waldstreicher, David, and Stephen R. Grossbart. "Abraham Bishop's Vocation; or, The Mediation of Jeffersonian Politics." *Journal of the Early Republic* 18 (1998): 617–57.

Williamson, Chilton. *American Suffrage: From Property to Democracy, 1760–1860*. Princeton, NJ, 1960.

Wood, Gordon S. *The Radicalism of the American Revolution*. New York, 1992.

2

John Wesley Young
Identity and Community among
"the People Called Methodist"

Ruth Alden Doan

The democratization of society and politics that began in the revolutionary era also affected organized religion. John Wesley Young, born into a Quaker family of modest means, took advantage of, and contributed to, the weakening of traditional forms of religious practice. Methodism, to which Young converted in 1777, was one of the many new sects that flourished in this emerging context of religious freedom and democratic culture. Its tenets challenged the assumption that regular church attendance was a measure of individual piety. Relying on circuit riders, such as Young, who lacked formal theological training to spread the Word and the faith, the Methodist church instead emphasized popular camp meetings that were characterized by religious frenzy and mass conversions. Although Young and other itinerant preachers stressed individual piety and personal responsibility for salvation, they also created through the camp meetings a sense of kinship among the spiritually committed. These communities provided stability and a collective identity in a young nation in transition and in a society and culture that were very much under construction. Moreover, the broad participation in religion that Young and other preachers promoted in a variety of established and recently formed denominations fostered a belief that commitment to a common Christian faith cut across different sects and systems of beliefs.

Ruth Alden Doan is associate professor of history at Hollins University, Roanoke, Virginia, and a member of the board of editors for the *Journal of the Early Republic*. The author of *The Miller Heresy, Millennialism, and American Culture* (1987), she is presently studying southern evangelicalism and narratives of religious experience.

M ethodist preachers carried both the message and the organization of Methodism across the United States with stunning speed and unmatched effectiveness between the 1780s and the 1850s. Elevated to the status of heroes by many ordinary Americans, circuit riders faced

The author would like to thank the North Caroliniana Society for support through the Archie K. Davis Fund.

physical hardship and intimidation as they rode the many miles between their preaching appointments. Traveling more limited circuits,
John Wesley Young faced those challenges with his Methodist brothers.
He preached in Virginia and North Carolina for more than fifty years—
longer than many of his fellow itinerants survived.

Young's writings dramatize both the emotional power of his spiritual life and the centrality of religious conversion to his identity. Yet he
also expressed his own sense of inadequacy in the face of the massive
task of bringing what he understood to be true religion to the many
people he met. Throughout his life, but especially as he grew older,
Young dwelt upon his feelings of alienation from his worldly self and
from a society that he perceived as drifting from its proper religious and
moral foundations. His reflections on such themes were set against the
background of a society in which white and black worshiped together,
Baptist and Methodist argued over theology, and evangelical Christians
built institutions out of which the future of the nation would grow.[1]

The Methodist movement grew out of the Church of England, or
Anglican Church, in England and in British North America. Methodism
emerged out of a religious culture and a society in which an ideal of
mutually reinforcing hierarchies held sway. Theoretically, the church
buttressed the state and vice versa; similarly, socioeconomic hierarchies
paralleled and reinforced religious hierarchies. The monarch was the
head of the Church of England. A local nobleman or gentleman often
had the right to appoint the local minister because gentry dominated
the financially powerful vestries. Sunday worship services began with
parishioners parading into the church building and seating themselves
in order of wealth and social standing. Worship services themselves centered upon the Book of Common Prayer, and short sermons expressed a
broad middle ground of Protestant theology.

When John Wesley, a founder of the Methodist movement, emerged
as a religious leader in England, the attitudes and practices that he proposed cut across the comfortably overlapping hierarchies of church and
society. Although Wesley remained a member of the Church of England
until his death, his movement threatened the unity of the church. He
asserted that a dramatic religious experience—an experience of the "heart
strangely warmed"—defined a genuine religious life. Wesley's own experience of conversion at Aldersgate set the pattern for other adherents
to the Methodist movement. The warm heart was not sufficient, however. Those who had gone through conversion would give evidence of
their spiritual state in their behavior. Methodists upheld rigorous moral

standards. To help ensure that such standards were met, Wesley gathered converts into class meetings—groupings outside regular Sunday worship—during which Christians would testify to their experiences and examine one another's failings. Conversion threatened to rise above attendance at regular church services as a measure of true religion, and the class leader threatened to compete with the minister as the true spiritual leader of the small Methodist bands.

Across the Atlantic a parallel movement emerged in the First Great Awakening. A series of religious revivals that began in New England in the 1730s and spread throughout British North America, the Great Awakening shared with England's Methodist revivals emphases on the conversion experience and on a voluntary adherence to a select, spiritually serious group. Adherents to the Great Awakening appeared in a variety of religious groups—what we would now call denominations: Congregational, Presbyterian, Baptist, and, of course, groups that would become Methodists. Wesley's friend George Whitefield, for example, amazed and entranced audiences in North America when he visited from England. No less a light than Benjamin Franklin commented on the huge crowd that Whitefield drew as well as upon the power of his outdoor preaching.[2]

By the time of the American War for Independence the small Methodist movement was poised for growth. Moreover, independence itself provoked a crisis in the Methodist movement. If the colonies were independent of the king, then colonists could no longer belong to a church with the king at its head. Methodists either had to become independent of the Church of England by joining with the new, American-based Episcopal Church, or they had to decide that the time had come to branch out on their own. They chose the latter, and the Methodist Episcopal Church, better known by the shorter term Methodists, was born.

Wesley sent two lieutenants, Francis Asbury and Thomas Coke, to America to lead the American group. The two officers headed a hierarchical organization that quickly moved to evangelize the land. Paradoxically the hierarchical organization of Methodism allowed the movement to take advantage of the new context of religious freedom and of democratic ideology.[3] Asbury and Coke were bishops; under their supervision, general conferences met every four years to decide major issues facing the denomination. Annual conferences covered geographical areas as large as a state or parts of two or three states; there, ministers gathered to renew themselves and to receive their preaching assignments for the coming year. Those preaching assignments—the circuits, on which rode the always-weary but spiritually intense riders—were the characteristic institution that citizens of the new nation came to associate with the upstart Methodist movement. Local preachers shared the spiritual intensity of the circuit riders and, along with class meetings, provided continuity and local grounding for converts to the new church.[4]

John Wesley Young, named for John Wesley, grew up with his father but lost his mother at only one year of age. His father had been raised in a Quaker household, but like many Virginians became loosely attached to the Church of England. John remembered his father as a good man, a man who did not swear or blaspheme, a man whom he never saw "toxicated with spirits." Reflecting back upon his childhood, John remembered his father as a moral man although he "knew nothing of being Converted or born again." Nonetheless he expressed his thankfulness for having had such a parent and such an excellent moral example. His father also made sure that John had a basic education in reading, writing, and arithmetic. That education was to go to some practical end, but John's father left it to his son what work he would follow: "Should I be a parson or a Doctor of Phisick or a Captain of a Ship"? At sixteen, John left home to become an apprentice to a carpenter. In his four-and-a-half years of "hard servitude," he did indeed hear blasphemy enough, and although he did not swear himself, he did indulge in "reveling gambling racing Cockfighting"—all evils that a man destined to be a Methodist preacher would live to regret.[5]

By the 1770s, Young had a household of his own. He had married and begun to father children. He also owned slaves—perhaps inherited from his father.[6] Young's first marriage lasted forty-four years, until the death of his wife in 1813. His second marriage followed quickly enough to give pause: his first wife died in October of 1813, and his second marriage took place in January of 1814.

Perhaps the serious duties of a husband and father or the life-and-death issues raised by the outbreak of hostilities with England overlapped with an inclination toward religious seriousness to draw Young increasingly to religious questions in the 1770s. In 1775, he heard a Baptist preacher for the first time. He was impressed: the Baptist spoke "Extempore"—that is, without a prepared written text but instead under immediate inspiration. As he later recalled the incident, he was also intrigued by a new notion of which he had not heard, "Conversion & the new birth." But he already knew that he had doubts about the theology of the Baptists; "Unconditional Election & Reprobation & Final perseverance of the saints" all sounded "strange" to Young, as indeed it might to anyone neither steeped in theology nor a Baptist.[7]

Young finally encountered his first Methodist preacher in 1777. John King had traveled from England to help spread Wesley's version of Christianity in the New World. His preaching left Young deeply impressed. King "opened the way & . . . Plan of Salvation to me that I never saw before," including the Methodist notion that Jesus Christ had opened the possibility of salvation for all people. On King's second visit, he was accompanied by one Mr. Long, who rode along with Young and "was free in conversing with me & Informing me of the People call'd Methodis [*sic*] & there [*sic*] doctrine." Young determined that at his first opportunity he would join and become one of "the People call'd Methodis."[8]

In January 1778, Young joined the Methodists. According to their understanding, however, it was not enough just to sign on and to show up for services. A true Methodist not only had to adhere to strict Methodist discipline for living and ordering one's religious life but also had to hope for an experience of rebirth or conversion. Young began with the first rule by instituting the regular practice of "famely worship" at home. In "famely," he included everyone in this household at any given time. When travelers stopped to take advantage of the hospitality of the Youngs, they were encouraged to join in prayer with the permanent residents of the household.[9]

Young had a more dramatic experience in his own effort to make private prayer a regular part of his routine. He went to a dark room, sank to his knees, and immediately had a sense that "the devil was there." For Young and his fellow Methodists, the Devil took dramatic, physical form. Frequently after that first, fearful effort at prayer, Young remembered, "the devil hath appeared to my Imagination in the form of a great monster something like a great black bull."[10] The Methodist world, split between good and evil, between God and the devil, demanded not just acquiescence but active wrestling in favor of God. Nor was the evil thus embodied just outside the person; the wrestling between good and evil took place first and foremost within the Methodist himself or herself.

The center of Methodist life—and of all evangelical life—lay in the moment of transformation known as conversion or the new birth. Young and his fellow itinerants knew that every person began life on the wrong side of the great divide and that every Christian therefore had to turn from those monstrous forces of evil and take on a new life. Belief in the centrality of conversion implied that life could properly be divided into three parts: the time before conversion, the process of rebirth itself, and the time after the turning.[11] No matter how outwardly good a Methodist's life before conversion, this first phase of existence went down in memory as somehow inadequate. For Young, who lived a relatively moral life, it was perhaps a stretch to find enough attachment to the world in his early years to demonstrate that he had something from which to turn away. Thus, when Young wrote of his attendance at such entertainments as cockfights, he was not just reciting the facts of his youth but also reconstructing the story of his life in such a way as to show that his preconversion life required transformation.[12]

Later, as he remembered the initial months in which he attached himself to the Methodists, Young emphasized the inadequacy of his faith. "I knew nothing of the power of religion," he wrote of those months. "I only had the form." The external requirements of religion—family prayer, secret prayer, attendance at preaching, participation at class meeting, fasting, resisting sinful activities—helped to prepare one for true religion, but they did not constitute true religion in themselves. Thus, it was possible for Young to worry that "I passt [*sic*] for a Christian among my Neighbours" and at the same time fear that he would "die & go to hell."[13]

When Young finally reached the crisis of his conversion, he did not pass through from sinner to saint in a single day. Throughout the winter of 1786, Young wrestled with himself. He thought he was born again but recognized that he needed "a deeper work of grace." He promised God greater devotion but fell into "my old form of duty." In a pattern that he shared with a number of other evangelicals, Young finally came to the crisis point when he fell ill. He faced the possibility of death and admitted that he might go to hell; indeed, he deserved to go to hell. Only when he threw himself upon God's mercy in that way, as Young saw it, could he pass through to genuine rebirth. "I felt the love of God shed abroad in my poor sin sick soul & I knew my sins forgiven," Young wrote, "my mourning was turned into joy, & it Appeared like I had got into a new world."[14]

Young's spiritual and personal struggles did not end with conversion. The postconversion phase of life required working in the world while maintaining distance from it. Still suffering from the illness that had brought on the crisis of his conversion, Young recognized that although "I loved my wife and Children equal to any man," he nonetheless "thought no more of leaving them then [*sic*] if I had them not."

Such was his devotion to "Glory"; such was his sense that he was "weaned from all below." Methodists recognized that they faced a constant challenge in seeking to maintain such a level of detachment from the world in which they lived. It was all too easy, conversion aside, to sink into a comfortable life or even to backslide. Among all evangelicals, Methodists put the greatest emphasis on the possibility of rising to another level of grace that they called holiness. Some Methodists even proposed that another spiritual experience beyond conversion was possible. As Young put it with reference to his own experience, "I hope I have somewhat advanced in the divine life," and because of the love of God, "I felt a Love to all mankind."[15]

Most Methodist converts sought to live a godly life in the context of the everyday round of farming, raising children, trading, nursing the sick, and attending religious services. Young merits attention in large part because, unlike the majority of Methodists, he made yet one more commitment to the religious life: he became a preacher. The call to preach typically followed a pattern of experience much like the pattern of conversion itself. Preachers remembered a growing sense—what they perceived as a message from God—that they should commit themselves to preaching.

Most preachers' response was to resist. With his compatriots, Young wondered, "How could such a weak and ignorant Creature as I was preach the Gospel"? In spite of his "bashfull" nature, Young was already doing everything short of preaching. He had been appointed a class leader. In the absence of an ordained preacher, he often led a religious meeting among local Methodists on Sundays. Those meetings included not only prayer but also the reading of a sermon (as long as Young read a sermon composed by someone else he was not, strictly speaking, preaching). Finally, Young reached the point at which he would read a chapter of the Bible and "Expound from it." A Baptist visitor reported him for preaching when he was not licensed to do so; although Young denied that what he was doing was preaching, the distinction was a fairly technical one. Having reached the point of virtually preaching anyway, Young had only to receive a final call. On August 14, 1786, Young stood by a work bench in his shop when he heard a voice—"an inward voice As though it had been human and Vocal"—that said "Preach the word." Just as the devil had threatened Young in almost embodied form, God spoke to Young in a voice almost human. Since Young took this to be a genuine message from the Lord, he received a license to preach at the next quarterly meeting.[16]

As a married preacher, Young's arrangements to carry out his calling differed somewhat from those of the classic circuit rider.[17] Instead of receiving a new appointment every year that might lead to moving across the full geographical area covered by an annual conference, Young stayed on a single circuit, or round of preaching appointments, for an extended period, and later he preached locally. He traveled the Roanoke circuit in Virginia from 1775 until 1788, then moved to the Tar River circuit in North Carolina. In contrast to the legendary circuit rider, after 1788, Young put down roots in a community. His life incorporated some balance between his family and his calling. Nevertheless, Young experienced many of the challenges faced by those who moved from circuit to circuit. Even after he settled in Franklin County, North Carolina, he often faced hard travel, rough weather, uncertainty over whether he might find a welcoming roof, and the pain and illness that often struck circuit riders.[18]

One of the greatest rewards offered by Methodism, to both preacher and layperson, was the promise of spiritual community. Those who sought conversion, those who had been converted but wanted to reaffirm their commitment, and sometimes even just the curious came together at religious services. Such services included not only Sunday preaching but also frequent weekday preaching, funeral services, and the larger gatherings known as camp meetings. Under the preaching of Young and others, they often reached heights of emotion and a sense of belonging that took them beyond the everyday. Young frequently commented that, if he preached with "liberty" or "power," he aroused "some tender feeling among the People" or the people "had a weeping time."[19]

The emotional power of Methodist preaching led, ideally, to a deep sense of community. Methodists often expressed their sense of joining together through the metaphor of "melting."[20] Methodists hoped for moments when the distances between people melted away in the furnace of God's love. A "cry among mourners [those who sought conversion]" and a "loud shout among professors [those already converted]" proclaimed the audible and visible rising of the audience toward such an emotional peak that they could feel themselves as one.[21]

With other believers and with his fellow preachers, Young reveled in the sense of community and of spiritual elevation that Methodist life and worship offered. But with such high expectations of the deepest sense of community and of spiritual commitment, he inevitably faced disappointment. Much of his experience was one of alienation: alienation from the wider society that did not accept the faith and discipline of Methodism; alienation from the changes that he perceived within the Methodist community; and ultimately alienation from his own body and self. Methodists in the eighteenth and early nineteenth centuries considered themselves a people who withdrew from the sinful world into a spiritual community of faith, experience, and discipline. Neighbors who met them with hostility and even violence reinforced the Methodists' sense of being different from them. Indeed, it was virtually a point of pride for Methodist preachers to face, and to face down, opposition. When preacher James Meacham wrote to Young that "the Messengers of Satan hath Scourg'd and Buffeted me well, with their Raged Tongues," he finished with some pride,"bless God he hath not Suffer'd them to lay their hands upon me."[22]

Young himself recounted several instances of attacks or potential attacks. One opponent, for example, "sent a very lusty fighting man to beat" Young, but the preacher "Reproved him very sharply," and, as proof that "power belongeth to God," the rude fighter "opened not his mouth."[23] When "the basor [sic] sort had ploted to beat" Young one day at Plank Chapel meeting house, he was protected by God and the magistrate. On another occasion, Young was preaching with great success— "there was a great shout"—so much so that "the devil got mad & an old man rose from his seat & turned into bawling as loud as he could & came to me I expected a blow," but once again Young escaped harm.[24]

One of the most significant ways in which Methodists set themselves apart from the society in which they lived was in their biracial community. They were far from alone in their practice of holding worship services attended by both blacks and whites. Following Wesley's tradition of challenging overlapping hierarchies, however, white Methodists in Virginia often went farther than their neighbors would allow in extending brotherhood and sisterhood to people of African descent. Thus, although Episcopalians might place blacks in the balcony of a church so that they might hear the word of God, Methodists not only heard preaching in biracial congregations but also went so far as to practice foot washing and love feasts across racial lines.[25] John Wesley Young, like other Methodists, accepted and participated in biracial fellowship. He frequently preached to congregations of blacks and whites together.[26] He found worship among African Americans uplifting, as, for example, when he "preached a funeral for a Coloured man that died happy in the Lord" and "felt greatly assured by the Lord" and "had a good time at the grave."[27] Occasionally Young found his relationships with African Americans a point of contention among some of his neighbors. "I suppose I gave some offence," he wrote in 1826, "because I asked a Colourd brother to go to prayer & did not ask a Mr H. who hath been excommunicated from the Church."[28]

Young was certain that spiritual status counted for more than race when it came to being included in the religious life of his community. For all of his sense of spiritual brotherhood with black Methodists, however, Young was no egalitarian in this world. He held slaves for most of his life. He also found lack of deference among black worshipers frustrating. Holding a "love feast for the Collord People" one day, he lashed out at the "dull" group and complained of the blacks' "preajudice against the white Preachers."[29] He could not, ultimately, see African Americans as true brothers and sisters. His expectation that blacks should respond to his efforts and his lack of self-reflection about his own position as a white slaveholder proclaiming "liberty to the captives" left him as alienated from his black neighbors as he was from white neighbors who disapproved of how much he accepted blacks into fellowship.[30]

Over the long decades of his service, Young also expressed alienation from the Methodist community itself—more specifically, from the internal strife and directions of change that Methodism followed. The Methodist movement was a great success in terms of numbers of converts. Methodism grew from a small movement within the Church of England to the largest Protestant denomination in the United States in less than a century.[31] By the time of Young's death, Methodism had spread to the North, South, and West and had gained tens of thousands of converts. Yet Young emphasized the failings of the faith. In part his disappointment arose from unsurprising levels of controversy among those in the church. Young advocated emphasis on holiness or sanctification; some of his fellows did not.[32] In the 1820s and 1830s, Young opposed the reformers within Methodism who would eventually form the Methodist Protestant Church.[33] Young believed that he stood for traditional and true Methodist doctrine and government; he was stung by the "reproach" that fell upon him for his views.[34] Camp meetings that should have renewed the sense of community instead became reminders of distance between Young and his fellow preachers.[35]

Young also expressed disappointment with his congregations. Although his preaching could still inspire "melting & weeping," he could no longer see such powerful experiences as typical. Instead he lamented, "alas it appears that all Preaching of late of no Effect."[36] His congregations remained "cold" far too often.[37] Young could not see in others the depth of experience that he had encountered in his own conversion, and he did not find in his community the emotional commitment and bonding that the ideal of conversion had promised. Perhaps his sense of alienation also reflected the changing place of Methodism in the wider society; the movement turned increasingly to institution building; education; acceptance of existing social arrangements, including slavery; and a new ideal of respectability over the span of Young's life.[38]

If evangelicals, including Methodists, were to live in, but not of, the world, they faced a similar dilemma with reference to the self. The process of conversion meant turning away from oneself and toward God; an essential aspect of evangelical religion was, thus, the denial of the self. At the same time, evangelicals believed that they had to tell the stories of their spiritual experiences, both to demonstrate to their peers the validity of their experiences and to provide models of Christian experience to others. Methodist Bishop Francis Asbury asked preachers, in particular, to write accounts of their spiritual experiences.[39] Thus, those who had to deny the self had also to celebrate the self—a tension that tormented John Wesley Young.[40]

Every year on his birthday, Young reflected on the year past and on his life as a preacher and as a Christian. His first such journal entry was May 10, 1815:

> This day I am 68 years old O what a mercy that so unworthy & Unprofitable a Servant as I am should be so long Spared in the land of hope & among the living when I look back on the past year & See how far I have lived below My previlige [*sic*] and how unprofitable I have been I have cause to blush before My God. O for grace for the time to come be my days many or few they may be spent to the Glory of God, I thank the Lord that I am what, I am. I am able to preach & my voice is nearly as loud and strong as it was ten years ago O that I could be more usefull to my fellow men, that I could be more holy & more than ever Glorify the name of the Lord.[41]

The last such entry, on May 10, 1837, was written when Young was approaching death. Again, he bemoaned, "how far I hav lived from the Lord & the Privelidge that I have been favoured with." His final entry was more typical than the first in its review of the spiritual experience that brought him to Methodism: "Thirty years I lived with very little concern about my pore Soul in the year 1778 I join'd the Methodis society but lived a Carless [*sic*] live . . . in the year 1786 I was brought on a bed of affliction wich proved a bless[ing] to my Soul the blessed of Grace was abundantly deepened in my Soul." In addition to his conversion experience, Young remembered his call to preach: "I thought it duty to my God to warn my fellow mrotels [*sic*] to flee the wrath to come . . . the August following I had such a Call from God that I thought I could not hold my peace & . . . Continued until the present."[42]

In these entries he wrestled with himself: Young could celebrate his commitment to God, but he always had to fall short. He was called forward for what he considered the most noble of work, but he had to deny that self-assertion played a role in that call. Part of Young's solution to the dilemma, posed by the requirement that he assert himself and deny himself simultaneously, was to attribute the motive force in his putting himself forward to God. He and other preachers understood the call to preach as coming upon them from God; the decision to preach was not a human decision but rather a requirement that descended from above.[43] Consistent with that understanding, Young often wrote of his power as a preacher as if it were not his own but rather a force that flowed through him from God. The "Spirit of God" made him able to "Speak with some degree of Power"; similarly, he "was Assisted to speak with Power & in the Spirit."[44] As he grew older, the gap between his physical ability to preach and the actual power of his preaching widened. At the age of eighty-one, he went to a preaching appointment with "such a swimming in my head" that he did not know whether he could fulfill his responsibilities to the congregation. When he went forward to preach, however, the "Lord Removed it all," and Young "Preached as an Alarming sermon as I had for months."[45]

Although Young always believed that his spiritual self was more significant than his physical self, that the eternal world held true omnipotence and this world only ephemeral power, his sense of the limitations of this life necessarily grew stronger as he aged. As he passed from his seventies into his eighties, Young's annual accounting to himself on each birthday not only looked back to his conversion and his call to preach but now also looked forward to the eternal life that he expected to come. Ten years and more before his death, Young began to anticipate that he was "shortly to appear in Eternity." In 1829, still eight years before his death, he wrote," I am now on the brink or margin of Grave, & nothing more Certain than a few more days my short Span of life will run out." As his body declined, his writing revealed more and more a wish to be finished with "the labours and toiles" of this world.[46]

The hard lives of Methodist preachers did not lend themselves to longevity. Many circuit riders never saw their fiftieth birthdays; preachers who "located" could not anticipate much more. John Wesley Young, through good genes, a hardy disposition, or, as he would have said, through the grace of God, followed his calling past his ninetieth birthday. By the time of his death the people called Methodist had grown from a disruptive movement within the Anglican Church to become one of the largest religious groups in the United States; had carried their ideas of faith, experience, and discipline to people who lived on the edges of the frontier as well as on the East Coast; had come to some accommodation with the society in which they lived; and had begun to have an institutional presence through conferences and colleges well beyond the little meeting houses and camp meeting grounds from which much of their energy had sprung. Tragically for Young, he could not see all of the energy, growth, and success of his own denomination as an unmitigated good. Instead, in his final years, he could only yearn to be set free of responsibilities in a world in which even Methodists seemed to have gone wrong. At the end of ninety years, he found his rest.

Notes

1. Major sources for the study of John Wesley Young are his Autobiography (1818) and his Journal (1814–1837) (hereafter cited as Autobiography or as Journal), both in the John Wesley Young Papers, Perkins Library, Duke University, Durham, NC (hereafter cited as Young Papers).

2. On the First Great Awakening and the introduction of evangelicalism in the colonies, see Wesley M. Gewehr, *The Great Awakening in Virginia, 1740–1790* (Durham, NC, 1930); and Rhys Isaac, *The Transformation of Virginia, 1740–1790* (Chapel Hill, NC, 1982).

3. Nathan Hatch, *The Democratization of American Christianity* (New Haven, CT, 1989).

4. See Elmer T. Clark, J. Manning Potts, and Jacob S. Payton, eds., *The Journal and Letters of Francis Asbury*, 3 vols. (Nashville, TN, 1958); Nathan Bangs, *A History of the Methodist Episcopal Church*, 4 vols. (New York, 1841); and Russell E. Richey, *Early American Methodism* (Bloomington, IN, 1991).

5. Autobiography [4]. John H. Wigger argues that artisan and small merchant backgrounds were common among Methodist preachers and allowed them to identify and communicate with their audiences. John H. Wigger, *Taking Heaven by Storm: Methodism and the Rise of Popular Christianity in America* (New York, 1998), 49.

6. Young owned seven slaves in 1790, the year of the first official U.S. census. "Halifax District, Franklin County, North Carolina, 1790 Census," ftp.rootsweb.com/pub/usgenweb/nc/franklin/census/frnk1790.txt.

7. Autobiography [7].

8. Ibid. [8–9]; the phrase was originally Wesley's.

9. Young refers in his Autobiography to his wife and to travelers joining him in prayer, but he does not mention either his children or his slaves. Ibid. [11].

10. Ibid. [11]. Also see Christine Leigh Heyrman, *Southern Cross: The Beginnings of the Bible Belt* (New York, 1998), chapter 1; and Wigger, *Taking Heaven by Storm*, 106–23.

11. Evangelical conversion is discussed in Virginia Lieson Brereton, *From Sin to Salvation: Stories of Women's Conversion, 1800 to the Present* (Bloomington, IN, 1991); Rodger Payne, *The Self and the Sacred: Conversion and Autobiography in Early American Protestantism* (Knoxville, TN, 1998); and Donald G. Mathews, *Religion in the Old South* (Chicago, 1977).

12. Rhys Isaac points to the significance of cockfighting as a ritual through which the values of the Virginia gentry were expressed, dramatized, and reinforced; Isaac argues that evangelicals posed a "countercultural" challenge to the dominant values of the Virginia gentry and symbolized their counterculture, in part, through rejecting such practices as the cockfight. Isaac, *The Transformation of Virginia*.

13. Autobiography [12].

14. Young made notes on his own understanding of conversion in his Journal in 1834. Under the heading "A Few Remarks on Conversion," he wrote, "Conversion is the turning or total change of a Sinner from his sins to God and is produced by the influence of divine grace on the soul. Conversion evidences itself by ardent love to God . . . delight in his people . . . Attendance on his Ordinances . . . Confidence in the Promises of God . . . ." Journal, July 27, 1834.

15. Autobiography [16].

16. Ibid. [16–18].

17. Although Young took a brief tour on a circuit after the death of his first wife, he concluded that he was unwilling to subject his aging body to the trials of full-fledged circuit riding again; and, he noted, he was not ready to "brake up housekeeping and put myself dependent on my Children or any one of them." Ibid. [26].

18. Young preached at Plank Chapel, Bethel, Rockspring, Jerusalem, Kingswood, Ebenezer, Antioch, and Shiloh, all in North Carolina, as well as at a number of homes and plantations; although not a circuit rider in the full sense during much of his life, he was certainly a traveling preacher. See Journal, passim, for the locations at which he preached.

19. Journal, June 25, 1820, and October 8, 1820.

20. For example, ibid., August 6, 1814, September 17, 1814, May 18, 1823, May 20, 1832, and May 3, 1835; Richey, *Early American Methodism*, 3.

21. Journal, January 23, 1823.

22. James Meacham to Dear Brother [Young], July 21, 1788, Young Papers.

23. Autobiography [22].

24. Ibid. [23].

25. Methodists frequently practiced segregation as well; class meetings were segregated by sex as well as by race, and camp meetings usually had an area reserved for black worshipers. Richey, *Early American Methodism*, 4–5; Heyrman, *Southern Cross*, 21–22 and 67.

26. For example, Journal, September 24, 1814, July 14, 1833, May 17, 1835, and August 2, 1835.

27. Ibid., April 13, 1823; see also October 28, 1827.

28. Ibid., March 22, 1826.

29. Ibid., June 25, 1826.

30. Donald G. Mathews applies the biblical injunction to antebellum evangelicalism in chapter 6 of his *Religion in the Old South* (Chicago, 1977). On the ambiguity

of Methodists' attitudes toward slavery and toward African Americans, see Donald G. Mathews, *Slavery and Methodism: A Chapter in American Morality* (Princeton, NJ, 1965); and Wigger, *Taking Heaven by Storm*, 139–146. On evangelicals more generally, see Sylvia R. Frey and Betty Wood, *Come Shouting to Zion: African American Protestantism in the American South and British Caribbean to 1830* (Chapel Hill, NC, 1998), especially 140–41, 176–78.

31. Edwin S. Gaustad gives the following figures on the growth of Methodism: 64,894 in 1800; 174,560 in 1810; 273,858 in 1820; 511,153 in 1830; about 1,000,000 in 1840; and 1,250,000 in 1850. Edwin S. Gaustad, *Historical Atlas of Religion in America* (New York, 1962), 79–82. John H. Wigger opens his recent work with a discussion of the growth of Methodism; idem, *Taking Heaven by Storm*, 3–6.

32. Autobiography [45], Journal, October 23, 1814, and October 17, 1815.

33. Journal, May 24, 1829, May 10, 1832, and September 30, 1833. The area where Young lived in the second half of his life had also seen the rise of the Republican Methodist, or O'Kellyite, schism in the 1790s.

34. Journal, May 10, 1832.

35. Ibid., August 15, 1829, August 10–13, 1833, and September 20, 1833.

36. Ibid., May 3, 1835, and June 14, 1835.

37. Ibid., February 15, 1835.

38. Such changes are discussed in Mathews, *Religion in the Old South*; idem, *Slavery and Methodism*; Anne C. Loveland, *Southern Evangelicals and the Social Order, 1800–1860* (Baton Rouge, LA, 1980); and Heyrman, *Southern Cross*.

39. Asbury to George Roberts, February 4, 1801, in Francis Asbury, *Journal and Letters*, ed. Elmer T. Clark, Manning Potts, and Jacob S. Payton, 3 vols. (Nashville, TN, 1958), 3:199.

40. This tension is explored in Rodger Payne, *The Self and the Sacred: Conversion and Autobiography in Early American Protestanism* (Knoxville, TN, 1998).

41. Journal, May 10, 1815.

42. Ibid., May 10, 1837.

43. For other accounts of the call to preach, see Virginia Conference Autobiographies, Duke University Special Collections; and Nathan Bangs, *A History of the Methodist Episcopal Church*, 4 vols. (New York, 1841), 4:15.

44. Journal, April 24, 1836, and April 27, 1834. On Methodism as a movement of the voice, see Richey, *Early American Methodism*, 82–83.

45. Journal, April 27, 1828; see also ibid., March 15, 1835.

46. Ibid., May 10, 1826, May 10, 1829, and May 10, 1835; see also ibid., May 10, 1833.

Suggested Readings

Bangs, Nathan. *A History of the Methodist Episcopal Church*. 4 vols. New York, 1841.

Boles, John B. *The Great Revival: The Origins of the Southern Evangelical Mind.* Lexington, KY, 1972.

Cartwright, Peter. *Autobiography of Peter Cartwright.* Edited by Charles L. Wallis. 1856. Reprint, Nashville, TN, 1984.

Frey, Sylvia R., and Betty Wood. *Come Shouting to Zion: African American Protestantism in the American South and British Caribbean to 1830.* Chapel Hill, NC, 1998.

Hatch, Nathan. *The Democratization of American Christianity.* New Haven, CT, 1989.

Heyrman, Christine Leigh. *Southern Cross: The Beginnings of the Bible Belt.* New York, 1998.

Isaac, Rhys. *The Transformation of Virginia, 1740–1790.* Chapel Hill, NC, 1982.

Loveland, Anne C. *Southern Evangelicals and the Social Order, 1800–1860.* Baton Rouge, LA, 1980.

Mathews, Donald G. *Religion in the Old South.* Chicago, 1977.

Payne, Rodger. *The Self and the Sacred: Conversion and Autobiography in Early American Protestantism.* Knoxville, TN, 1998.

Richey, Russell E. *Early American Methodism.* Bloomington, IN, 1991.

Schneider, A. Gregory. *The Way of the Cross Leads Home: The Domestication of Early American Methodism.* Bloomington, IN, 1993.

Wigger, John H. *Taking Heaven by Storm: Methodism and the Rise of Popular Christianity in America.* New York, 1998.

3

Trotter & Sons
Merchants and the Early West

Craig Thompson Friend

James Trotter and his sons took advantage of a growing frontier and the economic opportunities that flourished on it. As merchants in Kentucky, Trotter & Sons embraced the philosophy of self-interest that lay at the heart of modern, liberal capitalism and that challenged colonial republicanism's commitment to a common good. At the same time that Thomas Jefferson and like-minded republicans were arguing that an expansive and expanding country would ensure the permanence of a simple agrarian nation, Trotter and other opportunistic merchants were bringing capitalism to the farthest reaches of the republic. Yet the transformation and growth of a market economy produced strains in society that were no less dramatic than those seen and experienced in politics and religion. If the rudimentary condition of Kentucky's economy and society provided Trotter and others with the prospect of personal advancement and wealth, older ideas of community and mutual responsibility posed a challenge to, and placed limits on, their self-aggrandizement. In the end, James Trotter and his sons George and Samuel had to strike a balance between their pursuit of the main chance, on the one hand, and, on the other, their obligations as merchants and community leaders to their neighbors and customers. The Trotters' story demonstrates the opportunities, difficulties, and uncertainties of the market revolution.

Craig Thompson Friend is an assistant professor of history at the University of Central Florida, Orlando. He is editor and contributor to *The Buzzel about Kentuck: Settling the Promised Land* (1999). His current research project focuses on community, capitalism, and values along Kentucky's Maysville Road in the early republic.

In 1784, James Trotter moved his family—his wife, two sons, brother, and parents—to the Bluegrass region of Kentucky where, after a few years of farming, he turned his attentions to a mercantile business in Lexington. Thirteen years later, when he handed the enterprise over to his sons, they transformed it from a local store into the center of a commercial empire that stretched from the East Coast to New Orleans to the trans-Mississippi West. The notion that trans-Appalachian settlers lived in a geographically isolated commercial vacuum obviously misrepresents the reality and distorts their aspirations. Many Americans of the republic's early West wanted more than the self-sufficient lifestyle characteristic of a pioneer world, and they worked earnestly toward the day when they could have more.

In the 1780s, James Trotter was just one of thousands of migrants to wander into Kentucky. For most, Jeffersonian exaltations of the "richest & best poor mans Country in the World" fostered a land hunger that would never be satisfied. By the end of the century, only 49.2 percent of the state's heads of household owned land. Although Kentucky's landless rates approximated the national average, its land distribution was the least egalitarian of the western settlements and ranked with the more stratified societies of New York, South Carolina, and Georgia as having the most unequal apportionment of wealth and property in the new nation. Those without property found Kentucky to be more a quagmire than a republican garden. Consequently, the high land-to-labor ratio that originally enticed settlers to the region reversed to a high labor-to-available-land ratio, creating large numbers of tenant farmers and urban workers.[1]

Trotter was one of the fortunate, securing land and establishing a farm just west of Paris in Bourbon County. Still, despite his landownership, he was unsatisfied with the agrarian yeoman life. For men like Trotter, agriculture failed to satisfy their desires to profit from the maturing economic structures of Kentucky. As the grossly unequal distribution of land augured the failure of aspirations for an agrarian republic in the region, Trotter and other hopeful entrepreneurs turned their attentions to commercial development. Trotter chose merchandising as his career and procured enough credit from suppliers in Philadelphia and Baltimore to manage for twelve months, a sufficient length of time to determine whether his store would be sustainable and even profitable. In an economically expansive region like Kentucky, merchants faced little difficulty establishing their businesses; sustaining the enterprise was the real challenge. Just as land acquisition eluded many new settlers, so too did mercantile success often remain beyond the grasp of many entrepreneurs. "Kentuckey, is filled with Merchants, that know not what to Do with there [*sic*] goods," reported land speculator John May in 1796, "and it is the opinion of People in generall that more than two thirds of them will be ruin'd."[2]

Yet, because of his cultural background, James Trotter may have had a slight advantage over other merchants. Most settlers of Kentucky in the late eighteenth century migrated from the backcountries of North Carolina, Virginia, Maryland, and Pennsylvania. They brought with them cultural traditions quite distinct from those of Piedmont and Tidewater Virginia, or of eastern Pennsylvania and New Jersey, or of New England. Migrants from all these regions relocated to Kentucky, creating a cultural pluralism seldom acknowledged by historians. But the backcountrymen composed the largest population of Kentuckians.[3]

Still, they were not the most influential. Virginians from the Tidewater and Piedmont regions early came to dominate the political and social culture of central Kentucky. Virginian gentry like George Nicholas and John Breckinridge led the state's 1792 and 1799 constitutional conventions, respectively. And, despite some trends toward democratic participation found in those constitutions, the gentry's preservation of slaveholding, more oligarchical systems of local government, and the institution of voice voting (through which they heard exactly who voted for and against them) evidenced Virginians' conceptualizations of society in hierarchical terms of rank and deference based upon land ownership. Of course, the majority of Virginians who relocated to Kentucky were not the Old Dominion's greatest planters. In fact, much has been made of these Virginians' status as second and third sons of Tidewater gentlemen, desperate to escape the worn-out soils of the Piedmont. Still, they were members of a cultural group that emphasized hierarchy through symbol and action. Lower class people deferred to social elites; in return, the gentry responded with kindness and respect. Consequently, the goal of most Virginians, and thus their desires to control the political structures of the state, was to instill a genteel, hierarchical order on a frontier region.[4]

Even though they shared a Protestant faith and the English language with Virginians, backcountry people's perceptions of the world differed dramatically. Ethnically they were a blend of north Briton, Irish, and Scots-Irish. Before they migrated west of the Appalachians, backcountry folk had blended their cultures into a unique set of folkways. In contrast to Virginians' plantation-style brick and frame manors that arose amid the gently rolling hills of the Bluegrass, backcountry migrants settled in dispersed patterns of log cabins alongside creeks and springs to assure water accessibility, as they had done east of the mountains. Backcountry frolics, like cornhuskings and logrollings, became moments of rare revelry and sociability. Yet even as such contests strengthened the individualism that was characteristic of backcountry settlement patterns and culture, frolics often ended in drunken brawls and eye-gouging contests, thereby reinforcing a reputation for lawlessness and disorderliness—the "frontier" character of Kentucky that unnerved Virginians' sense of order.[5]

James Trotter arrived in central Kentucky as an elite backcountryman, a rewarding position as the region developed culturally. Clumsily situated between backcountrymen and Virginians, the backcountry elite of landowners and military officers provided a cultural bridge between the two worlds. Because education and heritage were not venerated by most backcountry folk, wealth and conspicuous consumption became more important as determinants of rank—circumstances that meshed nicely with Virginians' appreciation of refinement. Before emigrating west, therefore, those backcountrymen who enjoyed some wealth had risen to some social standing among their neighbors. Most would experiment with farming in Kentucky, but not as their primary occupations. One example, of course, was James Trotter of Augusta County, Virginia; others were Samuel Brown of the same county who became a prominent physician; John Postlethwait of Carlisle, Pennsylvania, who became central Kentucky's most successful tavernkeeper; and Nathaniel and Thomas Hart of Hagerstown, Maryland, who succeeded first as merchants, then as hemp manufacturers, and finally as bankers. Because they were elite backcountrymen, they commanded respect from the majority of people from the same region. Yet they also positioned themselves socially to mingle with the gentry and establish political and economic alliances that would prove beneficial later.[6]

Late-eighteenth-century Kentucky, then, because of its rudimentary economic and cultural development, appeared ideal for men of Trotter's status and ambitions. Yet the success of merchants depended as much on citizens' ideas about the place of commerce within a community as it did on merchants' efforts to draw customers. In that sense, Trotter's decision to relocate from Bourbon County to Lexington was wise. Within this center of Virginian gentility, a rage for refined goods bolstered the fortunes of merchants. Simultaneously, as the political and economic center of the region, Lexington drew backcountry people to its court days and market days, when they bartered agricultural and domestic products for goods that made them feel happier, warmer, or better looking. Although the need to live in independent self-sufficiency appealed to many, a desire to enjoy the fruits of their labors and achieve a higher standard of living encouraged commercial participation. The musings of a northern Kentuckian in the 1790s reiterated the point in a more lyrical manner: "May the Lord be praised/how I am a mased/to see how things have mended/hot cake and tea/for supper I see/When mush and milk was intended." Although the author clearly preferred the refined meal of hot cake and tea over the mush and milk of a less opulent life, more significant is the use of the term "mended," implying that mere subsistence was just a temporary consequence of relocation.[7]

Stocking their shelves with imported fabrics and wines, James Trotter and his brother opened a store along Main Street in Lexington, hoping to profit from others' desires for better quality goods and commercial opportunities. Like eastern merchants, Trotter attended to the one service that large numbers of customers demanded: accessibility to those commodities that settlers had not wanted to leave behind when relocating to a less developed area. The Trotter mercantile was more than just an import house, however. As a multifaceted merchant, James Trotter also exported domestic products, retailed, wholesaled, insured shipments, and offered loans from his store. His early success elevated his political status in the town. He served at the 1792 state constitutional convention; by 1805, he held a seat on Transylvania University's Board of Trustees; and he sporadically represented his district in the state assembly until 1823.[8]

Although the details of his financial status are unknown, Trotter undoubtedly not only survived but also excelled in his first years as a western entrepreneur. Yet his business acumen may seem successful only because of his political affluence. Still, that appearance offers hints about the relationship of merchants to community. Certainly, in order to draw political support, any aspirant had to demonstrate a sense of moral obligation and responsibility to his neighbors. Merchants earned such reputations by operating respectful economic households, a difficult goal indeed for some merchants.

For example, in 1793, Irwin & Bryson's mercantile opened in Lexington. Their Philadelphia sponsor was William Hunt, whose own son John Wesley would one day become the first millionaire west of the Appalachians. Bryson, whose first name has been lost to history, began squandering the store's profits almost immediately. In late 1793 local merchants urged Thomas Irwin to dissolve the partnership before his associate dragged the entire enterprise into debt. Fearful of acting without Hunt's consent, however, Irwin hesitated and, in November, left for the Ohio River port town of Maysville where he could oversee the unloading of shipments. Meanwhile, Bryson made daily appearances at the mercantile, spending one to two hours bossing around the employees and "Gambling and Paying his Losses out of the Store." On his return, Irwin fell into a rage and convinced Bryson that he could best repair the damage by accompanying a shipment to New Orleans. The latter eagerly agreed, but not for the reasons that Irwin assumed. When he arrived in the port city, Bryson sold the goods and spent the profit "aplaying at Billiards." The expenses for the trip exceeded the return. By April 1795, Bryson had foiled Irwin and Hunt's plans for a store in Lexington. "I blame you exceedingly for not destroying the partnership," Patrick Moore wrote to Irwin. As Bryson's uncle and a store creditor, Moore fumed that Irwin "should have done it instantly and secured the property for the payment of y[ou]r debts. . . . [When] I get a little more composed I will write you on other matters." Within two years, Hunt granted power of attorney to four Lexington merchants who disposed of the late Irwin & Bryson mercantile.[9]

As another example, in June 1796, John A. Seitz discovered that his partner, who was in Philadelphia supposedly procuring goods, instead spent his hours "in this infernall Practis of Gaming." "*For Godsake, be more prudent—more Just—towards our Creditors yourselfe & toward me,*" scolded Seitz; "reflect one minut on the Situation of J. Bryson & you cannot hesitate to quit gambling." And Bryson had brought a whole commercial enterprise crashing to the ground without consideration of the store or its customers! Indeed, merchants struggled with the temptation of gambling regularly.[10]

When conscientious merchants dealt with prodigal partners, the true nature of the mercantile business shone through. The shenanigans of their partners disparaged the values, particularly trustworthiness and industriousness, of the consumers that Irwin and Seitz hoped to entice into their stores. At stake was the merchant's socioeconomic relationship with the store's customers, a relationship that reflected a communal sense of moral obligation and responsibility. A successful merchant like Trotter was one who blended his own profit orientation with an attentiveness to moral accountability.

The issue became part of a larger debate taking place throughout America in the late eighteenth century about values and capitalism. Much of the discourse centered on the role of merchants, and for good reason. In tune with the social patterns of revolutionary America, early Kentuckians assumed men of commerce would act as economic patriarchs over households whose members became bound to mercantiles through networks of credit and barter. That they could not restrain their own partners suggested much about the management of the economic households that Irwin and Seitz headed. No wonder concerns about merchants' communal responsibilities arose. In 1798 "A New and True Friend" queried readers of the *Kentucky Gazette*, "Have the merchants in Kentucky arranged and conducted their plan of commerce as to enrich the state; and encreased the quantity of money in the country?" Why had Kentucky's entrepreneurs not created "a system as will combine in one point of view, and evidently promote the interests of the FARMER, the MANUFACTURER, the MECHANIC, the MERCHANT, and the PROPRIETOR OF LANDS"? "New and True Friend" did not refute that men of commerce had a role in agrarian society, for indeed they did and always had. Instead he questioned their apparent intentions to bind the local economy to a larger market network, a process that he perceived as driven by self-interested profit making. According to the editorialist, merchants ignored their moral responsibilities: they failed to incorporate all members of the economic community into their plans.[11]

Thus, while the initial risks involved in establishing a mercantile business were financial, the ultimate stake proved to be ideological. In 1797, therefore, when James Trotter retired from the family business and passed the ledger books to his sons, George and Samuel, the recent moral failures of other local merchants could not have escaped their attentions. But in a twist of logic, the sons' response was to do the very thing that "New and True Friend" feared—bind the local economy to a larger market network so that the store in Lexington merely served as the hub of an extensive commercial empire. In so doing, they proved themselves capable economic patriarchs.[12]

In the type of mercantile empire that George and Samuel Trotter endeavored to create, both distant and regional trade needed to be addressed. Suppliers in the East dictated the terms of distant trade with western merchants. The Trotters' suppliers, Bickham and Reese in Philadelphia, and their middleman, James Adams of Pittsburgh, shipped factory-manufactured goods down the Ohio River to Maysville, where workers unloaded the deliveries and sent them by wagon to Lexington. Imports ranged from unprocessed items, such as glass, dyes, and metals (including iron, tin, and copper), to semidurables and consumables, such as tea, Bibles, and queensware ceramics. Keelboats left every four weeks from Pittsburgh laden with merchandise from Baltimore, Philadelphia, New York City, and Alexandria. But the distance from eastern markets posed problems. In the winters, those goods might sit uselessly at Pittsburgh as shippers waited for the Ohio River to thaw. Or, when suppliers tried to send shipments overland, "bad men" in the Pennsylvania mountains often robbed caravans.[13]

If the goods sat uselessly upstream, so too did recent economic news. When John W. Hunt opened his business in 1795, his brother Abijah stayed in Philadelphia to purchase and transport merchandise. The siblings had expected to clear a 40 percent profit in Kentucky. In 1797 as diplomatic relations with France strained, Abijah panicked, cautioning his brother that economic conditions in Philadelphia demanded a speedy change in their business transactions. "Trade is much Stagnated— produce will not Sell, not a Merchant will Ship at this time," wrote Abijah, "the calls for money are as loud and as numerous as ever." He prophesied that the same would happen in Kentucky shortly and that, if his letter arrived in time, John could avoid the catastrophe by refusing barter sales; "to sell goods without money ought to be out of the question," Abijah warned.[14]

Exportation was as problematic as importation. In most cases, Kentucky's produce did not bear the expense of transportation to Philadelphia, but shipment to New Orleans could prove worthwhile. In 1802 the French tourist François André Michaux realized what almost every Kentuckian already knew about the Mississippi River: "twenty-five pounds weight would cost more expediting that way [to Philadelphia], even going up the Ohio, than a thousand by that river." In the 1790s the cry had gone out for better market connections. By 1793, hoping to push the federal government into securing export privileges through New Orleans, the Lexington Democratic Society pronounced that "the free and undisturbed use and navigation of the river Mississippi is the NATURAL RIGHT of the inhabitants of the countries bordering on the waters communicating with that river, and is unalienable except with the SOIL." In a 1798 congressional debate over taxation, Kentucky representative Thomas T. Davis explained how his constituents would gladly support a direct tax if Congress would aid them in opening the Mississippi River to greater trade. Kentuckians "had produce of every kind, in abundance," he declared, "but they want a market for it." The promise of Kentucky would enliven the national economy if only the market networks could be expanded. A Lexington merchant proclaimed that, in America, "five millions of people can raise more wheat than two millions [the number before the revolution] did formerly—and I can neither see, nor hear of any new markets." In the absence of federal efforts to establish markets and trade, merchants assumed responsibility for the process.[15]

As the primary problem facing aspiring merchants like the Trotters, the export of agricultural produce and domestic products to market commanded their monies and energies. They advertised relentlessly for "hands to work my boats." They also suffered substantial setbacks when Kentucky-crafted keelboats collapsed in the torrent of the mighty Mississippi. In 1805, John W. Hunt's shipment sank just north of New Orleans with $323 worth of flour aboard. Nothing was salvageable. If produce arrived safely in New Orleans, intermediaries normally purchased the goods "in order to Ship." In the 1790s a bribe to a Spanish official usually procured access through the port. By the early 1800s, wise merchants like Nathaniel Hart sent their sons to join New Orleans' middleman firms or even to form their own; Hart, Bartlett, & Cox became the principal exporter for Kentucky products by the eve of the War of 1812.[16]

Economic disasters like that which struck John W. Hunt inspired merchants to push the state assembly toward incorporation of the Kentucky Insurance Company. Chartered in 1803 for sixteen years as an insurer of river-trade vessels, the enterprise was enthusiastically received by Lexington's mercantile sector. In its first year, only seven men held stock in the company: Six were merchants in Lexington. And the enthusiasm persisted into 1804, when, at a sale of company stock, 143 shares sold at $105 each in less that ten minutes. Such institutions reeked of eastern corruption and favored certain sectors of society—those with fluid capital over those with land. By 1805, when the legislature chartered the Bank of Kentucky, many citizens voiced suspicion of the Kentucky Insurance Company and demanded that the assembly include a provision retaining the right to pack the bank's board of directors if, or when, it implemented policies contrary to popular or legislative opinions about how a financial institution should operate. Legislators hoped that this one principle, that of moral accountability to the larger society, would differentiate the bank from the increasingly less-than-popular Kentucky Insurance Company. Still, the establishment of the Kentucky Insurance Company and, later, the Bank of Kentucky erected a financial system that would enhance merchants' abilities to expand their individual enterprises.[17]

As the financial problems were addressed, Thomas Jefferson's orchestration of the Louisiana Purchase in 1803 theoretically should have solved the geographical problems. Instead, "it will be very difficult to do anything there [New Orleans] for 12 or 18 months," complained Wilson Hunt to his father; "from the quantities of goods and Adventurers that have gone there directly from England." After an influx of merchants into the lower Mississippi River valley ruined his plans to set up a store in Natchez, the younger Hunt opted to go west and establish a shop in Missouri Territory. Once again, his mercantile plans fell through: "too many goods here [St. Louis], and very little money." The opening of New Orleans exposed the entire Mississippi Valley to commercial expansion, flooding the settlements of the new West with people and products. And, in a pattern fairly familiar to many Kentuckians, every westerner whom Wilson Hunt met "is involved in debt beyond, far beyond their possessions." New Orleans middlemen, a flood of well-supplied entrepreneurs, the inability of customers to pay cash and ease the merchant's debt to his own creditors, and the trials of the Mississippi River itself—the Kentucky merchant had to navigate each of these or risk failure.[18]

George and Samuel Trotter also envisioned mercantile opportunity in the Mississippi Valley. Between 1805 and 1811 the brothers became the architects of an extensive western commercial network. In Kentucky, they had stores in Danville, Springfield, Russellville, Louisville, and Maysville, which they placed under the management of associates. They also sponsored stores in Ohio, Indiana, Tennessee, and the Missouri Territory. Most interesting about the Trotter empire were the patterns of exchange between the Lexington depot and the satellite stores. In return for cotton or promises of cash payment, stores to the west of Lexington received durable goods: linens, queensware, books, paper. When cash arrived in Lexington, it was forwarded to eastern suppliers. The cotton, however, was not sent east but to stores in Ohio and at Maysville, again in exchange for cash payments when they could be arranged. The Trotters also delivered hemp yarn to Hart, Bartlett & Cox, their exporting firm in New Orleans, as payment for shipping.[19]

In an ironic twist, the commercial empire of George and Samuel Trotter suggests the development of an economic sphere in the early West separate from the "national" market arising in the East. Before American control of New Orleans, Kentuckians clamored for ties to the national market; after all, congressman Thomas T. Davis's expectations had been that federal appropriation of the Mississippi River would enrich the United States (as well as Kentuckians' pockets) by drawing the West into a national economy. But after the Louisiana Purchase, a strong regional market arose along the Mississippi River. By the War of 1812 western financial and industrial developments had advanced to a point where they could support an independent regional market. Kentucky was at the forefront of this economic improvement, leading the nation in the production of hemp bagging, hemp rope, saltpeter, salt, and gunpowder, and second in maple sugar and blended cloth, all products largely financed by notes from the Kentucky Insurance Company or the Bank of Kentucky.[20]

What appears to have bound western merchants to the East, then, was not necessarily a need for manufactured goods (although such items certainly boosted profits) but the initial debt relations formed when westerners first established their enterprises. In fact, the only items that the Trotters sent eastward across the Appalachians were cash payments and promissory notes. Like other western merchants, the Trotters faced a serious shortage of cash payments, both in their Lexington store and in their commercial outposts. Eastern suppliers expected, indeed required, prompt payment in cash, preferably bank bills of the federal government. Convoys of fifteen to twenty horses carrying specie payments traveled from Lexington to Philadelphia regularly via the circuitous mountain passes of the Appalachians. But the very notes that subsidized industrial and commercial development in Kentucky were useless in the East. When the Trotters attempted to pay their Philadelphia suppliers Bickham & Reese in personal notes and notes drawn on the Kentucky Insurance Company, the Philadelphians returned the payment and demanded cash or a check drawn on the Bank of Baltimore.[21]

Likewise, the Trotters' Pittsburgh middleman, James Adams, only accepted payments from the Trotters in cash, although he acquiesced to payment in tobacco from John Armstrong, the Trotters' store manager in Maysville. Business between the Trotters and Adams was one of large-scale entrepreneurs communicating through intermediaries. But Armstrong was merely an associate, a small merchant who was often intimidated by the forceful demands of creditors and suppliers. Initially he attempted to satisfy Adams by appealing to the Trotters to send two bales of cotton "of the best kind, such as better than the last." Yet Adams rejected the payment, possibly hoping to exert greater influence over Armstrong in the future. After all, the store in Maysville, the first Kentucky port along the Ohio River, served as a depot for both Louisville and Cincinnati. Only by bartering directly with Adams was Armstrong eventually able to settle his debt with tobacco.[22]

Even though their business relationship with eastern suppliers was impersonal, the Trotters shared a much different relationship with their own associates. Although they also desired cotton and cash as payments, the brothers extended seemingly unlimited credit; indeed, months and years often passed without repayment. A sense of paternal obligation infused the transactions of this regional trade. As economic patriarchs, George and Samuel Trotter responded to the needs of their associates.

For example, John Armstrong's impotence in dealing with Adams arose from his sense that "I am in as much want of money as perhaps you." Although they were indeed desperate for cash themselves, the Trotters acted immediately (even if unsuccessfully) to satisfy their associate's debt. There was a sense that, as with any household, the problems of members should be resolved internally. When another associate, James Morrison of Maysville, could not collect on a customer's debt, the Trotters took up the endeavor without appeal to the courts, for "to do it as a Law Suit would be attended with trouble & Cost." With their careful management of the economic household came rewards; for example, associate Frederick Hite alerted the Trotters that "their [*sic*] is the greatest opening for selling goods at present in Russellville their is no course clothes of no kind their is no flannels no calico no muslins no knife & forks all sorts of house ware is a wanting. their is not cuttiers of no kind cotton Cards & groceries is a wanting." And yet, as a hint of the continued importance of neighborliness to traditional notions of economic patriarchy, Hise also expected the Trotters to "inform other merchants of the opportunity before it is too late."[23]

During the early republic, the distinctions between distant and regional trade revealed an emerging strain within American mercantile business. The reciprocal, mutually obligatory, commercial society of colonial America gave way to one characterized by specialization and detached avarice. But Kentucky and the West had yet to forsake that earlier notion of trade relations, at least within the economic household of George and Samuel Trotter. The reason may have been their strong connections to the culture of the backcountry citizenry: one in which trade implied reciprocity, in which mutuality permeated trade relations, and in which settlers strove toward the primary goal for which they had immigrated—collective economic improvement.[24]

Let there be no doubt, however, that the ones positioned best for economic improvement (and the accompanying political and social status) were merchants like George and Samuel Trotter. Their entrepreneurial pursuits not only created a western mercantile empire but led to a variety of peripheral activities, such as the production of gunpowder and Samuel's eventual role as director of the local branch of the Bank of the United States. In fact, when the War of 1812 erupted across the old Northwest, the Trotter's made a fortune from gunpowder sales, first to the U.S. Army and then to Indians in the Illinois Territory. Their success as economic patriarchs boosted their political aspirations; they had secured the respect of their clientele and appeared worthy representatives for the citizenry. Both men served as town trustees, positions that brought with them substantial influence over the economic development of Lexington, and George spent two terms in the state assembly.[25]

In 1815, just as the rewards of capitalism seemed most fruitful, George died. The loss of his brother and partner certainly had a profound effect on Samuel, who refused to change the name of the mercantile from S.&G. Trotter. For almost two more decades, Samuel continued the enterprises the two brothers had built upon the foundation laid by their father. By the mid-1820s, Samuel lost his father, wife, uncle, and younger brother as well. In 1833, as a cholera epidemic swept through central Kentucky, Samuel finally followed the family into death along with two daughters.[26]

The deaths of the Trotters, father and sons, serve as reminders that these men were merely human and subject to the same threats to life as the poorest tenant farmer or the lowliest slave. But the successes in their lives, from economic fortune to political clout, hint of their abilities to rise above the limitations of the early West. In a region where the dream of an agrarian republic foundered as most settlers could not secure a piece of land to farm and where the calls of urban opportunity were in the artisan shops or rudimentary manufactories of towns and villages, the Trotters exemplified the vanguard of a capitalist order that would transform the new nation during the early republic. Through the mercantile enterprises of entrepreneurs like James, George, and Samuel Trotter, the West became economically incorporated into the American nation.

Notes

1. R. C. Ballard Thruston, ed., "Letter by Edward Harris, 1797," *Filson Club Historical Quarterly* 2 (1928): 166 (quotation); Fredrika Johanna Teute, "Land, Liberty, and Labor in the Post-Revolutionary Era: Kentucky as the Promised Land" (Ph.D. diss., College of William and Mary, 1988), 632; James A. Henretta, "Families and Farms: *Mentalité* in Pre-Industrial America," *William and Mary Quarterly* 35 (1978): 6–9; Stephen A. Aron, "Pioneers and Profiteers: Land Speculation and the Homestead Ethic in Frontier Kentucky," *Western Historical Quarterly* 23 (1992): 179–98; Neal O. Hammon, "Settlers, Land Jobbers, and Outlyers: A Quantitative Analysis of Land Acquisition on the Kentucky Frontier," *Register of the Kentucky Historical Society* 84 (1986): 241–46; Thomas D. Clark, *Agrarian Kentucky* (Lexington, KY, 1977), 6–10; Patricia Watlington, *The Partisan Spirit: Kentucky Politics, 1779–1792* (New York, 1972), 11–34; Lee Soltow, "Kentucky Wealth at the End of the Eighteenth Century," *Journal of Economic History* 43 (1983): 632–33, and appendix; idem, *Distribution of Wealth and Income in the United States in 1798* (Pittsburgh, 1989), 77. For a discussion of the political consequences of landlessness, see Teute, "Land, Liberty, and Labor," 620–24.

2. François André Michaux, *Travels to the West of the Alleghany Mountains 1802*, in *Early Western Travels 1748–1846*, ed. Reuben Gold Thwaites, 36 vols. (Cleveland, OH, 1904–1906), 3:203; Howard C. Douds, "Merchants and Merchandising in Pittsburgh, 1759–1800," *Western Pennsylvania Historical Magazine* 20 (1937): 129–30; James A. Ramage, "The Hunts and Morgans: A Study of a Prominent Kentucky Family" (Ph.D. diss., University of Kentucky, 1972), 26; Thomas M. Doerflinger, *A Vigorous Spirit of Enterprise: Merchants and Economic Development in Revolutionary Philadelphia* (Chapel Hill, NC, 1986), 86; Dwight L. Smith, ed., *The Western Journals of John May: Ohio Company Agent and Business Advertiser* (Cincinnati, OH, 1961), 139 (quotation).

3. David Hackett Fisher, *Albion's Seed: Four British Folkways in America* (New York, 1989), 382–89.

4. James C. Klotter, *The Breckinridges of Kentucky 1760–1981* (Lexington, KY, 1986), 6, 25–27; Lowell H. Harrison, *John Breckinridge: Jeffersonian Republican* (Louisville, KY, 1969), 48–49; Gail S. Terry, "Family Empires: A Frontier Elite in Virginia and Kentucky, 1740–1815" (Ph.D. diss., College of William and Mary, 1992), 93.

5. Willard Rouse Jillson, *Pioneer Kentucky* (Frankfort, KY, 1934), 71–107; Frances L. S. Dugan and Jacqueline P. Bull, eds., *Bluegrass Craftsman: Being the Reminiscences of Ebenezer Hiram Stedman, Papermaker 1808–1885* (Lexington, KY, 1959), 15n3; Fisher, *Albion's Seed*, 760–63, 812–16; Bernard Bailyn, *Voyagers to the West: A Passage in the Peopling of America on the Eve of the Revolution* (New York, 1986), 27.

6. Robert V. Remini, *Henry Clay: Statesman for the Union* (New York, 1991), 14; Fisher, *Albion's Seed*, 755–56.

7. Richard L. Bushman, "Opening the American Countryside," in *The Transformation of Early American History: Society, Authority, and Ideology*, ed. James A. Henretta, Michael Kammen, and Stanley N. Katz (New York, 1992), 255; T. H. Breen, "Narrative of Commercial Life: Consumption, Ideology, and Community on the Eve of the American Revolution," *William and Mary Quarterly* 50 (1993): 483; inside cover of Mason County, Kentucky, Account Book 1797–1799, Filson Club Historical Society, Louisville (quotation).

8. Robert E. Mutch, "Yeoman and Merchant in Pre-Industrial America: Eighteenth-Century Massachusetts as a Case Study," *Societas* 7 (1977): 292. For examples and analyses of seventeenth- and eighteenth-century commercial societies, see Gregory Nobles, "The Rise of Merchants in Rural Massachusetts: A Case Study of Eighteenth-Century Northhampton, Massachusetts," *Journal of Social History* 24 (1990): 5–23; Jean B. Russo, "Self-Sufficiency and Local Exchange," in *Colonial Chesapeake Society*, ed. Lois Green Carr, Philip D. Morgan, and Jean B. Russo (Chapel Hill, NC, 1988), 389–432; Allan Kulikoff, *Tobacco and Slaves: The Development of Southern Cultures in the Chesapeake, 1680–1800* (Chapel Hill, NC, 1986); Christine Leigh Heyrman, *Commerce and Culture: The Maritime Communities of Colonial Massachusetts, 1690–1750* (New York, 1984); Carole Shammas, "How Self-Sufficient Was Early America?" *Journal of Interdisciplinary History* 13 (1982–83): 247–72; Winifred B. Rothenberg, "The Market and Massachusetts Farmers, 1750–1855," *Journal of Economic History* 41 (1981): 283–314; Robert D. Mitchell, *Commercialism and Frontier: Perspectives on the Early Shenandoah Valley* (Charlottesville, 1977); Michael Merrill, "Cash Is Good to Eat: Self-Sufficiency and Exchange in the Rural Economy of the United States," *Radical History Review* 3 (1977): 42–71; James T. Lemon, *The Best Poor Man's Country: A*

Geographical Study of Early Southeastern Pennsylvania (Baltimore, MD, 1972). For a review of this growing school of historians, see Allan Kulikoff, "The Transition to Capitalism in Rural America," *William and Mary Quarterly* 46 (1989): 120–44.

9. Thomas Irwin to Wilson Hunt, February 3, 1794, John Wesley Hunt Papers, Filson Club Historical Society, Louisville (quotation); Patrick Moore to Thomas Irwin, April 26, 1795, Abijah and John W. Hunt Papers, Filson Club Historical Society (quotation); Wilson Hunt to Abijah and John W. Hunt, April 15, 1796, John Wesley Hunt Papers, Filson Club Historical Society.

10. John A. Seitz to unknown, June 22, 1796, Sullivan-Gates Papers, Filson Club Historical Society (quotation).

11. *Kentucky Gazette* (Lexington), January 24, 1798 (quotation); Mutch, "Yeoman and Merchant in Pre-Industrial America," 292. Elizabeth A. Perkins and Stephen A. Aron provide the most recent explorations of the significance of market relations to the Kentucky frontier; Elizabeth A. Perkins, "The Consumer Frontier: Household Consumption in Early Kentucky," *Journal of American History* 78 (1991): 486–510; Stephen A. Aron, "The Significance of the Frontier in the Transition to Capitalism," in "The Transition to Capitalism in America: A Panel Discussion," *The History Teacher* 27 (1994): 263–288; and idem, "Pioneers and Profiteers," 179–98.

12. Gary A. O'Dell, "The Trotter Family, Gunpowder, and Early Kentucky Entrepreneurship, 1784–1833," *Register of the Kentucky Historical Society* 88 (1990): 395. Eighteenth-century merchants involved their sons in the business early in life and entrusted them with journeys to suppliers and with overseeing exports; see William Vincent Byers, ed., *B. and M. Gratz: Merchants in Philadelphia, 1754–1798* (Jefferson City, MO, 1916), 258. Only by extending into many markets through importing and exporting could an enterprise hope to be profitable in the late eighteenth century; see Thomas M. Doerflinger, "Commercial Specialization in Philadelphia's Merchant Community, 1750–1791," *Business History Review* 57 (1983): 20–49. For studies that demonstrate the multifaceted role of the merchant, see W. T. Baxter, *The House of Hancock: Business in Boston 1724–1775* (Cambridge, MA, 1945); Bernard Bailyn, *The New England Merchants in the Seventeenth Century* (Cambridge, MA, 1955); Edward C. Papenfuse, *In Pursuit of Profit: The Annapolis Merchants in the Era of the American Revolution 1763–1805* (Baltimore, 1975); and Doerflinger, *A Vigorous Spirit of Enterprise*. More specialized merchandising erased the pattern of the merchant-centered empire in the early nineteenth century; see Glenn Porter and Harold C. Livesay, *Merchants and Manufacturers: Studies in the Changing Structure of Nineteenth-Century Marketing* (Baltimore, MD, 1971), 7.

13. *Directory for Pittsburgh & Its Vicinity, 1813* and *Philadelphia Directory for 1808* in *United States City Directories through 1860* (New Haven, 1960–), microfiche; Meeker, Cockran & Co. to James Trotter, December 5, 1796; Bickham, Gellig & Co. to Samuel and George Trotter, September 9, 1803; James Adams to Samuel Trotter, January 12, 1811; and James Adams to Samuel and George Trotter, April 15, 1811, all in Samuel and George Trotter Company Business Correspondence, Cincinnati Historical Society; Victor Collot, *A Journey in North America* (Paris, France, 1826), 33; Fortesque Cuming, *Sketches of a Tour to the Western Country*, in *Early Western Travels 1748–1846*, 32 vols., ed. Reuben Gold Thwaites (Cleveland, OH, 1904), 4:169; Michaux, *Travels to the West*, 202; Byers, *B. & M. Gratz*, 245; Douds, "Merchants and Merchandizing in Pittsburgh," 129; William Lytle to John Breckinridge, January 10,

1797, Papers of the Breckinridge Family, Library of Congress, Washington, DC; Willard R. Jillson, ed., "Samuel D. McCullough's Reminiscences of Lexington," *Register of the Kentucky Historical Society* 27 (1929): 426.

14. Abijah Hunt to John W. Hunt, April 30, 1795, and Abijah Hunt to John W. Hunt, April 18, 1797, Abijah and John W. Hunt Papers (quotations).

15. Michaux, *Travels to the West*, 204 (quotation); *Acts Passed at the First Session of the Second General Assembly* (Lexington, KY, 1793), 54 (quotation); Thomas T. Davis debate over direct tax, *Annals of Congress*, 5th Cong., 2d sess, 1917 (quotation); Lowell H. Harrison, ed., "A Letter Concerning Economic Conditions in Kentucky in 1802," *Register of the Kentucky Historical Society* 53 (1955): 258 (quotation); Doerflinger, *A Vigorous Spirit of Enterprise*, 138; Soltow, *Distribution of Wealth and Income in the United States in 1798*, 83.

16. John Moylan advertisement, *Kentucky Gazette*, February 2, 1793 (quotation); John Clay to John W. Hunt, June 3, 1805, and Abijah Hunt to John W. Hunt, February 6, 1800, Hunt-Morgan Papers, Special Collections, Margaret I. King Library, University of Kentucky, Lexington (quotation); James A. Ramage, "The Hunts and Morgans: A Study of a Prominent Kentucky Family" (Ph.D. diss., University of Kentucky, 1972), 112; Bartlett & Cox to John W. Hunt, May 2, 1804, Hunt-Morgan Papers; Michael Allen, *Western Rivermen, 1763–1861: Ohio and Mississippi Boatmen and the Myth of the Alligator Horse* (Baton Rouge, LA, 1990), 62.

17. Dale M. Royalty, "Banking, Politics, and the Commonwealth, Kentucky, 1800–1825" (Ph.D. diss., University of Kentucky, 1971), 6, 9; William Littell, ed., *The Statute Law of Kentucky*, 5 vols. (Frankfort, KY, 1819), 3:25–31; Bray Hammond, *Banks and Politics in America from the Revolution to the Civil War* (Princeton, NJ, 1957), 33; Bank of Kentucky Records, Lexington Branch, Minute Book A, August 19, 1811, Kentucky Department for Libraries and Archives, Frankfort, KY; Basil W. Duke, *History of the Bank of Kentucky, 1792–1895* (Louisville, KY, 1895), 14.

18. Wilson P. Hunt to John W. Hunt, May 2, 1804 (quotation), and Wilson P. Hunt to John W. Hunt, September 14, 1804 (quotation), and Wilson P. Hunt to John W. Hunt, January 16, 1805 (quotation), Hunt-Morgan Papers.

19. *Kentucky Gazette*, January 4, 1794 (quotation); Michaux, *Travels to the West*, 203 (quotation); Christopher Clark, *The Roots of Rural Capitalism: Western Massachusetts, 1780–1860* (Ithaca, NY, 1990), 28–38, 163–79; Breen, "Narrative of Commercial Life," 471–501.

20. Tench Coxe, *A Statement of the Arts and Manufactures of the United States of America for the Year 1810* (Philadelphia, 1814), 2–43.

21. Michaux, *Travels to the West*, 204; Bickham, Gellig & Co. to Samuel and George Trotter, September 9, 1803, and James Adams to Samuel and George Trotter, July 3, 1810, Trotter Company Business Correspondence. Prompt, immediate payments undermined the personal nature of business, and such transactions also weakened the patriarchal structure of local communities; see Michael Merrill and Sean Wilentz, eds., *The Key of Liberty: The Life and Democratic Writings of William Manning, "A Laborer," 1747–1814* (Cambridge, MA, 1993), 12–13.

22. John Armstrong to Samuel and George Trotter, March 23, 1810, Trotter Company Business Correspondence. For further insight into the impersonal nature of distant trade, see Christopher Clark, *The Roots of Rural Capitalism*, 28–38.

23. John Armstrong to George and Samuel Trotter, March 23, 1810 (quotation), and James Morrison to Samuel and George Trotter, August 4, 1810 (quotation), and Frederick Hise to George and Samuel Trotter, November 4, 1812 (quotation), Trotter Company Business Correspondence.

24. See Clark, *Roots of Rural Capitalism*, esp. 28–38, 163–79; Breen, "Narrative of Commercial Life," 471–501; and Perkins, "The Consumer Frontier," 508.

25. O'Dell, "The Trotter Family, Gunpowder, and Early Kentucky Entrepreneurship," 419–28; Craig T. Friend, "Merchants and Markethouses: Reflections on Moral Economy in Early Kentucky," *Journal of the Early Republic* 17 (1997): 553–74.

26. *Reporter* (Lexington), October 18, 1815; Linda Ramsey Ashley and Elizabeth Tapp Wills, *Funeral Notices of Lexington, Kentucky, 1806–1887* (Rochester, MI, 1982), 87; *Kentucky Gazette*, August 10, 1827, July 27, 1832, July 6, 1833, August 14, 1833, and August 24, 1833.

Suggested Readings

Aron, Stephen A. *How the West Was Lost: The Transformation of Kentucky from Daniel Boone to Henry Clay*. Baltimore, MD, 1996.

———. "Pioneers and Profiteers: Land Speculation and the Homestead Ethic in Frontier Kentucky." *Western Historical Quarterly* 23 (1992): 179–98.

Doerflinger, Thomas M. *A Vigorous Spirit of Enterprise: Merchants and Economic Development in Revolutionary Philadelphia*. Chapel Hill, NC, 1986.

Douds, Howard C. "Merchants and Merchandising in Pittsburgh, 1759–1800." *Western Pennsylvania Historical Magazine* 20 (1937): 123–32.

Eslinger, Ellen. *Citizens of Zion: The Social Origins of Camp Meeting Revivalism*. Knoxville, TN, 1999.

Friend, Craig T. "Merchants and Markethouses: Reflections on Moral Economy in Early Kentucky." *Journal of the Early Republic* 17 (1997): 553–74.

Kulikoff, Allan. "The Transition to Capitalism in Rural America." *William and Mary Quarterly* 46 (1989): 120–44.

Mutch, Robert E. "Yeoman and Merchant in Pre-Industrial America: Eighteenth-Century Massachusetts as a Case Study." *Societas* 7 (1977): 279–302.

Nobles, Gregory. "The Rise of Merchants in Rural Massachusetts: A Case Study of Eighteenth-Century Northhampton, Massachusetts." *Journal of Social History* 24 (1990): 5–23.

O'Dell, Gary A. "The Trotter Family, Gunpowder, and Early Kentucky Entrepreneurship, 1784–1833." *Register of the Kentucky Historical Society* 88 (1990): 394–430.

Perkins, Elizabeth A. *Border Life: Experience and Memory in the Revolutionary Ohio Valley*. Chapel Hill, NC, 1998.

———. "The Consumer Frontier: Household Consumption in Early Kentucky." *Journal of American History* 78 (1991): 486–510.

Porter, Glenn, and Harold C. Livesay. *Merchants and Manufacturers: Studies in the Changing Structure of Nineteenth-Century Marketing*. Baltimore, MD, 1971.

Rohrbough, Malcolm J. *The Trans-Appalachian Frontier: People, Societies, and Institutions, 1775–1850*. New York, 1984.

4

Hiram Hill
House Carpenter, Lumber Dealer,
Self-Made Man

Gary J. Kornblith

Hiram Hill, like James Trotter, was a self-made man. The trajectory of his life from an apprentice carpenter to a wealthy lumber merchant reveals the possibilities for personal advancement in an expanding market economy. Additionally his personal life reflects the anxiety and uncertainty that were the price of success. Estranged from a father who was often away at sea, Hill lived with his grandparents, attended school intermittently, and spent an unhappy stint as an operative in a textile mill. At the age of sixteen he became an apprentice carpenter, and by twenty-one he had become a journeyman. A freak accident forced him to abandon his trade, and Hill decided to make a living selling lumber. He persevered and prospered. Hill's personal success, however, came at a cost. Although he thrived in this economically open society, Hill was plagued consistently with self-doubt about his headlong pursuit of wealth. Moreover, he soon discovered that affluence brought uncertainty about the future, not security. Hill's life demonstrates both the possibilities and the high psychological costs that the market revolution produced. If outwardly he championed modernity and success, inwardly Hill remained skeptical of their effect on his morals and commitment to family. His angst illustrates how economic opportunity could be both powerfully attractive and deeply disaffecting.

Gary J. Kornblith is professor of history at Oberlin College, Oberlin, Ohio, where he has taught since 1981. His recent publications include *The Industrial Revolution in America* (1998) and "Artisan Federalism: New England Mechanics and the Political Economy of the 1790s," in Ronald Hoffman and Peter J. Albert, eds., *Launching the "Extended Republic": The Federalist Era* (1996).

B y eliminating monarchical rule the American Revolution radically challenged traditional cultural assumptions about the sources of political authority and social respectability in the newly constituted United States. All claims to leadership based on custom, birth, and breeding came into question. Leisure and refinement, once considered prerequisites for disinterested civic virtue, suddenly appeared to be signs of decadence and corruption. Instead of the cultivated gentleman widely celebrated in the mid-eighteenth century, a new cultural ideal emerged during the early nineteenth century: the self-made man who, however lowly his origins and limited his formal education, achieved social distinction and material prosperity on the basis of his personal character, effort, and hard work.

The popular literature of the antebellum era portrayed the self-made man as a buoyant optimist, confident of his own abilities and eager to attain individual success and promote social progress by applying his natural talents. The life of Hiram Hill raises questions about this image. Hill was a Rhode Island house carpenter turned lumber dealer who "made himself" and acquired wealth and prestige but in the process experienced deep anxiety, self-doubt, and guilt. A personal memoir and diary he wrote over many years not only tells the particular story of Hill's success but also sheds light, more generally, on the private dilemmas that complicated self-made manhood in a rapidly developing democratic capitalist society.

Born in rural Smithfield, Rhode Island, on November 15, 1803, Hiram Hill was the fifth child of Marcy (Harris) and George Hill. A carpenter by trade, George Hill was also an adventurer and frequently absent from the household. The year before Hiram was born, George journeyed to China, and during Hiram's youth, he lived for extended periods of time in Boston (with a "person who it is not proper to name") and South Carolina. In 1811, he was arrested "for running goods" in violation of federal law, and he spent a number of stints in jail before the case was finally settled in 1815. Hiram later remarked of his father, "His family would have been much better situated had he remained at home with them, instead of roving the world over, and acquiring discipated habits, so common to all Sailors."[1]

Between the ages of nine and twelve, Hiram resided with his grandparents, who owned a sizable farm in Smithfield. He attended a school taught by his Aunt Deborah in the winter, helped out on the farm in the summer, and by his own account, chafed under his grandparents' caring but strict discipline. Meanwhile, in 1813, George Hill purchased three acres of land in Unity Factory Village—later renamed Manville—a mill community on the Blackstone River. He built a house and moved the family there in 1814. In 1816, Hiram rejoined them, and the following summer took a job under contract at the local textile mill. "I had always had a great anxiety to work in the Factory from seeing the pretty Machinery in operation," he explained in his memoir. But he soon grew disenchanted. "The business was to [*sic*] monotinous," and the overseer inflicted beatings unfairly.[2] By the time his contract expired the next winter, Hiram was glad to leave.

Shortly after his sixteenth birthday, "It was decided that I should go to a trade in the spring of 1820 provided a suitable place could be found." The choice of trade was left to Hiram, and he selected carpentry, his father's craft. George Hill had already taught his son some basic skills, and he now sought to place Hiram as an apprentice with John Holden Greene, the foremost master builder in Providence, Rhode Island's largest city. George and Hiram paid a visit to Greene in the summer of 1820 only to learn that business was slow and he "did not want any more apprentices at the time." A few months later, however, Hiram approached Greene again. This time "he said I might come and live with him as soon as I pleased." "On the 25th of September 1820," Hiram recalled, "I left home very early in the morning on foot for Providence with a small bundle of clothes, my chest was to be sent after me."[3] He arrived at Greene's house that afternoon and immediately began his apprenticeship.

Although Greene's operation was extensive by the standards of the day, it was still organized along traditional craft lines. Hiram resided in Greene's household with four other apprentices, and he worked under the direct supervision of both his master and his master's wife. At first, as the youngest apprentice, he was responsible for many domestic chores, including cutting firewood and caring for the family's horse and cow. Within a year, he was working as a member of Greene's building crew, which he enjoyed thoroughly. Celebrations and customary diversions interrupted the routine of labor. At one house raising, "They furnished lots of punch . . . which suited the apprentices very well." On another occasion, while helping build a barn in Smithfield, he "had a fine time eating cherries."[4]

During his apprenticeship, Hiram attended school intermittently and trained in the local militia. He also endured the emotional turbulence that later generations would label "adolescence." As his interest in the opposite sex increased, he had trouble concentrating on his work. The summer of 1822 proved particularly difficult. "I did not enjoy myself at all this summer," he recalled, "lost all my ambition, felt extremely dull and very unhappy. . . . I think it was the change from youth to manhood that caused the feeling."[5]

Fortunately for Hiram, Greene showed special concern for his professional and personal development. Hiram remembered his master as "a good Mechanic and architect, but rather a fractious man" who often scolded his apprentices. But Hiram escaped Greene's reprimands. "I got along with him very well, was a particular favourite and have no fault to find with the treatment I received during my apprenticeship."[6] Hiram adopted his master's religion (Universalism) and briefly "took a fancy" to one of Greene's nieces. Although Hiram "soon got sick of the business and cut the concern," he remained in Greene's good graces throughout his apprenticeship.[7] In his last year of service, Greene entrusted him with supervisory responsibility for two construction projects.

After four years of apprenticeship, Hiram possessed a broad knowledge of his craft. "I considered myself a good workman and capable of doing almost any kind of carpenter's work."[8] To supplement his training, he had attended "an architectural school, one evening a week" in the fall of 1823, and he boasted "considerable proficiency in architectural drawings."[9] On his own he "had studied the theory of Circular Stair building," which would later become his specialty.[10] Diligent and determined, Hiram Hill was ready to graduate from apprentice to journeyman status.

Upon turning twenty-one on November 15, 1824, Hill threw a party for his comrades to mark his freedom. He also moved out of Greene's household and took up residence at a nearby boardinghouse. Otherwise his transition from apprentice to journeyman barely changed his daily routine, at least in the short term. "Went to work for My old Master the day I was of age," he recalled, and he continued to perform the same tasks as he had done the day before.[11]

In theory Hill enjoyed more autonomy as a journeyman than he had as an apprentice. He was free to hire himself out to any master who would employ him, and he could begin accumulating the capital necessary to open his own enterprise. In practice he enjoyed less financial security. As an apprentice, he had received room and board from Greene. Now he was paid in money. But when Greene's business was slow, Hill had trouble collecting his wages and in turn had trouble paying his rent. He also had to procure his own set of tools to practice his craft. Soon Hill found himself in debt.

For more than a year after gaining his freedom, Hill worked mainly, though not exclusively, for Greene. Then in the summer of 1826, Greene went bankrupt. It "was a sad thing for me," Hill recalled, "for I lost nearly two Hundred Dollars by him which I had earned by days works and hard knocks."[12] Yet Hill survived Greene's failure. He promptly found employment with the firm of Cook and Brown, and at the end of 1826, he "took job of Tallman & Bucklin."[13] He was quickly gaining a reputation for building stairs, and in January 1827, he rented the upper floor of a shop on Planet Street in Providence to use as a workroom. Although he usually worked as a subcontractor and with another carpenter, he exercised significantly more control over the production process than did common wage earners. In a trade where distinctions between journeymen and small masters often blurred, Hill at the age of twenty-four was essentially his own boss and socially independent.

In a reflection of his rising status, he joined the Providence Association of Mechanics and Manufacturers, a group of civic-minded artisans and businessmen, and he took his first degree in Freemasonry. In August 1827 the Providence town meeting elected him to the post of surveyor of lumber. His main duty was to inspect lumber brought into Providence, and he received a handsome fee for his services. With his carpentry business also expanding, he grew prosperous. In the summer of 1828, he paid off all his debts, "had plenty of work . . . and employed three hands."[14] On turning twenty-six in November 1829, he calculated his worth at "$341 besides tools and clothing and felt quite rich."[15] In April 1832, he figured his total holdings at $1,175.

Along with prosperity came betrothal, marriage, and a son. In July 1829, Hill became engaged to Mary Ann Fowler, but he soon panicked at the prospect of making a lifelong commitment. By his own account, he "put off the time [of the wedding] as long as I consistently could"—nearly three years.[16] The ceremony finally took place on June 6, 1832, and five months later the couple "went to housekeeping" together in rented accommodations.[17] In November 1833, Mrs. Hill gave birth to their son George, namesake of Hiram's father, who had moved to Michigan in 1830. In 1835, with his father's encouragement, Hiram sold the family's Manville property, and Hiram's mother came to live with him in Providence. To provide better shelter for his expanding household, he purchased a lot on Power Street and began building a new residence. The Hills took occupancy in July 1836.

Speculative fever swept through much of the United States in the mid-1830s, and Hiram Hill caught the bug. In the spring of 1837, he decided to try his hand at importing mahogany into Providence and selling it at a profit. In April, he traveled by steamboat to New York

City and bought some lumber; in July, he went again and returned with a second allotment. Lumber dealing had an obvious appeal for Hill. It required few new skills and promised lucrative returns.

Yet it was an accident, not a well-developed business plan, that prompted Hill to forsake his craft for commercial enterprise. On August 5, 1837, while installing the frame for a staircase at Central Falls, he slipped, fell ten feet, and fractured his hip. The injury left him permanently lame. Although he completed the project at Central Falls, his career as a house carpenter and stair builder was over. In January 1838, he "gave up carpentry on account of my lameness, and concluded I would try to get a living by selling lumber of various kinds."[18]

The transition proved difficult, and Hill soon found himself "cramped some in making my payments, for want of sufficient Capital."[19] In December 1838, he placed an order for $600 in Caribbean mahogany only to lose $200 on the transaction. The economic turmoil of 1839 added to his woes. Early that year, he traveled to New York City and other places to purchase sizeable quantities of bed posts, table legs, and ash planks. During the summer, he commissioned the manufacture of a steam-powered veneer saw. Then business turned sour, and he was left with excess inventory and big bills to pay. To make matters worse, the saw "was not constructed in the best manner," and he had trouble arranging for the steam power necessary to run it.[20] All in all, 1839 proved "a disastrous year" for Hill.[21]

Yet he persevered. He made a "bargain with Tallman & Bucklin to put [the] saw in their building and operate it by their steam power."[22] He lured a sawyer from New York City to serve as his assistant, and he took long trips in search of quality woods for trading. Still, ambition and determination were not enough. He was repeatedly forced "to borrow a good deal of money for short periods, which kept me most of the time under excitement."[23] In the fall of 1840, he decided to cut back on his operations. He sent the sawyer packing and for the next two years carried on the business by himself.

At the same time that he was struggling to establish himself as a lumber merchant, Hill's family responsibilities increased. Daughter Helen was born in 1838, and Sarah arrived in 1842. Hill's mother continued to live with the family, and in 1840 his father-in-law moved in as well. When his father died in early 1841 in Pontiac, Michigan, Hiram had to make two journeys west to settle the estate.

Meanwhile a political crisis was brewing in Rhode Island. Whereas most states had adopted universal white manhood suffrage over the previous quarter century, Rhode Island retained a substantial property requirement for voting. In the fall of 1841, advocates of suffrage reform gathered for a convention in Providence to draft a "People's Constitution" that would extend the franchise to all adult white males who had resided in the state for at least one year. Although the convention lacked official standing, the constitution was duly ratified in a statewide referendum in December. Supporters made plans to install a new state government the following spring.

Many Rhode Islanders questioned the legitimacy of the People's Constitution, however. Hiram Hill, for one, upheld the authority of the existing state government, although he did not object to suffrage reform in principle. When the general assembly called another convention, which in turn proposed a compromise solution, Hill supported it. But staunch suffragists denounced the new plan as too little, too late. In combination with diehard defenders of the old order, they voted down the so-called Freemen's Constitution in a referendum held in March 1842. It was "a strange infatuation," Hill remarked, "that the Suffrage party should vote against the constitution presented to them, when it extended to them all the privileges or about all that they ask for."[24]

The stage was set for violent confrontation. On April 2 the general assembly passed a law making it a crime to vote in the forthcoming People's Election and a treasonous offense to hold office under the People's Constitution. Nonetheless, on April 18 more than six thousand Rhode Islanders cast ballots for Thomas W. Dorr, leader of the prosuffrage forces, for governor. Two days later seven thousand other Rhode Islanders went to the polls to reelect the incumbent governor under the provisions of the old charter. Both sides mobilized for armed struggle.

Denouncing the People's Legislature as a "spurious assembly," Hill rallied to the cause of the Law and Order Party.[25] He joined the local military patrol and was promptly elected third lieutenant. When the Dorrites advanced toward Providence in late June, with the goal of capturing the city arsenal, Hill was instructed to lead a hundred men to Woonsocket Falls to help repel the threat. Before he could execute the order, however, he was superseded as military commander. Feeling insulted, he promptly resigned his post, and he never fired a shot in the so-called Dorr War.

After the Dorr War ended in the Dorrites' ignominious defeat, the general assembly authorized yet another constitutional convention, which in turn proposed a new compromise plan. Dorr called on his supporters to boycott the ensuing referendum in late November, but Hill worked hard for ratification. His ward endorsed the proposed constitution by 302 to 0, and the statewide results were similarly lopsided. Conservative reform triumphed in Rhode Island.

The battle for political control of the state continued, however. No sooner was the constitution ratified than both Dorrites and their adversaries began preparing for the April 1843 state elections. It was a rough campaign. Employers pressured their employees to toe a partisan line. As Hill explained, "Those person[s] who employ many hands are determined to discharge such as will not agree to support the laws and constitution as now adopted."[26] He found no fault with such tactics. Having been elevated to surveyor general of lumber for Providence in 1842, he applied a political test to his own subordinates in 1843. At the behest of city officials, he dropped from his band of deputies "two of the old ones for being Dorrites, and otherwise unpopular."[27]

The victory of Law and Order candidates in the April elections brought an end to Rhode Island's political crisis. Hill refocused his attention on the lumber business. Between April and October 1843, he traveled to Boston three times, to New York City twice, and to Albany once. He again hired a sawyer to assist in his shop, and as surveyor general, he even "put on some of the Dorrites to help out" with the end-of-season rush.[28] Both sales and profits rose. By the end of 1843, Hill had entered a new phase of success in his career.

Over the remainder of the decade, Hill attained substantial wealth and social status. His lumber business proved so remunerative that in 1845 he could afford to build an addition to his residence and to hire a private nurse to care for his ailing wife. In 1847, he felt sufficiently secure to retire from his post as surveyor general, which over the previous few years had yielded roughly $1000 annually. "I felt that as I have business enough to support me handsomely, without the office," he explained, "and as there was other persons who . . . are qualified for the office, and needed the profits of it, being rather old to survey, I felt it my duty to decline a reappointment."[29]

Although he stepped aside as surveyor general, Hill remained active in local affairs. He enthusiastically supported the construction of railroads leading to and from Providence, and in 1847, running on the Law and Order and Temperance tickets, he won election as alderman for the third ward—a position he would retain for the next four years. In 1848, he was chosen senior warden of the Mt. Vernon masonic lodge, and three years later he was elected president of the Providence Association of Mechanics and Manufacturers. In 1853, he agreed to serve as president of the new Atlantic Bank. At midcentury, by all outward signs, Hiram Hill epitomized the antebellum American ideal of the self-made man. Born into modest circumstances and trained as an artisan, he now lived the life of an affluent businessman and solid, respectable member of the northern middle class.

Yet behind the facade of bourgeois success, Hill felt deep ambivalence about his constant pursuit of material gain. After an unusually profitable week in 1843, he wrote in his journal, "But money is not my sole object. I feel as though I wanted to enjoy life while it lasts, retired a little from the bustle and confusion of strife, for power or riches."[30] Likewise, following an unusually slow week three years later, he commented, "The almighty Dollar should not engross so much of our attention. [T]he pleasures and innocent amusements of life ought to attract more of our attention than it does, to mak[e] life agreeable and long."[31]

Such statements might be dismissed as wistful nostalgia had not Hill's inner conflict grown more severe over time. In 1847, he sent cotton goods worth several hundreds of dollars to Santo Domingo in the hope of exchanging them for mahogany to sell at a sizable profit back home. When the plan failed, he blamed his losses on the limitless scope of his ambitions. "Money making seems to be the principal object now aimed at by most people, and I should have made as much as any former year had I been satisfied when I was well off." He vowed henceforth "to try and be contented . . . with small and steady gains." Yet he felt unsure that he could keep to this pledge. "It may be hard to keep down the avaricious spirit, natural to the race which I belong to."[32]

In the fall of 1849, he began to worry incessantly about his sale of family property back in 1835. He had sold the Manville estate on his father's recommendation, and at the time the transaction barely occupied his attention. Fourteen years later, however, it became an obsession. For months, then for years on end, he reiterated his regret at having sold the Manville property. On one occasion he wrote, "I have the Horrors of the worst kind. [M]y head was not made quite clear enough for the situation in which I have been placed during life[. W]hy did I sell the Estate at Manvil[le?]"[33] On another occasion he observed, "Although it is probably for the best that it was sold but I cannot bring my mind to think so. . . . The estate would have been a nice place to retreat to from the noise and bustle of the city occasionally, but it cannot now be helped and if . . . I could get the thoughts from my mind I should be very glad."[34]

At the conscious level, Hill's psychological crisis manifested itself as a conflict between the pursuit of wealth and loyalty to family identity. The Manville property represented his family of origin, and Hill felt guilty for having broken his ancestral ties by selling it. Likewise, when his mother died in August 1854, Hill castigated himself for his selfishness. "My disposition is too selfish a great deal and it has been a great fault in my life, but I have not discovered it until it is too late to make amends in a great many cases."[35] When his sister Jane took mortally sick shortly thereafter, he again blamed himself. While she lay on her deathbed, he wrote, "O! horrible have I been the cause of her death. I would give half of my fortune to make her well and sound and insure her 20 years of life."[36]

Hill's personal crisis deepened when his wife's health, which had long been poor, deteriorated markedly in the fall of 1855. He had just moved into a new, custom-built office and was looking forward to having his son join him in business as a bookkeeper. When the doctors offered little hope for his wife's recovery, he was overwhelmed by "the horrors of a guilty conscience. . . . She wanted sympathy and I did not give it, but was cold towards her."[37] "I have thought too much of [business] and have neglected my family," he lamented.[38] "I would give all I am worth could I restore [my wife] to health."[39]

After twenty-four years of marriage, Hill buried his wife on June 12, 1856. In his grief, he stopped keeping his journal. Consequently the last twenty years of his life are relatively obscure. Yet surviving R. G. Dun and Company records reveal he remained financially secure. His credit rating rose from "good" in 1856 to "good beyond doubt" in 1858 and "first rate" in 1860. In 1864, he was termed "A1 rich," and his business continued to thrive after the Civil War. Although he went into semiretirement in 1870, he was said to be worth nearly $100,000 in 1873. In 1875 the R. G. Dun and Company correspondent described him simply as "Safe and sound."[40] Hiram Hill died on April 20, 1876, at the age of 72.

Over the course of Hill's life, the United States had developed from a profoundly agrarian society into one of the world's leading industrial powers. In a process that recent scholars have termed the "market revolution," money and impersonal commercial transactions rapidly displaced customary forms of face-to-face and in-kind exchange. Many Americans actively resisted this transformation. They voted against so-called internal improvements and undertook strikes, riots, and other forms of collective protest.

Hiram Hill, by contrast, embraced the opportunities offered by economic modernization. He supported Law and Order politicians and made his fortune by pursuing his self-interest according to the rules of a capitalist economy. Yet privately Hiram Hill felt uncomfortable about the social priorities of the emerging economic order. If he behaved outwardly as a champion of modernity and progress, inwardly he brooded about the moral choices he had made in chasing profits rather than engaging fully with his family. Whether Hill was in any genuine sense a "representative figure" of his era is open to question. Undoubtedly some self-made men did not suffer from such intense neurotic conflict. Yet it remains significant that Hill did. His experience suggests that even for those who supported the market revolution, it could prove traumatic. Capitalist development not only generated conflict among social classes, it also triggered struggles within individuals over how to approach a new way of life that was both powerfully alluring and deeply alienating at the same time.

Notes

1. Hiram Hill, "Incidents in the Life of Hiram Hill," Manuscript Collection, Rhode Island Historical Society, Providence. According to the inside cover of this bound, unpaginated manuscript, Hill began writing it on January 5, 1842. Some of the account was probably based on an earlier diary, however, since events from September 1822 forward are often precisely dated.

2. Ibid., n.d.

3. Ibid., n.d.

4. Ibid., n.d.

5. Ibid., n.d.

6. Ibid., n.d.

7. Ibid., October 5, 1823.

8. Ibid., November 15, 1824.

9. Ibid., September 23, 1823.

10. Ibid., November 15, 1824.

11. Ibid.

12. Ibid., July 31, 1826.

13. Ibid., December 16, 1826.

14. Ibid., June 1828.

15. Ibid., November 15, 1829.

16. Ibid., July 19, 1829.

17. Ibid., August and September 1832.

18. Ibid., January 1, 1838.

19. Ibid., September 1838.

20. Ibid., July 1839.

21. Ibid., March 1840.

22. Ibid., September 1839.
23. Ibid., October 1840.
24. Ibid., March 23, 1842.
25. Ibid., May 2, 1842.
26. Ibid., December 31, 1842.
27. Ibid., February 28, 1843.
28. Ibid., November 13, 1843.
29. Ibid., January 15, 1847.
30. Ibid., August 19, 1843.
31. Ibid., October 10, 1846.
32. Ibid., December 31, 1847.
33. Ibid., December 30, 1850.
34. Ibid., March 4, 1852.
35. Ibid., August 14, 1854.
36. Ibid., October 28, 1854.
37. Ibid., November 30, 1855.
38. Ibid., January 26, 1856.
39. Ibid., February 2, 1856.
40. Rhode Island, Vol. 9, p. 145, R. G. Dun and Company Collection, Baker
Library, Harvard University Graduate School of Business Administration, Boston.

Suggested Readings

Blumin, Stuart M. *The Emergence of the Middle Class: Social Experience in the American City, 1760–1900.* Cambridge, England, 1989.

Burns, Rex. *Success in America: The Yeoman Dream and the Industrial Revolution.* Amherst, MA, 1976.

Coleman, Peter J. *The Transformation of Rhode Island, 1790–1860.* Providence, RI, 1963.

Gilje, Paul A., ed. *Wages of Independence: Capitalism in the Early American Republic.* Madison, WI, 1997.

Gilkeson, John S., Jr. *Middle-Class Providence, 1820–1940.* Princeton, NJ, 1986.

Kimmel, Michael. *Manhood in America: A Cultural History.* New York, 1996.

Rock, Howard B., Paul A. Gilje, and Robert Asher, eds. *American Artisans: Crafting Social Identity, 1750–1850.* Baltimore, MD, 1995.

Rorabaugh, W. J. *The Craft Apprentice: From Franklin to the Machine Age in America.* New York, 1986.

Rotundo, E. Anthony. *American Manhood: Transformations in Masculinity from the Revolution to the Modern Era.* New York, 1993.

Ryan, Mary P. *Cradle of the Middle Class: The Family in Oneida County, New York, 1790–1865.* Cambridge, England, 1981.

Sellers, Charles. *The Market Revolution: Jacksonian America, 1815–1846.* New York, 1991.

Stokes, Melvyn, and Stephen Conway, eds. *The Market Revolution in America: Social, Political, and Religious Expressions, 1800–1860*. Charlottesville, VA, 1996.

Wood, Gordon S. *The Radicalism of the American Revolution*. New York, 1992.

Wyllie, Irvin G. *The Self-Made Man in America: The Myth of Rags to Riches*. New Brunswick, NJ, 1954.

5

Senator John Smith
The Rise and Fall of a Frontier Entrepreneur

Andrew R. L. Cayton

If the market revolution marked an ideological shift from the traditional republican emphasis on a common good to Lockean self-interest, Senator John Smith's extensive business dealings with the U.S. Army reveal that in this emerging capitalist ethos the line between public and private interests was often indistinct. Initially, Smith became a hot commodity as a preacher, but his real interests were of this world. Smith quickly discovered that economic and political self-interest on the Ohio frontier were overlapping and reinforcing—not mutually exclusive. Smith parlayed his life (or lives) as a U.S. senator and a merchant into a lucrative business enterprise in which the U.S. Army was his main customer. Although the army was stationed in Ohio to protect the public, Smith quickly discovered that he could exploit his position and connections as senator to promote his own private wealth. The same interconnected relationship between the public's interest and economic self-interest that provided the context and opportunity for Smith's rapid rise to prominence also proved to be his undoing. When he became entangled in the web of the Burr conspiracy, his fall from eminence and power was swift, certain, and complete. Smith's life makes a clear, convincing case for the hazards of new fortunes.

Andrew R. L. Cayton is professor of history at Miami University in Oxford, Ohio. He is the author of several books and articles dealing with the history of trans-Appalachian North America, including *The Midwest and the Nation: Rethinking the History of an American Region*, with Peter S. Onuf (1990); and *Frontier Indiana* (1996).

In 1805 and 1806, Aaron Burr, recent vice president of the United States, spent a great deal of time talking with prominent men in trans-Appalachian North America about some kind of a filibustering expedition west of the Mississippi River. No one knows Burr's exact plans, if he ever had any. Like any astute person who is considering a potentially illegal or controversial action, Burr kept his own counsel. Among the dozens of men with whom he conversed was Senator John Smith of Ohio. Smith's brief meeting with Burr eventually cost him his seat in the U.S. Senate and destroyed his burgeoning commercial empire. It is hardly surprising that consorting with a man who was arrested and tried for treason against the United States got Smith into trouble. More interesting is why a man as successful as Smith would become involved with Burr in the first place. Answering that question reveals a great deal about economic and political relationships in trans-Appalachia, in particular the extent to which personal calculation informed national loyalty.

Difficult as it is for us to imagine, many people had doubts about the permanency of the United States in the early republic. History warned that such a huge and loosely organized nation could not last long unless it could win and hold the loyalty of its most influential citizens. Nearly everyone agreed that attachment to the federal Union had to be the product of personal choice. In a democratic republic with a limited government, men had to opt to support and defend the Constitution of 1787. Self-interest, broadly conceived, was at the heart of their decision. Nationalism was a dynamic mixture of affection, benevolence, and a shared sense of commitment to basic republican notions of personal independence and social equality—all of which rested to a great extent on a sense of calculation. Indeed, the attachment of John Smith and many powerful men like him in the Ohio and Mississippi Valleys to the U.S. government grew and ebbed according to their sense of where their loyalty would do the most for them personally.

The federal government was small in the early republic. Its resources were meager, its bureaucracy tiny, its military capabilities limited. Its officials were charged with protecting and governing millions of diverse people spread out over a vast terrain extending from Maine to Georgia and New York to Louisiana. Size, however, was not a reliable guide to power. The national government awarded military contracts and political appointments that were highly prized by ambitious citizens, in no small part because demand far exceeded supply.

The national government was particularly important on the nation's frontiers. Outside of the original thirteen states and the ones formed directly from them—that is, Vermont and Kentucky—federal officials appointed and supervised territorial governments, surveyed and sold federal lands, directed military operations against Indians, and established critical institutions such as courts and post offices. Because of its limited resources, the national government depended, as European and colonial governments had for centuries, on powerful local figures to conduct its basic business. The relationship between national and personal interests was symbiotic. Whether they were Federalists or Jeffersonian Republicans, federal officials not only gained legitimacy by awarding contracts and appointments to local notables but also entrusted the nation's business to men who could get things done. Meanwhile the recipients of federal largess acquired both money and the social imprimatur of an imperial government. National and personal interests were intertwined in ways that were often profitable for both sides. The United States provided ambitious men with the liberty to pursue their main chance for gold and glory, and its government became their main chance. For many of the most powerful residents of trans-Appalachia, loyalty to the federal government was a matter of loyalty to their livelihood.

We do not know when or where John Smith was born. We do know that in May 1790 he appeared in the new settlement of Columbia in the Northwest Territory, a few miles east of Cincinnati. A small Baptist congregation invited him to become their preacher, and he agreed. The next year he brought his wife, Elizabeth Mason Hickman, and their seven children to the three-year-old settlement. It was as a Baptist elder that Smith first achieved local prominence. In addition to serving the people of Columbia, he guided the construction of the first Baptist church north of the Ohio River, ordained other ministers, and helped found the Miami Baptist Association in 1797.

The energetic Smith was just as active in secular affairs. In the late 1790s, Smith emerged as a leading critic of the administration of Northwest Territory Governor Arthur St. Clair. Elected to the first territorial legislature in 1798 as a delegate from Hamilton County, Smith was unwavering in his support of statehood for Ohio. Smith received his reward for loyalty when, after serving as a member of the 1802 Ohio Constitutional Convention, he became one of Ohio's first two U.S. senators in March 1803.

As successful as Smith was in politics, he made his name in commerce. He started with a warehouse in Columbia, which, according to a visitor, consisted "of but one room, where he brings down the river such articles of European manufactory as are most in demand."[1] By 1796, he owned over $2,600 worth of property in Columbia (ranking second in a male population of 282, of whom 48 owned no property) and had two male laborers living with him. Soon, he owned stores in both Columbia and Cincinnati. In Cincinnati, he entered into a partnership with James Findlay, a Pennsylvanian who became one of Cincinnati's most prominent citizens in the early nineteenth century.

Smith also owned two mills near the Little Miami River, which he operated with John Cleves Symmes, the largest landowner in the region; on
occasion, he acted as a land agent for Symmes.

Like many of his contemporaries, John Smith was willing to take
risks to achieve greater wealth and influence. Calculation was at the
heart of his character. He had little interest in becoming a man of leisure. Refinement did not matter to him. What he cared about was getting ahead. According to a local historian, Smith "yielded to the
fascination of fame and was led from one step to another, farther and
farther from his pledge to preach the Gospel, to which he had felt, and
always believed, he had been specially called." Ignoring the pleas of his
wife Elizabeth, Smith ended up in "the vortex of worldly business and
ambition, until he found himself overwhelmed with a storm which he
could neither escape nor control."[2]

Hardly the denizen of some isolated frontier, Smith was at the center of American economic development in the early republic. He spent
much of his time in Natchez, New Orleans, Philadelphia, and Washington, DC. He talked with men all over eastern North America. He
learned Spanish so that he could do business in the Mississippi Valley.
He and his colleagues shared little of the ambiguity about market capitalism that recent historians have discovered in the early republic. To
the contrary, markets were Smith's life. In this sense, he was no different
from hundreds of other men who lived less in Ohio or Louisiana or the
United States than within a trans-Appalachia commercial web, men who
were less localists or nationalists than capitalists, men whose imagined
community was a world of profit and contacts.

Illustrative are the peregrinations of Major William Stanley, a veteran of the War for Independence, who started as a clerk in Cincinnati
in 1790 and entered into a mercantile partnership with Daniel and Benjamin Stites Gano of Columbia in 1793. In February 1792, Stanley
took the balance of a Cincinnati store to Frankfort, Kentucky; over the
next few months, his business carried him to Cincinnati, Lexington,
Danville, Bardstown, and Louisville (more than once); another trip included stops at Cincinnati, Lexington, and Nashville. In December,
Stanley left with three boats for New Orleans. Fighting sandbars and
other natural obstacles, not to mention the Chickasaw and Arkansas
Indians who stole his clothes, a barrel of whiskey, and some tobacco, he
did business in New Madrid, Walnut Hills, and Natchez. By the end of
March 1793, Stanley was sailing along the coast of Cuba on his way to
Philadelphia to sell tobacco. Two months later, he arrived in Pittsburgh.

Floating down the Ohio toward Columbia, Kentucky, Stanley was soon selling goods directly out of his boat at Limestone, Kentucky.

This was the commercial world in which John Smith operated. It was essentially a triangular trade, with major corners at Cincinnati, New Orleans, and Philadelphia. Trans-Appalachian merchants sold agricultural products in New Orleans and bought finished goods in Philadelphia. More complex was the market in Cincinnati.

Neighbors and travelers provided business, but hardly enough for men as ambitious as Smith, Stanley, or Gano. Looking for markets, they found the most promising one in the U.S. Army. To a considerable extent, the military expenditures of the United States made Cincinnati the major commercial center west of the Appalachian Mountains in the 1790s. Its early rivals—Maysville, Kentucky; and Marietta and Columbia in the Northwest Territory—were worthy competitors for the position of the chief entrepôt of the upper Ohio Valley. Cincinnati's great advantage was Fort Washington, the political and military headquarters of the United States in the West and the point of departure for expeditions against the Indians in the Maumee valley. Built in 1789, the large fort sheltered around its perimeters a great number of small buildings. According to lawyer Jacob Burnet, the military gave "character to the manners and customs of the people." Bored soldiers and their officers spent much of their time and money on "the bottle, the dice-box, and the card-table." Burnet did not mention prostitution, but it also flourished around the fort.[3]

Providing food—beef, pork, flour, and whiskey—to military posts was potentially the fastest track to profit for trans-Appalachian merchants. Both collectively and individually, armies were the most reliable sources of money. Soldiers not only had to be fed, on regular occasions they also had money they wanted to spend. According to the agent of one partnership, "The soldiers expresses a Thousand wants but at the same time intimate that Nothing will supply them but mony and when that comes They will supply themselves."[4] When Anthony Wayne and his troops were near Cincinnati in 1793, William Stanley exulted that "we purchase [*sic*] & deliver considerable produce & do considerable business."[5] In 1796 the partnership of Smith and Findlay collected almost $300 from four companies of troops; most of the men owed between three and six dollars for goods purchased in May and June 1795. The partners invested in a distillery and sold whiskey for a dollar a gallon. In the late 1830s, storekeeper John Bartle recalled "little or no specie or bank notes in circulation" in early Cincinnati. Instead, "Orders or drafts on Government, drawn by the officers, were principally used as a circulating medium."[6] No wonder, then, that the quartermaster general's home, a two-story yellow frame house, "was the most commodious and best finished edifice in Cincinnati."[7]

Benjamin Van Cleve, the young nephew of contractor Robert Benham, earned his keep by doing everything from leading pack horses to Fort Jefferson to carrying messages to Secretary of War Henry Knox in Philadelphia. On one occasion, Van Cleve spent almost $155 traveling to the nation's capital, but he lost the bill and had to wait months to get reimbursement. Meanwhile, he and his uncle formed partnerships with friends to make money from transporting salt and selling goods and liquor to the army. As early as 1794, Van Cleve was working with a contractor who was supplying troops at Fort Massac on the Illinois River. When his horse was stolen in the same year, the young man recorded his belief that "this was a rascally world[,] that an honest man had no business in it, that without sharp elbowing no man could get through life." He "determined for the future to fight my way like others with force of hand."[8]

Nowhere were the camp-following entrepreneurs of the Ohio Valley in the 1790s more brutal than in their pursuit of information. Success in the army trade depended on the cultivation of well-informed contacts. Where were troops going to be? When would forts be abandoned or new ones constructed? In late 1794, Stanley and Gano's agent at Fort Jefferson, Aaron Reeder, wrote to Stanley because he wanted butter. He mentioned that liquor, flour, and bacon had been selling well; not so moccasins. In addition Reeder praised Lieutenant Andrew Marschalt "for his kindness to the store at Large." Marschalt had heard that Kentuckians "had arrived at Greenville." He "imediately gave me word of it," and Reeder "got the Baker to Bake some bread," which he sold "the next morning in about fifteen Minutes."[9]

In 1795 the signing of the Treaty of Greenville, which secured the lower two-thirds of what is now the state of Ohio for the United States and effectively ended hostilities between Indians and Americans in the upper Ohio Valley, brought an end to the commercial boom times in Cincinnati. Facing reduced military spending in the new city and its environs, traders and merchants had to expand their interests throughout the Ohio and Mississippi Valleys. The growing population of the Miami Valley kept them busy, especially when they could combine store keeping with tavern keeping. But it was never enough for the city's ambitious entrepreneurs. Like children behind the pied piper, they followed the U.S. Army in pursuit of its money and contracts. In May 1798 the ubiquitous William Stanley bid his partner Gano farewell and took a load of their goods and some purchased from Smith & Findlay down the Ohio. At Louisville, he contemplated going to Vincennes in the Northwest Territory but decided against it. Instead he pinned his hopes on the string of posts established by the United States on the lower Ohio and the Mississippi Rivers.

Smith & Findlay was not far behind Stanley. An employee informed the partnership in September 1798 that he had "arrived" in Lexington "from a d——d fatiguing journey from Natchez." There was "no sale for" the "Truck" of "Monogahala lads" at New Orleans, so he had sold his load in Natchez and promptly got the fever. Most of the people Smith & Findlay's man talked with in Natchez were army officers. Among them was Lieutenant John Steele, who gave him ten dollars to pay to Smith & Findlay for "a certain verbal order; be pleased to call on [Griffin] Yeatman [a Cincinnati tavern keeper] who will pay you that sum on my acct."[10]

As the attention of the U.S. Army turned away from the Northwest Territory to the lower Mississippi and as the Jefferson administration reduced the military budget, information and contacts became more important than ever to entrepreneurs like Smith and Findlay. While Smith was in the Senate, his partner enjoyed federal patronage with appointments as receiver of public monies in the Cincinnati land office (1801) and as U.S. marshal for the District of Ohio (1802).

Politics—on a national or even international level—was a necessary corollary to commerce. Not for nothing did John Smith seek a role in the U.S. government. Where better than Washington, DC, to obtain the information and forge the network of people so vital to the profits of Smith & Findlay? Or to affect the policy of the powerful U.S. government? What are politics about anyway, if not acquiring, keeping, and using power and influence?

In March 1802, Congress and President Jefferson reduced the size of the U.S. Army from an authorized level of 5,438 to 3,312 troops and officers. These numbers did not change until the end of the Jefferson administration. Most of the army was scattered in posts in trans-Appalachia. The same act that cut the number of troops also eliminated the position of quartermaster general. Thenceforth, the military supplied itself by contracts made between the secretary of war, Henry Dearborn, or his designated agents, and entrepreneurs such as Smith and Findlay. The system, haphazard and inefficient, was revised during the War of 1812. Before then, army officers and their government were largely at the mercy of local and regional merchants. Basically unregulated and irregularly audited, the supply system created by Jeffersonian frugality was a boon to the likes of John Smith.

Senator Smith easily obtained government contracts to supply food and gunboats to the western posts. Smith & Findlay did business across a huge area, from Cincinnati to St. Louis and south to Natchez and New Orleans. The senator was constantly on the go, reliving the early travels of William Stanley on a grand scale. Smith was hardly a frontier yokel, coyly ambivalent about the culture of the marketplace. Like many of his friends and competitors, he was exploiting the intersection of business and politics in the early republic. These Jeffersonians supported a weak national government only to the extent that it benefited them; they wanted money with as little regulation as possible. Their concern was less with a strong or impotent United States than with an accessible one.

Smith and Findlay were as interested in governmental policy as in contracts. Not surprisingly, the free navigation of the Mississippi obsessed them, and on several levels. They desired unimpeded use of the Mississippi and unregulated right of deposit at New Orleans. Smith and Findlay also had an economic interest in seeing the United States government assert itself with a display of force, that is, to spend money in trans-Appalachia. In March 1803, Findlay told Meriwether Lewis, President Jefferson's private secretary, that the people of Cincinnati, "from the oldest citizen to the shoeblack," were talking about the recent shutting of the port of New Orleans. "God forbid we should have to fight" the French or the Spanish, but if the United States did, Findlay hoped that the government would not rely on militia alone.[11]

At the same time, a Natchez correspondent of the Cincinnati *Western Spy* (probably Smith) urged the residents of trans-Appalachia not to wait for "forms, ceremonies and etiquette" before deciding "whether it will be best to drive the miscreants from these waters or not."[12] The simple fact was that war was good for Smith and Findlay. Trans-Appalachian merchants needed officers with money for supplies and soldiers eager to spend their pay. Zebulon Pike, at Kaskaskia, urged Findlay to be for "War with Spain." He hoped that "it would add to the Numbers and respectability of the Members of our Profession."[13] Smith was more direct. In urging the taking of New Orleans, he warned that "no time . . . ought to be lost. The Western Country has become an object of importance, by her Geographical, Commercial and political situation."[14]

Although the Louisiana Purchase of 1803 put an end to the war talk—temporarily—Smith and Findlay could not afford to terminate their relationship with the national government. Eager for some kind of military engagement, they continued to nurture their government contracts. Sometimes Senator Smith relied on an agent, such as Findlay's quarrelsome and incompetent nephew Jonathan. More often than not, he dealt directly with military officers in the Mississippi Valley.

The most important of these men was James Wilkinson, commander of the U.S. Army. In August 1805, Wilkinson wrote from St. Louis to offer his services to Smith. He described the extent of the troops in the lower Mississippi Valley and warned Smith that with the contract for sixteen forts, "it is possible you might make a trifle, but most probable you will lose."[15] In October when he learned that Smith was definitely a contractor, he wrote to Smith "by a private Hand . . . to apprise you of my ready disposition *to enter into your Service & of my determination to do it well for you.*" Wilkinson was full of suggestions about how Smith should handle his business.[16]

The spectacle of a military officer putting himself in the service of a merchant may strike us as astonishing. Wilkinson did it in part from necessity; after all, he had troops to feed. He also did it to cement both his economic and social relationship with Smith. Such an arrangement was not unusual in trans-Appalachia. Regional, large-scale entrepreneurs needed the agents of the national government, and vice versa. When Wilkinson enclosed inventories of the St. Louis area posts, including the number of rations needed of whiskey, flour, salt, vinegar, pork, and beef, he was giving Smith both information and access. In return, the general expected prompt and efficient service from the contractor. Wilkinson was no fool, even if personal integrity was a concept with which he was unfamiliar. He knew that this relationship was awkward. (How could he not when he told Smith that he acted "With every disposition to serve you & to promote yr Interests, as far as I can, consistently with my Duty to the public"?) But Wilkinson also knew that it was necessary, given the evolution of regional commerce along intertwined political and economic lines.

Wilkinson had told Smith in November 1805 that "the Conduct & measures of the Spaniards" would "force" military movements down the Mississippi.[17] In January, Smith positively salivated about the prospects for war. "High toned measures" were in the air. "If the Belligerent Powers persist in these depredations War is inevitable."[18] In virtually his only speech before the U.S. Senate, Smith ardently supported a resolution asking that President Thomas Jefferson demand the return of property seized by British warships. The senator talked at length about freedom of the seas and the need to protect citizens from being "robbed and plundered on the high seas, while sailing under the American flag and engaged in a lawful trade." He was eager for war. Smith "would make a provisional declaration of war" against any country that refused to "redress our wrongs. . . . Rather than see the honor and the rights of my country violated, I would wade through rivers of blood and fight till doomsday in their defence."[19] No doubt Senator Smith would also have been willing to sign whatever contracts were necessary to supply as many men as possible for as long as possible.

In 1806, John Smith was at the peak of his career. He and his family lived in a large house in Terrace Park to the east of Cincinnati; he owned extensive property in the Miami valley and in Louisiana. The president of the United States apparently sought his advice on matters regarding the West. He was well known all over the western and southern United States, his credit secured by his reputation for reliability. Then, in the fall, Aaron Burr visited Cincinnati and spent time at Smith's home. This meeting destroyed Smith's world. Accused of conspiring with Burr and denounced by politicians in both Ohio and Washington, Smith resigned his Senate seat, and his trading empire disintegrated almost overnight.

There is no need to rehash the details of the Burr Conspiracy, if anyone can figure out exactly what they were. Suffice it to say that Burr was planning an expedition somewhere in the Southwest, and he needed supplies. Where else would an intelligent man seek them but from John Smith? The former vice president, who Senator John Quincy Adams believed had courted Smith in the Senate with "a very studied attention" and "a peculiar respect," was paying Senator Smith a compliment by coming to him when in need of boats, provisions, and possibly arms.[20] The senator talked with Burr and perhaps made promises. The details of their meeting are unknown.

In a sworn deposition, taken in April 1807, Smith claimed that Burr had only asked him for a pack saddle, two bear skins, and "some flour and pork." "[The] Deponent told Col. Burr that It was not in his power to enter into any Contract with him and he positively Refused to do it as he had Large arrangements to make to supply the troops of the United States with provisions."[21] Smith's protestations aside, it is clear that he did agree to supply Burr in some way. It is highly likely, however, that the conversation involved commerce more than politics. Smith probably did not consider the possibility of treason because he was concentrating on closing a deal.

By coming at Smith and other prominent western figures trapped in the Burr Conspiracy with questions of treason and character, historians have missed the significance of the event. What was at issue was less the dismemberment of the Union—why would a man such as Smith risk all that he accumulated?—than the emergence of a regional economy built on long-distance commerce and a complex relationship among entrepreneurs and government officials. The United States was the best customer of Smith and Findlay. It was their market. And they needed military expeditions to make it bigger.

If Burr talked of provisions and boats with Smith, he was only testifying to the workings of the trans-Appalachian mercantile world. As state and federal officials began to swarm down on Burr and his alleged conspirators, where was John Smith but in the lower Mississippi Valley? He surrendered to federal authorities in Nashville. On the very same day, he wrote to Secretary of War Henry Dearborn to arrange for payment for provisions he had purchased for Mobile. Always the businessman, John Smith was solid and persevering during the greatest crisis of his life. "You are certainly a man of firmness," wrote one friend reassuringly. "It is your character."[22]

Smith devoted most of 1807 and 1808 to efforts to clear himself of charges of treason, for which he was tried in Richmond, Virginia, and later in the U.S. Senate. Without reputation or contacts, labeled a deceptive traitor, John Smith, merchant, could no longer exist. Friends and allies in Cincinnati rushed to the senator's defense with resolutions and depositions. Smith called on his son to attend his trial at Richmond. However, he had to send letters to Natchez and Fort Adams as well as his address at New Orleans to find the young man. As always, the Smiths were a far-flung family.

Meanwhile, James Findlay and John S. Gano proved to be fair-weather friends. Gano had also met with Burr, but he claimed to have heard and done nothing illegal. Although Findlay took a leading role in squashing anyone associated with Burr, he seems to have ignored Smith. Other Cincinnatians—political opponents and competitors—did their best to ruin Smith with vague accusations. The bottom line was the basis of personal loyalty. Cincinnati merchants sacrificed Smith in order to keep one of their biggest customers happy. Caught up in the hysteria of the moment, the Ohio legislature demanded that Smith resign his Senate seat.

A stunned Senator Smith refused. Bitterly, he accused the legislators of having given currency to "malicious" insinuations. The resolution condemning him was "highly calculated to wound my feelings, and injure my character." Although Smith wanted to resign, he could not now do so. Such a "step" would be "at present, incompatible with my feelings, my duty & my honor."[23] Rallying his resources and friends, Smith decided the best defense was a good offense. If someone was trying to destroy his good name, he would reply in kind. And so he attacked his Cincinnati critics as deceitful and dangerous men.

Smith's defense had some impact. He was never convicted of treason. In April 1808 the Senate failed by one vote to expel him, in part because of the vigorous defense by his lawyer, Francis Scott Key, who asked what Smith could possibly have gained from treason and a dismemberment of the United States. After all, the chief witness had himself denounced Smith as "a damned army contractor and gunboat-builder." "No man in the whole Western Country would have been more certainly ruined by this project than Mr. Smith," pointed out Key. Smith enjoyed an almost unparalleled amount of the government's "patronage and favor," added Senator James Hillhouse of Connecticut. Given the arc of Smith's career, one is inclined to agree with his other attorney, Robert Goodloe Harper, that Smith was not interested in breaking up the United States but in using "his connexions and situation" to get "a large share" of the trade with whatever expeditions or settlements Burr had in mind.[24]

Despite his narrow victory, Smith resigned anyway. Not only had he lost the confidence of his constituents, but he also had to devote all his time to saving his trading empire. Over the next few years, Smith worked to restore his previous social and economic standing. He tried to organize a Farmer's Exporting Company, although the former merchant and senator was now in the position of begging for the attention of his former colleagues. He sent his son Lewis and a crew of four with the brig *Compromise* loaded with cargo to his other son in New Orleans to sell for the benefit of his creditors in Philadelphia.

The War of 1812 briefly revived Smith's career as a contractor. Settling in St. Francisville, Louisiana (near Fort Adams), he labored to resolve the interlocked social and financial entanglements created by his brief encounter with Aaron Burr. His fondest wish was to be free of his debts. In 1819, as financial panic struck Cincinnati, New Orleans, and points in between, dramatically and painfully demonstrating to the people of trans-Appalachia just how much they were enmeshed in the international marketplace, Smith suffered personal losses. Both his wife Elizabeth and his daughter Ann died en route to Louisiana.

The ever-adaptable Smith soon remarried; with his new wife, Margaret Wisdom, he had four children in quick succession. Part of the time the "renegade Senator," as he was known in Louisiana, lived with the family of a Baptist minister. According to his daughter, Smith's "last days were his best days. His return to the fold from which he had long strayed was accompanied with bitter repentance and deep humility." Smith preached again, first among African Americans and then in Texas. He taught the children geography, astronomy, chemistry, and Spanish and professed regret at not following his first wife's advice to renounce politics for religion; had he done so, he "would have prevented all misfortunes." As he told his children in 1818: "I have tried many conditions of life, and . . . it is only in Religion I can find peace & Happiness."[25] In August 1823, he seemed at last to be at peace. All he wanted now was to be remembered to granddaughters, family, and friends with great affection. He died while walking home on July 30, 1824. Smith left a considerable amount of property, all of which was sold at a probate auction to cover his debts.

Smith's world was one in which the U.S. government was a major player, in which public reputation, private piety, personal profit, and professional politics could scarcely be disentangled from each other. The tragedy of his life was his own doing; when he talked with Burr, he gambled with the slippery line between public and private interests once too often. Still, Smith's career is not without larger significance. If nothing else, it demonstrates both the naked ambition of many trans-Appalachians and the centrality of the federal government to the realization of their dreams. Much as many of us today would like to celebrate resistance to or ambivalence about the capitalist transformation of trans-Appalachia, what is most startling about the region in this period is how eagerly hundreds of men like John Smith put their lives, their fortunes, and their sacred honor directly and deliberately into the maelstrom of a government-supported marketplace.

Notes

1. Francis Baily, *Journal of a Tour in Unsettled Parts of North America in 1796 & 1797*, ed. Jack D. L. Holmes (Carbondale, IL, 1969), 92.

2. A. H. Dunlevy, *History of the Miami Baptist Association* (Cincinnati, OH, 1869), 109, 114.

3. Jacob Burnet, *Notes on the Early Settlement of the North-Western Territory* (Cincinnati, OH, 1847), 36.

4. Aaron Reeder to William Stanley, October 27, 1794, John Stites Gano Papers, Cincinnati Historical Society, Cincinnati, OH.

5. "Diary of Major William Stanley, 1790–1810," *Quarterly Publication of the Historical and Philosophical Society of Ohio* 14 (1919): 22.

6. "John Bartle's Recollections, taken down at Dr. Drake's," in Beverley W. Bond, ed., "Dr. Daniel Drake's Memoir of the Miami Country, 1779–1794," *Quarterly Publication of the Historical and Philosophical Society of Ohio* 18 (1923): 116.

7. Burnet, *Notes*, 34.

8. Beverley W. Bond Jr., "Memoirs of Benjamin Van Cleve," *Quarterly Publication of the Historical and Philosophical Society of Ohio* 17 (1922): 53–54.

9. Aaron Reeder to William Stanley, October 27, 1794, Gano Papers.

10. W. McCluney to John Smith and William Findlay, September 4, 1798, in "Selections from the Torrence Papers, v. the Transfer of Louisiana and the Burr Conspiracy, as Illustrated by the Findlay Letters," ed. Isaac Joslin Cox, *Quarterly Publication of the Historical and Philosophical Society of Ohio* 4 (1909): 96–97.

11. William Findlay to Meriwether Lewis, March 7, 1803, ibid., 98–99.

12. Ibid., 98n.

13. Z. M. Pike to William Findlay, March 11, 1803, ibid., 99.

14. John Smith to William Findlay, April 13, 1803, ibid., 101–2.

15. James Wilkinson to John Smith, August 11, 1805, John Smith Papers, Cincinnati Historical Society.

16. James Wilkinson to John Smith, October 9, 1805, ibid.

17. James Wilkinson to John Smith, November 26, 1805, ibid.

18. John Smith to John William Findlay, January 27, 1806, in Cox, "Selections from the Torrence Papers," 114, 115.

19. Speech of John Smith of Ohio, February 1806, *The Debates and Proceedings in the Congress of the United States*, 9th Cong., 1st sess., 111, 111–12.

20. John Quincy Adams, Speech to the Senate, April 1808, *The Debates and Proceedings in the Congress of the United States*, 10th Cong. 1st sess., 249.

21. John Smith, Affidavit, April 13, 1807, Smith Papers.

22. Henry Carberry to John Smith, September 7, 1807, ibid.

23. John Smith to Edward Tiffin, January 12, 1807, ibid.

24. Francis Scott Key, James Hillhouse, Robert Goodloe Harper, Speeches to the Senate, April 1808, *Debates and Proceedings in the Congress of the United States*, 10th Cong., 1st sess., 205, 276, 227.

25. E. Challen to Mary Gano, n.d., quoted in Dunlevy, *Miami Baptist Association*, 115, 117.

Suggested Readings

Abernethy, Thomas Perkins. *The Burr Conspiracy*. New York, 1954.

Appleby, Joyce. *Capitalism and a New Social Order: The Republican Vision of the 1790s*. New York, 1984.

Aron, Stephen. *How the West Was Lost: The Transformation of Kentucky from Daniel Boone to Henry Clay*. Baltimore, MD, 1997.

Cayton, Andrew R. L. *Frontier Indiana*. Bloomington, IN, 1986.

——. " 'Separate Interests' and the Nation-State: The Washington Administration and the Origins of Regionalism in the Trans-Appalachian West." *Journal of American History* 79 (1992): 39–67.

Cunningham, Noble E. *The Process of Government under Jefferson*. Princeton, NJ, 1978.

Downes, Randolph C. "Trade in Frontier Ohio," *Mississippi Valley Historical Review* 16 (1930): 467–94.

Faragher, John Mack. *Daniel Boone: The Life and Legend of an American Pioneer*. New York, 1992.

——. *Sugar Creek: Life on the Illinois Prairie*. New Haven, CT, 1986.

Gilje, Paul A., ed. *Wages of Independence: Capitalism in the Early American Republic*. Madison, WI, 1997.

Hurt, R. Douglas. *The Ohio Frontier: Crucible of the Old Northwest*. Bloomington, IN, 1996.

Kohn, Richard H. *Eagle and Sword: The Federalists and the Creation of the Military Establishment in America, 1783–1802*. New York, 1975.

Perkins, Elizabeth A. "The Consumer Frontier: Household Consumption in Early Kentucky," *Journal of American History* 78 (1991): 486–510.

Ratcliffe, Donald J. *Party Spirit in a Frontier Republic: Democratic Politics in Ohio, 1793–1821*. Columbus, OH, 1998.

Sellers, Charles. *The Market Revolution: Jacksonian America, 1815–1846*. New York, 1991.

Stokes, Melvin, and Stephen Conway, eds. *The Market Revolution in America: Social, Political, and Religious Expressions, 1800–1880*. Charlottesville, VA, 1996.

6

Arsène Lacarrière Latour
Immigrant, Patriot-Historian,
and Foreign Agent

Gene A. Smith

As the experiences of James Trotter and John Smith plainly prove, opportunities abounded on the frontier in the early republic. Adventurers, no less than the industrious, were drawn to it. Arsène Lacarrière Latour, a ruined French aristocrat, emigrated to the New World to reconstruct his fortunes—economic and personal. There he adopted many personas: advance agent for Napoleon's new empire in the Caribbean; architect and businessman in Louisiana; aide to General Andrew Jackson at the Battle of New Orleans; and Spanish operative in the American Southwest following the war. Like many citizens of the early republic, Latour wore many social masks and spoke in a variety of cultural dialects. His shifting political allegiances also reveal the tenuous hold that the government of an expansive and expanding republic had on its citizens. In the end, Latour's loyalty was less to the masters and governments he served than to himself. Propelled by the same self-interest that obsessed the sober-minded, this French adventurer exploited the competing empires and rival nationalities in the Gulf Coast to achieve personal success if not eternal glory. His many careers and the cycle of his successes and failures suggest the seemingly endless possibilities and the many perils of life on the periphery of the United States.

Gene A. Smith teaches early American history at Texas Christian University in Fort Worth. He is author or editor of numerous publications, including *Filibusters and Expansionsists: Jeffersonian Manifest Destiny, 1800–1821*, with Frank L. Owsley Jr. (1997); *Arsène Lacarrière Latour's Historical Memoir of the War in West Florida and Louisiana in 1814–15, with an Atlas* (1999); and *Thomas ap Catesby Jones: Commodore of Manifest Destiny* (2000).

On January 8, 1815, General Andrew Jackson's hastily assembled army—consisting of regulars, Kentucky and Tennessee volunteers, Louisiana Creoles, French refugees, Baratarian privateers and pirates, Choctaw Indians, and African American slaves and freemen—confronted a superior force of British veterans seasoned by long service in the Napoleonic Wars. When the sun burned off the lingering fog that morning,

British general Sir Edwin Pakenham arrogantly ordered his troops to make a frontal assault, expecting that the American troops would flee, as had happened some months earlier at Bladensburg, near Washington, DC. But in this instance Jackson's army had the advantage of terrain, determined leadership, and a strongly constructed earthen-covered cotton-bale rampart designed by the French-trained engineer Major Arsène Lacarrière Latour. Within thirty minutes some two thousand Redcoats, including Pakenham himself, lay dead in front of the American line on the Plains of Chalmette.

The American victory at the Battle of New Orleans has been the subject of considerable study and debate since 1815. Jackson has been both praised for his military talent and accused of stealing victory from the jaws of defeat. Regardless, the battle represented one of the watershed events of U.S. history: no other military engagement between George Washington's victory at Yorktown and the Confederate attack on Fort Sumter did more to intensify American patriotism or ensure independence. In its aftermath many authors eulogized Jackson and the men who served with him and praised the glorious triumph as a pivotal event in the young country's history. The battle came to represent the American ability to persevere and prevail despite overwhelming odds.

Perhaps no one praised Jackson as much or offered a more fitting and lasting tribute than did the Frenchman Latour, who wrote the first historical account of the battle. The engineer-turned-historian celebrated Jackson's defense of New Orleans in glowing terms. He related "in detail, with the utmost exactness and precision, the principal events which took place in the course of this campaign." Latour also substantiated his story with copies of original letters, reports, and documents that provided "the vouchers [evidence] of the facts which [he] related." Throughout his memorial, or what Latour called his "inadequate tribute," he insisted that the victory at New Orleans was "due to the energy, ability and courage of a single man." According to Latour, Jackson had preserved the country, and the "voice of the whole nation" acknowledged his selfless sacrifice and service. Latour's book told the American people in no uncertain terms that Jackson had saved their country and was their hero.[1]

Major Latour appears to be a shadowy figure of the past, with very little information about him available upon first examination. History has told us that he was a Frenchman, the "Principal Engineer of the Seventh Military District" during the Battle of New Orleans, and the

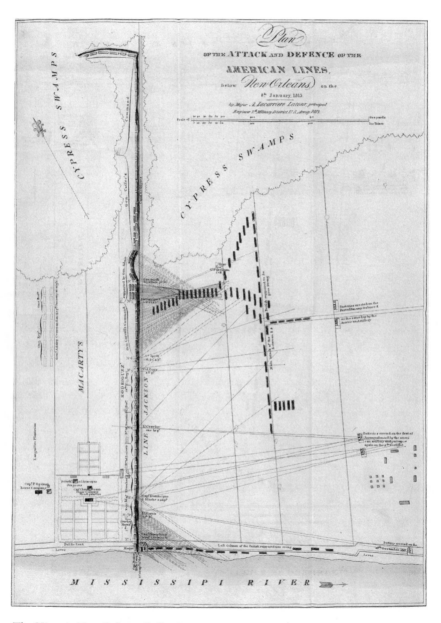

The Historic New Orleans Collection, accession no. 73-13-L. *Courtesy of the Historic New Orleans Collection*

author of *Historical Memoir of the War in West Florida and Louisiana in 1814–15* (1816). Yet other than this basic information, his life before and after January 8, 1815, has remained an untold story. Had he not written his book it is quite probable that Latour would have fallen between the cracks of time, to be completely forgotten.

Géraud-Calixte Jean-Baptiste Arsène LaCarrière was born in the French village of Aurillac on October 13, 1778, to Guillaume LaCarrière (Seigneur de Latour and Falhiés) and his wife, Louise Marguerite Daudin. Being the oldest son, Arsène would have inherited the family's title and lands had it not been for the French Revolution that began in May 1789. During that summer the price of grain, the grist of ordinary people's diet, soared to prohibitively high levels. Worse, unemployment became rampant in both cities and countryside. Across France, peasants soon rose against their manor lords, and chaos prevailed. Although by the fall of 1789 a brief period of calm had returned to the countryside, France soon found itself at war with Austria and Prussia; by 1793 the Reign of Terror swept the country. The world Arsène had known crumbled before his eyes. His uncle Antoine, the priest of Lascelle, suffered deportation in the fall of 1793, and by early 1794 a guillotine had been erected in the public square of Aurillac.

Upheaval and disruption in France provided opportunities for many young men to advance. Accordingly, in 1799, Latour accepted an apprenticeship with a local architect—Citizen Lallié—who designed and built houses in Aurillac. Within two years, he had enrolled at the Academy of Fine Arts, where he studied with the noted architect Charles Percier, who designed the original Arc de Triomphe as well as additions to the Louvre and the Tuileries. Latour's engineering and architectural training in Paris taught him valuable skills that would be useful for his future. His new career, however, was not the reason for his emigration to the New World. Motivation to seek new opportunities in new lands came after his arranged marriage to Marie-Anne Caroline de Montal in January 1798. The union brought Latour a sizable dowry, including an estate in Saint Domingue that ten years earlier had made a profit of 10,000 francs.

Though the marriage appeared to be amicable—it produced the birth of son Emile in 1799 and daughter Coralie in 1800—Latour apparently did not have a deep, loving relationship with his wife. In early September 1802, he happily boarded the ship *L'Alphonse* bound for Saint Domingue, where he planned to recover the property belonging to him and his wife's family. Unhappily, Saint Domingue did not provide the prosperity or stability that Latour had hoped for. The island already had suffered a twelve-year insurrection in which slaves ultimately defeated the local whites. They also conquered French General Victor Emmanuel Leclerc's 34,000-man expeditionary force sent by Napoleon Bonaparte to retake the island. Thus, when Latour arrived in Cap François in late October 1802 the country had been ravaged by years of fighting. As a result he found himself plagued by the same financial problems that he had experienced in Paris. His fortunes soon improved. On Christmas day 1802, Latour informed his wife that General Donatien Rochambeau—who had recently arrived to take command of French forces on the island—had offered him a position in the Corps of Engineers. Latour eagerly accepted the appointment, convinced that it would solve his financial problems.

Rochambeau soon escalated the island's racial war in his attempt to subdue the population. French troops burned, hanged, drowned, and tortured blacks in a policy of terror that by March 1803 had driven the island's population again to insurrection. Two months later Napoleon decided to break the Peace of Amiens and renew his war with Great Britain. He amassed men and ships along the English Channel for a planned invasion of England while Rochambeau begged for additional troops, supplies, and relief. Black insurgents in the southern part of Saint Domingue, supported by the British, waged a devastating guerrilla war that slowly decimated and demoralized the French army and terrified the white population, who expected to suffer an exacting revenge. Every night, privateers sailed from the island with wealthy white refugees bound for Cuba and Louisiana. Having lost control of the countryside, Rochambeau sought refuge in the fortified port city of Le Cap, where he was quickly surrounded by black insurgents and British warships off the harbor. Having no choice, on November 29, 1803, Rochambeau surrendered to the British the remnants of his force. French soldiers soon languished in English prisons.

Latour, however, escaped the horrors of those last days in Saint Domingue. In May 1804, he wrote his son that he had been working in the United States for a few months. How Latour arrived in the United States remains a mystery. Most likely, he fled the island with General Charles François Antoine Lallemand aboard a privateer for Cuba and remained with the general in Havana for a short time before emigrating to Louisiana. While in Havana, Latour apparently met several French privateers and exiles—including Jean Lafitte and the engineer Barthélemy Lafon—who would soon play important roles in Louisiana's history as well as in Latour's life.

Exactly when Latour arrived in Louisiana is also subject to speculation. In the introduction to his *Historical Memoir*, Latour declared that he had helped Lafon prepare maps of New Orleans and its Gulf Coast environs. The two most likely acted as advance agents for Napoleon's projected occupation of the Louisiana territory in 1803. The following year, after the Louisiana Purchase, he and Lafon turned over the maps that they had prepared to General James Wilkinson of the U.S. Army, who had arrived in New Orleans with the acting governor of Louisiana, William C. C. Claiborne, to receive the territory for the United States. Unknown to Claiborne or other American officials, Wilkinson also worked for the Spanish. His trip to New Orleans gave him a chance to renew his foreign connections and to receive back pay.

Wilkinson's intrigue while in Louisiana ultimately delayed his departure to Washington by weeks, and to cover his tracks, he informed Secretary of War Henry Dearborn that he was collecting material for a report on the territory. That report took the form of Wilkinson's essay, "Reflections on Louisiana," and his monograph, *The Topography of Louisiana*, which combined hard-to-get reliable information about the territory with a number of excellent maps prepared by Latour and Lafon. The general gave copies of his work to Secretary Dearborn, who passed it along to a grateful President Thomas Jefferson, and to the Spanish governor of West Florida, Vicente Folch, who paid him handsomely. Wilkinson's report provided sensitive information about the contested boundaries of the territory, the military situation in the region, and the U.S. government's intentions concerning the Gulf Coast. Wilkinson also secretly warned Spanish officials to maintain control over the Floridas because they were the key to American commerce in the Gulf: Latour's maps vividly illustrated this point.

Latour subsequently left Louisiana to pursue business opportunities in the North. After a short and unsuccessful partnership in a New York City trading business, Latour returned to Louisiana in the summer of 1806. The young French engineer, who had recently arrived in the remaining Spanish territory of Louisiana, decided to tackle an important project. For Elias Toutant Beauregard, the retired military captain of Spanish Louisiana, he drafted a city plan for Baton Rouge. Laying the city out in the classical French tradition, Latour's design used grid and radial streets around a proposed cathedral square. With the Mississippi River on the West, he surrounded the city to the north, south, and east with boulevards. The Spanish commandant of the district, Carlos Grand Pré, a former French commandant who had gained recognition as a fair-minded administrator, approved Latour's plan and began construction.

During the years 1806 to 1810, while Louisiana experienced the growing pains of a new territory, Latour spent much of his time moving between Baton Rouge and New Orleans making land surveys for both Beauregard and prominent attorney Edward Livingston. Latour also worked for the Marquis de Lafayette, to whom Congress had voted a sizable land grant; he spent weeks locating and surveying a suitable tract of land for the French hero of the American Revolution. Although these jobs brought him into contact with the most respected members of Louisiana society, they did little to improve materially his financial well-being.

By the fall of 1810, Latour decided to devote himself full-time to architectural projects in New Orleans. On September 22, 1810, the newspaper *Gazette de la Louisiane* reported that he and Jean-Hyacinthe Laclotte had opened an engineering and architectural firm at the corner of Royal and Orleans Streets. According to the notice the partners would draw plans and offer estimates, oversee construction, and erect both public and private buildings. In addition, on September 20, they had opened a day and evening school that taught drawing, painting, architecture, and carpentry, as well as interior design and decoration. Their business initially prospered as the two purchased office space, designed Tremoulet's Hotel, began constructing the first Orleans Street Theatre, and renovated extensively the house of doctor Yves Lemonnier. Their success quickly brought new projects, including a house on Bourbon Street and several other buildings in the city's French Quarter.

In but a few years Latour had become one of the most successful architects in New Orleans. He designed and constructed many of the most important buildings in the now bustling city, and he moved easily between the established French Creole elite and incoming Anglo-American entrepreneurs. Latour also understood the opportunities that Louisiana provided for a businessman who could bridge the cultural gap between the two disparate groups, gain and maintain the confidence of each, and promote his business in good times as well as bad. Initially he was successful doing it all: he spoke French and English fluently, became a citizen of the United States during the spring of 1812 (without repudiating his French heritage), and chose jobs that did not overtax his financial resources. Despite a seemingly auspicious beginning, on May 7, 1813, Latour and Laclotte filed a petition for bankruptcy. When they offered an inventory a month later, it revealed that the two architects owned only their office, a slave, construction tools, and an assortment of building materials.

Their demise did not result completely from their financial mismanagement, but rather from the economic problems caused by the War of 1812. The war between Britain and the United States brought tremendous disruption and uncertainty to Louisiana and the Gulf Coast because it hindered commerce there. Economic inactivity forced many businesses into bankruptcy and virtually closed the port of New Orleans to trade. Bales of cotton piled up on the city's wharves as British warships constantly patrolled and blocked the mouth of the Mississippi. Another problem that made life on the Gulf Coast uncertain was the problematic allegiance of Louisiana's inhabitants. The territory had become the eighteenth state of the Union in 1812, but the true loyalty of Louisiana's mixed population remained a perplexed and unresolved question. Spanish and French Creoles appeared reluctant to sacrifice or become involved in what was to them an apparently foreign war that brought them nothing but further hardship. To worsen matters, rumors circulated throughout the region that should England win the war (as seemed to be happening), Louisiana would be returned to Spain. Given these circumstances, it was no surprise that American officials questioned the fate of New Orleans and the Gulf Coast and the loyalties of their peoples.

For the French émigré Latour, however, the war provided a new opportunity for him to demonstrate his talents. Even though he had no strong loyalty to the United States, he hated the British. Latour had trained as an engineer and had applied his trade in Saint Domingue; the war gave him another chance to practice his craft. When the war moved to the Gulf of Mexico in the fall of 1814, Latour volunteered his talents to General Andrew Jackson, commander of the Seventh Military District. On November 21, Edward Livingston heartily recommended Latour as a "man of perfect honor and integrity [who] speaks both French and English fluently."[2] When Jackson arrived in the city a few days later, he met with his old acquaintance Livingston and appointed Latour as principal engineer of the district.

Latour possessed the qualities that Jackson needed to bridge the linguistic and cultural gap between French Louisiana Creoles and Anglo-Americans as he prepared the city for an attack. In addition, Jackson desperately needed Latour's engineering services because most West Point-trained military engineers already had been sent to the northern frontier or were superintending coastal defenses. Jackson knew that Latour and Lafon had prepared maps in 1805 for Wilkinson and again in 1813 for General Thomas Flournoy (then commander of the Seventh Military District). Jackson also recognized that these maps were both accurate and the best available.

By the time the two men met in early December, Jackson's strategic situation appeared perilous. It became more critical when Latour informed him that there were seven possible water routes for a British attack, including Bayou Lafourche, Barataria Bay, River Aux Chenes and Bayou Terre aux Boeufs, the Mississippi River itself, and three routes via Lake Borgne. Latour assured Jackson that of the possible routes Lake Borgne, with its three approaches, offered the most feasible alternative for a British attack. Not surprising to Latour, the British ultimately used Bayou Bienvenu, which drained the area east of New Orleans and stretched from Lake Borgne to within a mile of the Mississippi River. From there the British proceeded north nine miles along the river levee,

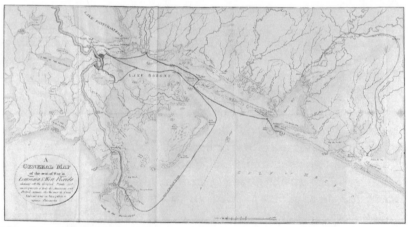

The Historic New Orleans Collection, accession no. 73-13-L. *Courtesy of the Historic New Orleans Collection*

a narrow strip of land through the region's sugar plantations, toward New Orleans. Though this approach had appeared to be the path of least physical resistance, Latour assured Jackson that it had many obstacles. The route was shallower than expected, which prevented British ships from entering the estuary and limited gunfire support to cover their barges' advance. Moreover, he went on, the distance from Cat Island, at the mouth of Lake Borgne, to Bayou Bienvenu spanned sixty-two miles, and it took thirty-six hours of hard rowing to reach it.

Soon after his consultation with Latour, Jackson, now emboldened, ordered all of the water routes to the city blocked. Early on the morning of December 4, he joined Daniel Todd Patterson, commander of the New Orleans naval station, and Latour as they traveled down river to Fort St. Philip. En route, Latour provided Jackson with diagrams of the bastion—which appeared to be in good shape—and explained its strengths and weaknesses. After heeding Latour's advice, Jackson ordered only minor alterations, instructing the engineer to destroy the wooden barracks within the fort and add more artillery on both sides of the river. During their return, Latour pointed out to Jackson that marshes and swamps dominated the landscape and thus afforded the British only a few locations to land troops below New Orleans.

On December 15, Jackson received news that an overwhelmingly superior British force had captured the Navy's gunboat flotilla stationed on Lake Borgne the previous day. The enemy's victory placed Jackson at a severe disadvantage because it allowed the British to choose their point of attack. This distressing news was made worse by reports of more than eighty British warships off the Louisiana coast. The situation had become desperate for Jackson. He declared martial law and, on December 18, reviewed troops in the square at the cathedral. Jackson needed men and at this point accepted any help, including two battalions of free men of color and Jean Lafitte's "hellish banditti" of pirates and privateers, who brought their important cache of powder, shot, and flints. At first Jackson had been unwilling to seek help from the black troops or Lafitte's pirates, but he could not refuse their assistance when facing such a critical state of affairs. To his credit and Jackson's subsequent relief, Latour most likely arranged the meeting in which Lafitte offered to help Jackson and the Americans.

On the evening of December 22, 1814, Jackson learned that British sails had been sighted off the three bayous behind Terre aux Boeufs. The following morning, he sent Latour and Howell Tatum to investigate the report that the British were within striking distance of the city. As they traveled south along the river, Latour encountered several people rushing toward New Orleans. He was told that British forces occupied General Jacques Villère's plantation and had captured the general's son. Tatum immediately returned to tell Jackson of the recent developments, while Latour continued south to reconnoiter Villère's plantation. Cautiously approaching "within rifle shot of those troops," Latour estimated that the British had between 1,600 and 1,800 men.[3] He immediately returned, and by the early afternoon Latour had provided Jackson with precise information about the enemy's disposition, location, and strength.

Latour's report prompted Jackson to launch a surprise attack later that evening. In the nighttime operation against the British position some seven miles below the city, Jackson lost more than 10 percent of his force (24 killed, 115 wounded, 74 missing or captured) and had to retreat without destroying the British advance guard. Jackson's surprise attack, although not completely successful, did force the British to exercise caution and to delay their operations. The attack bought Jackson extra time, and as such, it was a turning point in the New Orleans campaign. During that important operation, Jackson reported that "Major Latour, having no command, volunteered his services, and was of great assistance to me."[4]

On December 24, 1814, the same day that American and British diplomats signed the Treaty of Ghent ending the war, Jackson moved his army north along the river levee to the old Rodriguez Canal millrace. Here Latour supervised the emplacement of artillery and the construction of earthen ramparts on the north side of the canal. After four days of backbreaking, nonstop work, Latour's "intrenchments on Rodriguez's canal" were ready for use.[5] To strengthen the defenses further, Jackson ordered Latour to cut the levee south of the canal, which flooded the ground in front of the American line. Jackson also instructed Major Lafon to do the same below the British lines, surrounding the British with water. Although the temporary swell of the river quickly subsided, the torrent provided a week's worth of protection as Jackson's troops bolstered their defenses. The water eventually saturated the ground and created a quagmire that hindered future British operations.

On that same day, Jackson also received an alarming report from the Chef Menteur. Apparently British troops had landed, and this news prompted Jackson to reevaluate enemy operations south of the city. Wanting to corroborate the story before he acted, Jackson sent Latour and two hundred Tennesseans to erect batteries at the confluence of the Bayou Sauvage and the Chef Menteur Pass. When Latour arrived, he did not find a full-scale enemy assault but rather news that British sailors had set fire to the dry grass of the peninsula; smoke and flames had forced the withdrawal of American forces. Latour returned immediately to New Orleans and told a now-relieved Jackson that the news had been false: there was no British attack.

Latour, however, had arrived at Jackson's headquarters south of the city just as the British launched a frightening rocket attack against the American line. For the better part of a day the British fired Congreve rockets with the expectation, as Latour recounted, that the "noise would strike terror" into the inexperienced Americans. Although the rocket attack only wounded ten men and destroyed two caissons, it convinced Jackson that the main British army lay before him and that he should strengthen his defensive position. To that end, Latour widened the ditch, raised the height of the rampart, and placed more guns along the length of Jackson's line.

Although Latour had played a critical role during preliminary operations, he left the center of activity just as the British intensified their efforts against Jackson's main line of defense. On December 28, Jackson sent Latour to the west bank of the Mississippi, where he started building another defensive line stretching from the river west to a cypress swamp. After quickly surveying the area, Latour chose Boisgervais's canal some three miles south of New Orleans, and for six days he supervised 150 African Americans as they worked on the parapet.

The line was never completed. Latour did not have enough time to build redoubts or bastions at Boisgervais's canal before General Jackson requested a more advanced position. Apparently Jackson wanted a line more parallel to the one constructed on the east side of the river. Latour quickly examined a series of advanced positions—far inferior to the one he had almost finished—before finding a suitable location on a plain between Raguet's and Jourdan's canals. Although the distance between the river and a thicket of woods to the west spanned nine hundred yards, Latour believed this position could be adequately manned with General David B. Morgan's limited number of troops and light artillery.

This defensive line was never completed. Morgan wanted a position a mile south of Jackson's line, closer to Daniel Patterson's naval batteries on the river. According to Latour, Morgan made a poor decision, and the subsequent "disaster might perhaps have been avoided, had another point for defense been adopted."[6] Morgan's site was a plain about 2,000 yards wide, or about twice the length of Jackson's line and the initial line Latour had chosen. When the British finally launched their main assault on January 8, only 200 yards of Morgan's line had been completed. The remaining 1,800 yards had only an undefended canal ditch, which could not be held by Morgan's 500 Louisiana militia and his recently arrived 400 Kentucky troops—only 250 of whom had arms.

Latour had played an important contributing role during the events leading up to the major British operation on January 8, 1815. On that fateful day, Latour apparently was with Jackson at Chalmette. In his book, Latour proclaimed that "all of us who were at Jackson's line" during the battle felt concern and fear because of the disaster on the west bank.[7] The disaster of which Latour spoke occurred when Morgan's feeble force broke and ran when attacked by the British. Although the untrained Kentucky and Louisiana troops ultimately secured a safe cover at Latour's unfinished line at Boisgervais's canal, this event became the most controversial of the entire campaign. When Latour examined the episode, he did not impugn the bravery of the troops but instead insinuated that the affair on the west bank—which could have spelled defeat for the entire army—was Morgan's fault. Even so, Latour decided to leave the verdict of the affair on the west bank "to the judgment of the reader."[8]

On the morning of January 9, British naval vessels began bombarding the still-unsupported Fort St. Philip downriver. Jackson immediately sent Latour to recruit skilled laborers from the army and proceed to Fort St. Philip; all who volunteered for this hazardous duty received extra pay. The workmen, despite enemy shells and a nonstop driving rain, built covers between the guns to shelter the soldiers and strengthened the powder magazines with additional dirt. While British forces withdrew after an unsuccessful nine-day siege, Latour continued inspecting the bayous around New Orleans and offering plans for their defense. Those plans were never implemented because Latour's tenure as an American patriot ended on March 17, 1815, when Jackson discharged him from the service. Jackson now believed that the British posed no immediate threat to New Orleans, and he released all assistant engineers and troops from military service.

Latour began to fade again from public view in the months after the Battle of New Orleans, and had it not been for his *Historical Memoir*, he might well have been overlooked altogether. During the spring and summer of 1815, he gathered information for his book. By September that "little sharp looking frenchman," as architect Benjamin Henry Latrobe described him, was traveling through Baltimore on his way to Philadelphia, where his book appeared in early March 1816.[9]

In late May 1816, Latour had returned to New Orleans to begin a third professional life—this one as an agent for Spain. Latour, the evidence suggests, joined the Spanish service during the fall of 1815 while in Philadelphia. Latour's constant money problems, the uncertain nature of loyalty in this era, and the prospect of adventure and personal gain all played a role in his decision. During his stay he met with his former comrade in arms Jean Lafitte, who probably introduced him to Spanish minister Luis de Onís. Latour asserted that he met at least twice with Secretary of State James Monroe and the two discussed a second edition of his book and the territorial ambitions of the United States in the Southwest. Latour passed this information along to Spanish officials, who immediately dispatched him on a special expedition into the "Internal Provinces."

From June to November 1816, Latour and Jean Lafitte made a trip on which they supposedly examined the gold region of Arkansas. In reality the two agents traveled extensively throughout the Southwest, surveyed the region, and prepared maps. They visited the headwaters of the Red, Sabine, Arkansas, and Colorado Rivers. Latour wrote an exhaustive report concerning American designs on the region. After returning to New Orleans, he presented his report to Father Antonio Sedella, head of the Spanish spy network in Louisiana, who forwarded the information to his superiors. In March 1817, Latour, alias John Williams, traveled to Cuba to meet with the Spanish captain general and intendant of the Army.

While in Cuba, Latour provided Spanish officials with a copy of his *Historical Memoir* and two reports on conditions within the Spanish empire. The first report discussed American plans to foment a slave insurrection in the West Indies as well as pirate and privateer operations in the western Gulf of Mexico. This information offered nothing new to the Spanish. His second report, the lengthy account of affairs in the "Internal Provinces," warned that should Spain not do something "the time will come, and unfortunately is not . . . far off, when the Americans . . . will pour in myriads into Mexico."[10] This information, substantiated by reports from other agents, was soon disseminated to Madrid, to the Spanish minister in Washington, to the viceroy of Mexico, and to provincial governors of Mexico's northern frontier. Latour's report received careful consideration and produced considerable commentary. However, the second report proved to be as ineffective as the first. Spanish officials did not have the power to counter the threat Americans presented in the borderlands.

The Cuban captain general was nonetheless impressed with the thoroughness of Latour's report and offered him an opportunity to serve

Spain as consul in New Orleans. Latour declined, preferring instead to relocate to Cuba. By 1818, he had moved to Havana, where he continued his association with Lafitte, Lafon, and with French operatives such as Charles François Lallemand, who planned a colony for Napoleonic émigrés in Texas. Latour opened an architectural firm in Cuba that built the famous Neptune fountain, paved roads and squares, constructed a sewer system in Havana, and erected bridges over the Canimar and Almendares Rivers. He also proposed a steamship company to operate between Havana and Pensacola, Florida.

Latour prospered. Or so it seemed. In January 1829 his business suddenly went into liquidation. A court finally resolved his case five-and-a-half years later in June 1834, and shortly afterward Latour returned to his native country. When he arrived in France, his friend, the governor of Corsica and new peer of the Kingdom of France, Charles Lallemand, invited him to become his assistant. Although honored by the loyalty of his friend and former associate, Latour declined. His health was deteriorating, and, more important, he wanted to rejoin his son Emile and daughter Coralie in Aurillac. For the next two years, Latour enjoyed a quiet and peaceful reunion with his family. Ironically, the man who had experienced some of the most exciting and tumultuous events of the age died quietly and unremarkably. On March 21, 1837, while at the house of an old aunt in LaCombaldie near Aurillac, Latour—engineer and architect, businessman, soldier and American patriot, historian, and foreign agent—succumbed to a flu epidemic that also killed hundreds of others in the region.

Arsène Lacarrière Latour was representative of the type of adventurer who flocked to Louisiana in the early nineteenth century. The Gulf Coast became a nexus of competing empires with rival nationalities vying to determine the fate of the region. French Creoles wanted to maintain their identity. Spaniards yearned to regain control over an area that had been stolen from them. Anglo-Americans wanted to incorporate Louisiana into the United States both politically and culturally. Each group worked diligently to secure its ends, which provided soldiers-of-fortune like Latour with a chance for adventure and personal and financial success. But shortly after the War of 1812, Latour saw the handwriting on the wall. Louisiana began changing socially, politically, and economically. Anglo-Americans incorporated Louisiana into the American union and began migrating to Spanish/Mexican Texas, shifting the nexus of empires to the west. As that expansion occurred, opportunities for adventurers such as Latour vanished. So did he.

Notes

1. Arsène Lacarrière Latour, *Historical Memoir of the War in West Florida and Louisiana, 1814–15*, ed. Gene A. Smith (Philadelphia, 1816; reprint ed., Gainesville, FL, 2000), 5, 13, 14.

2. Edward Livingston to Andrew Jackson, November 21, 1814, Andrew Jackson Papers, Library of Congress, Washington, DC.

3. Latour, *Historical Memoir*, 68.

4. Andrew Jackson to James Monroe, December 29, 1814, in ibid., 229–30.

5. Latour, *Historical Memoir*, 83.

6. Ibid., 116.

7. Ibid., 114.

8. Ibid., 120.

9. Benjamin H. Latrobe to Henry Latrobe, September 18, 1815, Benjamin Henry Latrobe Papers (Maryland Historical Society, Baltimore, MD).

10. Edwin H. Carpenter Jr., "Latour's Report on Spanish-American Relations in the Southwest," *Louisiana Historical Quarterly* 30 (1947): 730.

Suggested Readings

Bardon, Martine. "Arsène Lacarrière Latour: His Life in Paris in 1802." Unpublished paper presented at the Historic New Orleans Collection, January 1997. Manuscript now in possession of the Historic New Orleans Collection, New Orleans, LA.

Carpenter, Edwin H., Jr. "Arsène Lacarrière Latour." *The Hispanic American Historical Review* 18 (1938): 221–27.

———. "Latour's Report on Spanish-American Relations in the Southwest." *Louisiana Historical Quarterly* 30 (1947): 716–37.

Cullum, George W. "Louisiana Campaign of 1814–15; with a Biographical Sketch of Major A. Lacarriere Latour." In *Campaigns of the War of 1812–15, against Great Britain*, 305–41. New York, 1879.

Garrigoux, Jean. *Un aventurier visionnaire: L'étrange parcours d'un Français aux Amériques*. La Haute-Auvergne, 1997.

Hodges, Dr. and Mrs. T. L. "Jean Lafitte and Major L. Latour in Arkansas Territory." *Arkansas Historical Quarterly* 7 (1948): 237–56.

Latour, Arsène Lacarrière. *Historical Memoir of the War in West Florida and Louisiana, 1814–15*. Edited by Gene A. Smith. 1816. Reprint ed., Gainesville, FL, 2000.

Smith, Gene A. " 'A Little Sharp Looking Frenchman' and his Battle of New Orleans." *The Historic New Orleans Collection Quarterly* 16 (1998): 2–6.

7

Thomas Sidney Jesup
Soldier, Bureaucrat, Gentleman Democrat

Samuel J. Watson

The career of Thomas Sidney Jesup makes evident the many paths to individual success in the early republic. Rising to the rank of major during the War of 1812, Jesup remained in the service of his country the rest of his life. As a professional soldier, he found the U.S. Army in the Jeffersonian era to be small, disorganized, and fraught with personal and personality conflicts. Taking advantage of his political connections, Jesup became quartermaster general of the army. From that position he imposed a system and a regularity on the army's business transactions. Yet his later conflicts with General Winfield Scott and other military leaders too plainly prove that despite his reforms the army was neither fully modern administratively nor wholly removed from politics. His unhappy experiences during the Indian wars in the South reveal both the blurred line between professional responsibilities and personal gain and a conflict between the values of the military elite and the democratic government that controlled it. Jesup's involvement in the removal of Indians from their homelands exposed Jesup to and laid bare the tensions between the spirit of egalitarianism that characterized the early republic and the racism that flatly contradicted and ultimately undermined it.

Samuel J. Watson is assistant professor of history at the U.S. Military Academy at West Point. His publications include "Flexible Gender Roles during the Market Revolution: Family, Friendship, Marriage, and Masculinity among U.S. Army Officers, 1815–1846," *Journal of Social History* 29 (1995): 81–106; and "United States Army Officers Fight the 'Patriot War': Responses to Filibustering on the Canadian Border, 1837–1839," *Journal of the Early Republic* 18 (1998): 485–519. His research lies in the social, political, and professional roles of early army officers, and of the officer corps as a whole, and he is working on a manuscript that will address these roles in the context of U.S. state formation and territorial expansion.

Thomas Sidney Jesup was born in western Virginia late in 1788, the son of a Connecticut farmer and an Irish woman. After considering law as a career, he received a commission as a lieutenant in the U.S. Army in 1808. During the War of 1812, he served as both staff officer and combat commander, rising to the rank of major and receiving honors for leadership and bravery at the hard-fought battles of Chippewa and Lundy's Lane. President James Madison then sent him to report on the proceedings of the Hartford Convention, at which the New England states were rumored to be considering secession. Jesup served as the army's commander in Louisiana in 1816 and 1817, feuding with fellow officers and proposing that the United States seize Cuba. He exploited institutional and political connections to secure the new post of quartermaster general (the army's chief supply officer) in 1818. Jesup spent the next eighteen years improving the army's administrative procedures, fostering unprecedented "system and regularity" (a phrase common among officers of that period) in the army's supply and accounting.

While quartermaster general, Jesup yearned for a combat command. In 1836, he was sent to join in the removal of the Creek Indians from Alabama and Georgia, and his success there led to appointment as commander of the forces fighting to dispossess the Seminole Indians in Florida. Jesup found this task deeply frustrating, especially after he became embroiled in controversies with abolitionists and local planters over the status of African Americans who had found shelter from slavery with the Indians. Jesup also was drawn into an acrimonious dispute with Winfield Scott over their roles in the capture of the Creeks. As a soldier with a growing national profile, Jesup gradually became identified as a Democrat, but he refused to consider suggestions that he stand for that party's vice presidential or presidential nomination in 1844.

Relieved from command in Florida at his own request, Jesup returned to the quartermaster department in 1838. He later directed the U.S. Army's supply effort in the war with Mexico and served until his death in 1860—having spent fifty-two years in the army, forty-two as quartermaster general. In the process he built perhaps the largest and certainly the most complex "business" in the nation, supplying his "customers" on a then unparalleled scale while developing systems of accountability unequalled outside the army.

Jesup's career as soldier, bureaucrat, and public figure illustrates the army's role in U.S. territorial expansion, the manifold civil-military and local-national conflicts this engendered among citizens, and the army's increasing bureaucratization, professionalism, and military capability. In his disputes with fellow officers, his quest for systematic administration and professional accountability to the national government, and his reluctance to become involved in partisan politics, Jesup stands as representative of the army officer corps in a formative era of its development. A fixture on the Washington scene, Jesup's overlapping social and professional relationships illustrate the intersection of public office holding, private elites, and "genteel" social values in the government (particularly its appointment and personnel policies) of both the early republic (when the nation was still dominated by a class of landed gentlemen) and the supposedly more democratic antebellum years.

Professionally, Jesup directed a supply effort without precedent in U.S. history to sustain the invasion of Mexico; the margin for error was much slimmer than American victories on the battlefield indicated, and the conquest of northern Mexico would probably have been impossible were it not for Jesup's reforms. Though little known today, Thomas Sidney Jesup played a significant role in the professionalization of the army, the institutional development of the U.S. nation-state, and the extension of its borders and sovereignty.

Jesup rose to this status from rather humble beginnings, through ambition, talent, and a chain of good fortune that began with being in the right place when an opportunity came. The Jesup family moved to Kentucky early in 1793. Thomas's father James rented land and built a cabin, while his mother Ann bore three more children. James died when Thomas was eight, compelling him to assume new family responsibilities. Jesup's early employment included work as a store clerk. Although little is known of his reasons for seeking an army commission, his behavior and letters later in life suggest that a desire for fame and recognition was as significant as the need for financial security. He secured an appointment at the junior rank of second lieutenant in the military build-up of 1808, along with such future comrades as fellow Kentuckian Zachary Taylor and Virginian Winfield Scott. Three years of peace, experience as a quartermaster (an officer responsible for the distribution of supplies), and a War Department attempt to charge him for expenses incurred by his commander gave rise to Jesup's belief in fiscal accountability. Yet these experiences also frustrated his expectations of recognition and promotion, and he came to learn that political connections often mattered more than military expertise. So great was his feeling of disappointment that Jesup wrote of "regretting that I have lived," and he thought of leaving the army to "court danger and distinction" with South Americans rebelling against Spanish rule.[1]

This frustrating inactivity ended when the United States declared war on Britain in June 1812. Jesup immediately volunteered to join William Hull's invasion of western Ontario and was appointed the expedition's adjutant (the chief administrative aide, responsible for personnel records). Jesup found himself in service alongside future secretary of war and Democratic presidential nominee Lewis Cass. The offensive quickly went awry, and Jesup was captured along with the rest of the American force when it surrendered to the British in August. Soon released, Jesup at first believed that his services had gone unnoticed, and he considered turning to the legal profession. But Jesup had not been forgotten; he received two quick promotions (to major) and served as both quartermaster and combat officer in the counteroffensive that recaptured Detroit.

Jesup was transferred to the Niagara front in 1814, where the primary American offensive was to take place under General Jacob Brown. There he secured regimental command and finally was able to distinguish himself, not just as a conscientious officer and an able adminstrator but as a combat leader and tactician. In the first major engagement (and Jesup's first major battle) at Chippewa on July 5, Jesup's Twenty-Fifth Infantry skillfully mixed musketry and bayonet charges to drive the enemy's right wing from a strong position before attacking their flank, pressure that ultimately forced the more numerous British to retreat from the field. Jesup's commander, Winfield Scott, commended his decisiveness and skill, for which he received a brevet (honorary) promotion to lieutenant colonel.

On July 25, Brown's army advanced and engaged the British a second time. Once again Jesup struck the enemy flank, maneuvering his soldiers through woods to surprise the British and take hundreds prisoner. He then moved his small unit to the support of the main body, which rebuffed three British assaults between 9 P.M. and midnight. Standing shoulder to shoulder and exchanging fire at point-blank range for up to half an hour at a time, both sides took tremendous casualties (about a third of the American force was lost). In this era, officers led from the front lines. Generals Brown and Scott were both wounded and forced to leave the field. Jesup was hit by bullets or fragments four times, taking a lead musket ball through his shoulder, and he had two horses slain beneath him, but he remained at his post. One fragment permanently disfigured his right hand, forcing him to become ambidextrous in order to carry out his administrative duties.

The Americans withdrew after the last British attack. The Battle of Lundy's Lane was a tactical draw but a moral victory for the United States, coming against a highly professional British army amidst a summer of battlefield disasters elsewhere. Jesup was given a second brevet (to colonel) "for gallant conduct and distinguished skill." The officers of Brown's army, especially the "Left Division" commanded by Scott, became the core of the professional officer corps after the war, leading the army until 1861. Only twenty-five years old, Jesup had made his reputation and forged the connections that would take him to the top of the army's hierarchy.

With the onset of winter and the cessation of active operations, Jesup was sent to Hartford, Connecticut, on a dual personal and political mission. He was to recruit for his regiment while observing the convention being held there to discuss the relationship between New England and the national Union. Jesup was certain that the convention's "real object will be . . . resistance to the laws of the Union"; he reported to Secretary of War James Monroe that he would respond to direct insurrection by raising "such a storm as this country has never witnessed . . . [to] overwhelm all those turbulent D[e]magogues who are labouring to overturn the Government." Despite his outrage at local interference with his recruiting, Jesup awaited further instructions, while the Hartford crisis blew over as the war came to an end. Jesup's assignment to this sensitive mission displayed the esteem in which the most senior Republican leaders held him. In turn, his belief in the Federalists' "hostility . . . to every thing American" both reflected and reinforced his nationalism and his identification with the national government.[2]

Jesup was next ordered to the southern frontier as commander of the Eighth Military Department, headquartered in Baton Rouge with responsibility for the defense of Mobile and New Orleans, outlets for the booming trade of the Mississippi Valley and the Old Southwest. There he became enmeshed in a web of civil-military intrigue centering on the future of Spanish Florida and Mexico. Jesup reported that the local authorities were aware of neutrality law violations by Americans who were helping Mexican revolutionaries. Although the governor of Louisiana was attempting to shift the blame for these violations onto the army, Jesup confidently assured Andrew Jackson (the commander of the army's Southern Division) "that soldiers are not to be outgeneralled by Politicians."[3]

Though determined to enforce the law against private foreign policy initiatives, Jesup was unwilling to observe the conflict between Spain and its colonies in passive silence. His opinions hardened by war and formed by military ambition and republican political beliefs, Jesup now believed in the desirability of territorial expansion by the United States. Driven by ambition, impetuosity, and a growing strategic foresight, Jesup held expansionist hopes that extended beyond Florida to Cuba, as he reported to Jackson that Havana lay "in a defenseless state." Jesup professed to fear a Spanish attack on Mobile or New Orleans, but his contingency plan in such an event was offensive: If attacked he would "take immediate possession of Cuba," certain "that the better way to defend a country is to carry war into that of the enemy." Like most American leaders, Jesup believed that Cuba constituted the geographic and strategic key to New Orleans and the Mississippi Valley. He, like many others, believed that Spain was too weak to hold on to the island and that the United States should forestall any British action there through its acquisition. He immediately asked the naval commander at New Orleans for assistance, claiming that he could mobilize several thousand men within a few days. Two days later he wrote to Jackson and President James Monroe outlining a plan to seize Cuba. Jesup also sought personal orders to spy on the defenses, even as he reported a rumor that the Spanish intended to attack New Orleans.[4]

Jesup aborted his plans when his superiors refused their support. Nonetheless, he continued to send warnings about the danger of Spanish or British attack—undoubtedly exaggerated but representative of the professional soldier's sense of responsibility for national defense. Meanwhile, Jesup's subordinates continued to grapple with private attempts by American citizens to outfit illegal expeditions against Mexico. Yet they were hampered in their efforts by the need to secure the sanction of civil authorities, who proved unsympathetic, before intervening. Other officers in the district reported on the defenses of the United States and Spain along the Texas-Louisiana border and chased the pirate-adventurer Jean Lafitte.

When General Eleazar Ripley was transferred to command the Eighth Military Department, Jesup faced a new set of personal problems. Jesup had supported Generals Brown and Scott in their dispute with Ripley over who was responsible for the American retreat after the Battle of Lundy's Lane. More to the point as far as Jesup was concerned, Ripley was in overall command when the withdrawal took place, a withdrawal that gave the British a claim to victory. Ripley attempted to justify his action by declaring that the troops under Jesup's command had been near collapse. In effect, Ripley had blamed Jesup for the withdrawal. Though their relations began amicably, one of Ripley's staff soon threatened Jesup with violence. In return, Jesup fired a volley of letters critical of Ripley's command to the War Department.

Jesup's predicament was not uncommon in the postwar army, as ambitious officers fought verbally—and sometimes literally—for preference, refusing to submit to any compromise of their claims or to any slight against their "honor" (which meant both reputation and integrity) and arresting subordinates on the slightest pretext. Junior officers responded to criticism by demanding time-consuming investigations to justify their conduct. As a result, the officer corps became divided among an array of shifting, sometimes overlapping, factions. Jesup was not above this infighting, pronouncing Ripley "a most contemptible . . . malignant villain," and threatening to "make the whole establishment tremble before I have done with them." When Ripley offered Jesup's regimental command to another officer, Jesup considered challenging Ripley to personal combat. Persuaded against challenging Ripley by Edmund Gaines (a fellow veteran of the Niagara campaign), Jesup escaped Ripley's command in the fall of 1817, when Jacob Brown asked Jesup to serve as adjutant general (chief staff and personnel officer) of the Northern Division. Once safely transferred, he boldly declared his unwillingness to serve under Ripley in the future.[5]

Brown's request for Jesup suggests many of the essentially civilian social values held by army officers in this era. Brown sought "a gentleman," "most distinguished during the late War" for "my confidential friend." After speaking with President Monroe, Brown concluded that the adjutant general's position would not be jeopardized by any further reductions in the army's strength. Therefore he assured the anxious Jesup that it would "elevate you to a higher station with as much certainty as any situation you can at present fill." Connections like that between Brown and Jesup ensured that men whose status and income were based on lives of national service could make careers in the postwar army. Conversely, less professionally committed or more locally oriented men— especially those who prized financial opportunity over security—returned to civilian life as planters, lawyers, land speculators, and politicians.[6]

Jesup's adjutant appointment was short-lived, for the vagaries of politics and individual preference led reformist Secretary of War John C. Calhoun to appoint Jesup (his second choice) to the newly permanent position of quartermaster general in April 1818. Jesup was awarded the prestigious rank of brigadier—the only staff officer so ranked, and one of only four generals in the entire army after the second postwar reduction in force in 1821. Jesup spent the rest of his life working hand-in-hand with fellow Niagara veterans Brown, Scott, Gaines, and, beginning in 1825, Adjutant General Roger Jones. Jesup's principal assistants were appointed with him in 1818: Henry Stanton and Thomas F. Hunt both served continuously in the department until their deaths in 1856, and Trueman Cross, who had attached himself to Jesup in the factional struggles in the Eighth Military Department less than a year before their quartermaster appointments, served until his death in Texas in 1846. Though saddled with inflated egos and plagued by personal quarrels, this cadre of experienced veterans provided the army with a dedicated professional core that reformed its structure and enhanced its ability to serve national objectives. They would also act as an important force for national cohesion along contested borders and frontiers while making possible the victory over Mexico in 1848.

Immediately, Jesup began developing regulations for quartermaster operations, basing them on his study of those of the British, French, and Prussian armies and of American logistics in the Revolution and the War of 1812. He introduced uniformity by eliminating competing offices and establishing a centralized hierarchy. Jesup eventually came to function as the army's chief accountant, creating a "regular chain to a final accountability at the treasury" through "a uniform system of returns" (monthly tabulations of all expenditures) channeled through the quartermaster general's office. He demanded individual account books and duplicate sets of receipts for every soldier's clothes and equipment. Subordinates who failed to furnish their accounts promptly and regularly were to be replaced. He successfully proposed that the quartermasters be drawn from the army rather than from civilian contractors. The latter lacked "military responsibility": subordination to military discipline and devotion to national rather than personal pecuniary interests. These reforms embraced the same values of personal integrity and patriotic duty instilled (along with expertise in mathematics and record keeping) at the Military Academy by other military reformers. He entered these rules into the 1821 Army Regulations.[7] Jesup also created standardized printed forms to list, categorize, and summarize all expenditures, and he later developed a separate set of quartermaster regulations that laid down standard procedures, enabling him to enforce fiscal accountability with unprecedented consistency and rigor.

In addition, Jesup demanded greater accountability from unit commanders. He ordered quartermasters—who were given autonomy from the line chain of command to ensure their subordination and accountability to the Quartermaster Department (much to the irritation of field commanders)—to report "all orders . . . requiring the expenditure of money contrary to regulations." He demanded that "extraordinary expenditures" be justified with written certificates of necessity. Jesup's emphasis on precision and accountability soon became the hallmark of the

Quartermaster Department, and by 1836 the quartermaster's ideal of efficiency had spread throughout the army. Fellow reformer Winfield Scott placed logistical ability at the forefront of military identity by admonishing his army in Florida that "to handle and preserve the supplies . . . [is a duty] required of every good soldier." In an era of limited budgets and civilian suspicion of the military, these reforms provided Congress with convincing evidence of the army's fiscal reliability and discouraged some members' attempts to replace the regulars with the militia.[8]

Throughout his career, Jesup never ceased to stress his belief that the effectiveness of military operations depended on the efficiency of their supply. His efforts at rationalizing logistical procedures significantly enhanced the army's ability to project power over long distances. Ultimately this efficiency would ensure the success of campaigns, such as the invasion of Mexico, that would have been impossible with the convoluted staff structure of the 1810s. The results of Jesup's efforts to supply the war against Mexico speak for themselves. Never before had a North American army projected its force in such numbers over such distances with so few logistical problems; the contrast with the campaigns of 1812–1814, when the United States was unable to concentrate the men and supplies needed to seize Quebec, was decisive. Indeed, though the procedures developed and experience gained by the army supply bureaus under Jesup's administration have been neglected by scholars, they were almost certainly of more value during the Civil War than the often-vaunted experience gained by the future generals in their Mexican battles, where they employed Napoleonic shock tactics— densely massed formations charging the enemy with bayonets—that would prove disastrous against rifles and entrenchments fifteen years later.

Jesup was a gentleman—defined economically by substantial land and slave holdings—as well as an officer. Though not among the uppermost economic elite, he probably ranked among the wealthiest 5 percent of Americans. Beginning in the mid-1820s, shortly after his marriage to Kentucky heiress Ann Croghan (made possible by his connections from the War of 1812), Jesup's personal correspondence with important figures in that state grew. They discussed land values, rents (one of the major sources of Jesup's income) and their collection, and opportunities for purchasing new land throughout the Ohio and Mississippi Valleys. Jesup's investments prospered despite his near-permanent absence in Washington, so that by 1824 he was pondering the sale of a thousand acres while receiving reports on land for sale in Indiana and Illinois.

Unfortunately for Jesup, the expenses associated with keeping homes in both Washington and Kentucky were multiplied by the gambling debts accumulated by his brother-in-law George Croghan, an alcoholic war hero. Jesup employed his influence to help Croghan get a post as inspector general in 1825. Croghan, however, never escaped debt, and Jesup was often forced to raise cash to stave off his brother-in-law's creditors. Jesup considered a variety of options to pay these expenses, including land speculation, stock raising, and "a carding & spinning establishment." Despite these difficulties, by 1826 he held more than 8,000 acres in Kentucky worth $10,000. Jesup seems to have left the management of his land and workers to others, but he both bought and sold slaves, planning in 1832 to take a year's leave and "transfer my force [the slaves] to either Arkansas or Mississippi."[9]

Despite his success as quartermaster, Jesup never really was satisfied with his deskwork in the department. He always yearned to resume a line command but was twice passed over when opportunities appeared at the deaths of generals Brown and Alexander Macomb. In 1836, he received the chance he had been waiting for, after both of the army's line brigadiers—Edmund Gaines and Winfield Scott—botched offensives against the Seminole Indians of Florida, whom the U.S. government sought to move west of the Mississippi. Jesup, now away from the desk and in the field, first moved against the Creek Indians in Alabama. His assault was so speedy and decisive that he captured large numbers of Creeks without causing substantial casualties on either side.

Jesup's success led to an order to do the same in Florida. Winfield Scott (later known as "Old Fuss and Feathers") became aggrieved, however, hindering Jesup's ability to command effectively. First, he resented Jesup's nimble field maneuvers, which had upstaged and embarrassed the more cautious Scott (who was, ironically, waiting to build up his supply depots before moving). Second, Scott misperceived the sequence and causes of his dismissal from and Jesup's appointment to the Florida command. Easily irritated in the best of circumstances, Scott became convinced that Jesup had maneuvered to supplant him. Whig politicians, who saw Scott as a rising star in their party, saw an opportunity to bolster him and criticize the Jackson administration. Jesup's problems were aggravated further when Scott and Gaines—whom Jesup had alienated a decade before when he refused to take Gaines's side in an earlier dispute with Scott—prefered court-martial charges against each other over their performances in Florida. In their defense of Gaines, his supporters attributed his defeat to a lack of supplies that were Jesup's responsibility as quartermaster general.

Surrounded by professional controversy, Jesup grimly pressed the offensive against the Seminoles. Their guerrilla tactics and the swampy terrain quickly convinced him that a war of removal was futile. Therefore, in March 1837, he signed the first truce intended to spur the Indians' emigration west. Jesup recognized that the most determined Seminoles were men and women who had escaped from slavery in Georgia. He attempted to break down their resistance to removal by guaranteeing their freedom, trading emigration west for protection against reenslavement. As a result of this strategic gambit, Jesup came under intense pressure from local whites and their congressional allies, who saw Florida as a promising frontier for plantation slavery. They demanded the refugees returned. Despite his earlier guarantee, the ever-wary Jesup remained suspicious of the Seminoles' intentions. Public criticism and private doubts led him to allow whites to return to southern Florida (where they hunted black refugees), while he attempted to divide Indians from their black allies by encouraging the former to turn in the latter. Militant Seminoles who got wind of this double-dealing rescued a large proportion of those Jesup had captured. This counterattack forced Jesup to resume the war, which encouraged northern abolitionists (especially antislavery Whigs) to assail him for serving the interests of southern slaveholders.

Unable to satisfy any—much less all—sides, Jesup became increasingly frustrated by this political crossfire. His distaste for the aggressive materialism of the white settlers in Florida—widely shared throughout the army, whose officers tended to blame frontiersmen for intruding upon Indians' lands—came to the fore. "I will not make negro-catchers of the army," he exclaimed to the secretary of war, though the practice was in fact government policy.[10] Refused the relief that he requested and determined to succeed in his mission and vindicate his reputation, he adopted and adapted the Seminole strategy of alternately fighting and negotiating. Jesup brought innovation to this tactic as he blended negotiation with treachery on an ever-increasing scale, seizing Seminole leaders under truce flags. All the while he continued to work assiduously to divide blacks and Indians. Offering Afro-Seminoles freedom west of the Mississippi, he treated them as prisoners of war subject to military control in pursuit of national interests, rather than as slave property subject to local civil control as the War Department had directed.

Abetted by increasing military pressure that deprived the Seminoles of food and rest, Jesup's strategy succeeded in capturing or inducing the surrender of more Seminoles (including the Afro-Seminole core of the resistance) than any of his many predecessors or successors in command had captured.

Still leading from the front at the age of forty-nine, Jesup received his fifth war wound when a bullet shattered his glasses and tore open his cheek. He was finally relieved of command at his own request in April 1838. Jesup returned to the Quartermaster Department satisfied that he had done his duty but glad to be done with it. All three of his successors (including his friend Zachary Taylor) would pursue similar strategies, come to similar conclusions, and like Jesup request relief. Collective war weariness led in 1842 to a unilateral declaration of peace that allowed a number of Seminoles to remain in Florida. Criticized by slaveholders and abolitionists alike, Jesup had become embroiled in a series of controversies that tarnished his reputation and hounded him for life. Yet he was certainly the most effective U.S. commander in the conflict, and he made sincere efforts to secure the freedom of the Afro-Seminoles years after the war had ended.

The constant stress of maintaining the army's accountability repeatedly endangered Jesup's health. Health considerations had already led him to consider resignation in 1832, when he suffered internal bleeding due to an inflammation of the lung. As early as 1824, he was encouraged to leave the army by sympathetic friends in the Kentucky elite, who reported that he "would not fail to meet with a sincere welcome by the better part of society." Though normal business hours lasted from only 9 A.M. to 3 P.M., Jesup was often in his office from 5 A.M. to 11 P.M. He took leaves of about three months in 1822 (upon his marriage), 1827, and 1832. In 1838, he received six months leave upon the conclusion of his Florida command. In 1845, he secured a two-month leave en route to an inspection of the army's western posts (during which he made preliminary plans for supplying the invasion of Mexico) by noting that he had been on duty for nearly six years without a significant break. In the end the permanence and national prestige of his commission combined with his sense of public duty and personal reputation (which would suffer if it appeared that he was leaving the army under any sort of cloud, as would always be the case given the complexity of army finances) kept Jesup in the service until his death in 1860.[11]

Throughout this long, distinguished military career, Jesup tried, often unsuccessfully, to give politics a wide berth. A gentleman and public officer of national standing, Jesup was linked to a variety of social and political networks, frequently receiving news of candidates and elections from fellow officers and Kentucky associates. As a man dependent on the unified nation-state, a product of the "Second War of Independence," and an observer of the highly partisan and potentially secessionist Hartford Convention, Jesup developed over time a distaste for partisan activism, which he believed threatened both the officer corps' direction over American military forces and uniformity and accountability in public administration. In 1827, at a time when other senior officers were lining up behind Andrew Jackson or John Quincy Adams for the next election, Jesup wrote to James Monroe that "under no circumstances would I permit my name to be used for party politics, or for party purposes."[12]

Yet his efforts to remain aloof from, and untouched by, politics failed. Jesup was inextricably connected to the same networks of gentry and patronage that had assisted his own rise, and those seeking federal appointments often called upon him for assistance. His national reputation was enhanced by his success in the Creek and Seminole wars but tarnished by questions about his performance as Whigs sought ammunition to attack the Jackson and Van Buren administrations' conduct of these campaigns. In defending his personal reputation against Generals Scott and Gaines, Jesup acquired recognition as a war hero of sorts. As a consequence, his partisan identity was defined not by himself but by his defenders. That is, at precisely the moment when Jackson alienated Gaines by criticizing his operations in Florida and Texas and when Scott was becoming associated in the public mind with the Whigs (and eyed as a potential presidential candidate), Jesup by default became the sole option for Democrats looking for a recognized military leader—whether as presidential candidate or as defender of administration policy in Florida.

By 1840, Democrats were attempting to make political capital of Jesup's reputation. The general, though, resisted becoming entangled in the election, despite his fears that the Whigs would appoint an enemy to head the War Department, "the signal, necessarily, of my separation from the service." Although the Whigs carried the election, no such enemy was appointed. Nevertheless, the Whigs continued to attack Jesup's record, and by 1842 he was being considered as a potential Democratic candidate for the presidency. Encouraged to seek the nomination by a prominent party committee in New York, Jesup responded that he had been resisting similar intimations for nearly a decade. Jesup's refusal to leave the army to join in political combat suggests both the professional officer's growing sense of political neutrality and his intimate familiarity with the genteel republican ideal of public service. The constitutional separation of civil and military functions was to Jesup "a matter of high principle." "As a matter of military propriety," he observed, "I never meddle with party operations (nor concern myself with party interests)." Still, he concluded, "were I not a soldier I should take an active part in public affairs."[13] The moment of his popularity quickly passed amid the war against Mexico, in which the leading field commanders were Whigs.

Jesup's attitudes and actions were politically and culturally representative of military officers and civilian men of his social class, representative of the bureaucratization of the army that took place during the years between 1815 and 1846, and exceptional in the degree of his managerial success and in some of his policies as an agent of U.S. imperialism in the war to dispossess the Seminoles. As a gentleman, he was thoroughly a man of his time—public-spirited yet vain and jealous of his rank and reputation. Because of his personal qualities, which were enhanced by the financial "independence" secured by his personal fortune, other gentlemen who held the authority to appoint and promote him thought Jesup capable of "disinterested" public administration and accountability. Jesup's politics exemplified the balance career military officers had to craft (as they do today) between their professional responsibility for effective national defense and their constitutional accountability to the elected civil government. Expected as gentlemen to play public roles, members of this professional officer corps became nationally prominent during a period of party formation. Yet they also became increasingly conscious of the dangers partisan allegiance posed to the military's subordination to civil government. Jesup was drawn reluctantly into partisan debates only by the need to defend his professional integrity, his reputation, and the credibility and effectiveness of the army bureaucracy.

As a slaveholder, Jesup shared the prejudices of his society. As a military officer, he was an active agent in—though hardly the initiator of and in practice a moderating influence on—the dispossession of Native Americans throughout the Southeast. In this service to his government ("duty," as constitutionally defined), he blended a sense of personal good faith ("honor") with a genteel distaste for the greed of white settlers and a desire to accomplish his mission as efficiently as possible. These sentiments led him to offer guarantees of freedom and a means of escape to hundreds of refugees from slavery. As a bureaucrat, he was one of the foremost innovators of his era, one of a small cadre of dedicated reformers who introduced powerful systems of accountability and efficiency into army administration and supply, distributing the foundations of bread and bullets on which Manifest Destiny thrived and an ocean-bound Union was built.

Notes

Unless otherwise stated, all quotations come from the Thomas Sidney Jesup Papers, Manuscript Division, Library of Congress, and are to or from Jesup.

1. Thomas Sidney Jesup to Ethane A. Brown, February 17, 1812, Thomas Sidney Jesup Papers, Library of Congress, Washington, DC.

2. Thomas Sidney Jesup to James Monroe, January 20, 1815; Thomas Sidney Jesup to James Monroe (?), February 4, 1815, ibid.

3. Thomas Sidney Jesup to Andrew Jackson, August 12, 1816, ibid.

4. Thomas Sidney Jesup to Andrew Jackson, August 18, 1816, ibid.

5. Thomas Sidney Jesup to ————, August 4, 1817, ibid.

6. Jacob Brown to Thomas Sidney Jesup, October 1, 1817, ibid.

7. Thomas Sidney Jesup, February 9, 1824, file Q-130, Office of the Secretary of War, Letters Received, Registered Series, Record Group 107, National Archives and Record Service, Washington DC (first quotation); Thomas Sidney Jesup to John C. Calhoun, July 17 and June 5, 1818, in *The Papers of John C. Calhoun*, ed. Robert L. Meriwether, W. Edwin Hemphill, Clyde N. Wilson, and Shirley Bright Cook, 25 vols. to date (Columbia, 1963–) 2:391 (second quotation) and 2:330 (third quotation). The July 17 letter contains the outline for Jesup's quartermaster regulations.

8. Thomas Sidney Jesup to John C. Calhoun, July 17, 1818, in Hemphill et al., eds., *Papers of Calhoun*, 2:392; Scott, Order No. 1 of the "Army of Florida," February 22, 1836, printed in *Army and Navy Chronicle* 2 (March 17, 1836): 168.

9. J. R. Underwood to Thomas Sidney Jesup, July 7, 1824, Thomas Sidney Jesup Papers; Jesup to John Croghan, March 24, 1832, ibid.

10. Thomas Sidney Jesup to Joel Poinsett, May 8, 1837, in the Jesup Papers (Florida War), Adjutant General's Office, Letters Received, Registered Series, Record Group 94, National Archives.

11. J. R. Underwood to Thomas Sidney Jesup, March 21, 1824, Jesup Papers, Library of Congress.

12. Thomas Sidney Jesup to James Monroe, October 7, 1827, ibid.

13. Thomas Sidney Jesup to James L. Cantis, March 22, 1843, ibid; Thomas Sidney Jesup to John R. Sherburne, September 24, 1842, ibid.

Suggested Readings

Crenson, Matthew A. *The Federal Machine: The Beginnings of Bureaucracy in Jacksonian America*. Baltimore, MD, 1975.

Giddings, Joshua R. *The Exiles of Florida*. Columbus, OH, 1858.

Hoskin, Keith W., and Richard H. Macve. "The Genesis of Accountability: The West Point Connections." *Accounting, Organizations, and Society* 13 (1988): 37–73.

John, Richard R. "Governmental Institutions as Agents of Change: Rethinking American Political Development in the Early Republic, 1787–1835." *Studies in American Political Development* 11 (1997): 347–80.

Kieffer, Chester L. *Maligned General: The Biography of Thomas Sidney Jesup.* San Rafael, CA, 1979.

Littlefield, Daniel F. *Africans and Seminoles: From Removal to Emancipation.* Westport, CT, 1977.

Mahon, John K. *History of the Second Seminole War, 1835–1842.* Gainesville, FL, 1967.

Porter, Kenneth Wiggins. *The Black Seminoles: History of a Freedom-Seeking People.* Revised and edited by Alcione M. Amos and Thomas P. Sutter. Gainesville, FL, 1996.

Risch, Erna. *Quartermaster Support of the Army: A History of the Corps, 1775–1939.* Washington, DC, 1962.

Skelton, William B. *An American Profession of Arms: The Army Officer Corps, 1784–1861.* Lawrence, KS, 1992.

Sprague, (Captain) John T. *The Origin, Progress, and Conclusion of the Florida War.* 1848. Reprint, Gainesville, FL, 1964.

Watson, Samuel J. " 'This Thankless . . . Unholy War': Army Officers and Civil-Military Relations in the Second Seminole War," in *The Southern Albatross: Race and Ethnicity in the South.* Edited by P. David Dillard and Randal L. Hall, 9–49. Macon, GA, 1999.

———. "The Uncertain Road to Manifest Destiny: Army Officers and the Course of American Territorial Expansionism, 1815–1846," in *Manifest Destiny and Empire: Essays on Antebellum American Expansionism.* Edited by Christopher Morris and Sam W. Haynes, 68–114. College Station, TX, 1997.

8

John Ross
Cherokee Chief and Defender of the Nation

Mary Young

In his first term as president, Thomas Jefferson predicted that over the course of time Indians would either be absorbed and amalgamated into American society or removed beyond the Mississippi River. By the 1830s most Americans had long abandoned any commitment to the former possibility, concluding that Native Americans were "savages" incapable of civilization or being civilized. Contempt for Indians as a people, a desire to have no contact with them, and, above all, an insatiable hunger by whites for the valuable lands of Native Americans were melded together into a powerful movement for removal. White encroachment on Indian territory and the forceable removal of tribes from their lands began at the state level. Removal became the official policy of the U.S. government in 1830 when Congress passed, and President Andrew Jackson signed, the Indian Removal Act that appropriated federal money to fund negotiations with eastern tribes that had as their goal relocating them to the West. John Ross, Principal Chief of the Cherokees, took exception to (and proved wrong) whites' insistence that Indians were neither intelligent nor civilized. Although he consistently fought against further loss of Cherokee land, Ross's efforts were subverted through a collusion of federal officials and political rivals within the nation. Nonetheless, Ross's resistance proves that Indians were neither passive about, nor complicit in, their removal from their native lands.

Mary Young has worked on southeastern tribal history and historiography as well as on the history of the U.S. public lands and the historiography of the American West. Her many publications include *Redskins, Ruffleshirts, and Rednecks: Indian Allotments in Alabama and Mississippi, 1830–1860* (1961). She is also past president of the Society for Historians of the Early American Republic. Until her retirement in July 2000, she was professor of history at the University of Rochester, Rochester, New York.

In 1828, shortly after the Cherokees chose John Ross (1790–1866) as Principal Chief—a post he would hold for the final half of his life—word went out from Washington that he was not a "real Indian." From 1817 to 1827, he had been chairman of the Committee, or upper house of the tribal legislature. He had a Cherokee great-grandmother, Ghigooie, who married interpreter William Shorey at the British Fort of Loudoun

115

in what is now east Tennessee. Their daughter, Anne, married Scots trader John McDonald; their daughter, Molly, married McDonald's fellow Scot, protégé, and trading partner Daniel Ross. John was the third Ross child and first son. White officials in Georgia who denied Ross's viability as a Cherokee had no difficulty defining individuals who were one-eighth African as people of color, entitled to all appropriate disabilities. Yet, John Ross, one-eighth Cherokee, was no "real Indian" to Georgia. This conclusion conveniently enabled them to deny his authority as a tribal leader when he proved insufficiently pliant.

Unlike white officials, the Cherokees who elected Ross had no trouble identifying him as Cherokee. Although the Cherokees developed racist attitudes toward African Americans who had no clans, they generally categorized people not by race but by matrilineal descent. Hence, John Ross, known as Tsan Usdi or Little John as a child, became Kooweskoowe, of his mother's Bird Clan.[1] Such "Indians" were in fact common in John Ross's generation. For example, three Ross associates trace their lineage to Nancy Ward, Beloved Woman and chair of the women's council from her elevation to War Woman in 1755 until her death in 1822. Ward had married several times and was the great-grandmother of Richard Taylor, a Ross loyalist; James Starr, champion of the removal treaty of New Echota and sworn enemy to Ross and his party; and Jacob West, a friend of Starr's hanged for his role in the murder of a Bushyhead politician. Hundreds of English, Irish, Scotch, and German traders, officials, soldiers, and mechanics settled in the Cherokee Nation beginning in the 1720s. With the loss of Cherokee husbands in tribal wars and the way wives like Nancy Ward changed mates, the proportion of mixed-bloods might have been larger still had those of mixed heritage not tended to marry each other.

By the time John Ross came of age, old chiefs were seeking less advice from priests or warriors and more from the sometimes wealthy, literate, numerous, English-speaking, ambitious, and loyal young men of mixed heritage. In 1820 the National Council wrote a set of constitutional laws dividing the Nation into eight districts, supplanting a national council chosen by clan councils in each of their fifty-odd towns with a national council openly elected by male voters in each district. It kept an upper house, or "committee," on which John Ross had already served for three years. Initially the committee was designed to give trusted mixed-bloods control of tribal finances and a voice in diplomatic negotiations. Although both committee and council contained significant full-blood representation, increasing numbers of mixed-bloods served on both bodies. By Jacksonian standards, therefore, the Cherokees' elected government had few "real" Indians.

In 1827, John Ross chaired a convention that drew up a formal constitution, providing for an elective committee and council, a Principal Chief and assistants selected by the two governing bodies, and a supreme court to decide cases appealed from the eight district courts. Though the Cherokee people ratified it, three sets of critics took aim at the constitution. In their very first article, the authors of the Cherokee Constitution asserted in detail the Nation's right to territorial claims, which included ten million acres in the Appalachian summit regions of Alabama, Georgia, North Carolina, and Tennessee. President John Quincy Adams objected, contending that the U.S. Constitution would not permit the creation of a sovereign state within a state; thus, the Cherokees' new government could be merely municipal.

Seven million acres of the Nation were in Georgia. The people of Georgia, the constitution's second set of critics, found this Indian state within their state presumptuous and intolerable. When Andrew Jackson, a long-standing supporter of Indian removal, was elected president in 1828, Georgians responded by extending their jurisdiction over the Cherokee Nation. Over the next five years, they created counties, with courts, in Cherokee territory, substituted their law for that of the Cherokee Nation, and made it a penal offense to make or execute a Cherokee law. The state surveyed the territory into lots, held a lottery, and put winners into possession of every lot not actually occupied and improved by a Cherokee.

Attacking the "near-white" Cherokee aristocracy, the state of Georgia eventually limited the holdings of each Cherokee to a single lot and dispossessed those who had received personal reservations of land under earlier treaties or who had even hired an overseer. In the fall of 1835 the legislature proposed to put white Georgian winners into possession of all the lots, including those where Cherokees still somehow managed to live. A group independent from the official tribal government agreed the Cherokees would sign a treaty of removal by the end of 1835. Only that promise postponed the forcible dispossession of Cherokees by impatient white Georgians.

The third set of critics were traditional Cherokees who thought the constitution the work of people who were changing their world too fast. The political changes adopted in 1820 had imposed on them not only a system that made local councils and the matrilineal clans who chose them politically irrelevant but also laws designed to please missionaries by prohibiting polygamy, infanticide, drinking at ballgames, and all-night dances.[2] The new laws of the Cherokee Nation might suit white businessmen who wanted trading licenses, turnpike monopolies, and prompt debt collection, but they hardly reflected the reciprocity, egalitarianism, and generosity traditional Cherokees valued.

Just before the constitutional convention, White Path, who had been expelled from the council in 1825 for intemperate criticism of innovation, held a council of these disaffected Cherokees. John Ross, then acting chief, refused to take strong measures to oppose this initiative. Instead he invited the rebels to a special council and worked out a compromise to which most agreed. By its terms, critics would resort to petitions rather than to clandestine meetings calculated to disturb the peace. White Path subsequently won election again to the council and remained a loyal if occasionally fractious statesman until his death a dozen years later on the Trail of Tears.

The unauthorized delegation that sent the Cherokees down that trail were tribesmen who thought themselves more realistic patriots than John Ross. They also disagreed with him on the race question. John Ross, an olive-skinned, dark-haired, dark-eyed man a little over five-foot-six-inches tall, looked, some said, like Martin Van Buren. Ross believed race to be irrelevant to intelligence and accomplishment. He concluded that the Cherokees' accomplishments proved them not only civilized but a people equal in stature to whites. By the time of removal, perhaps one-tenth of the Cherokees adhered to Protestant churches, making them, like the United States, a Christian nation as well as a nation of laws. Ross wrote his daughters in the Moravian Academy and his nephew, William Potter Ross, whom he was grooming for leadership at Princeton, of their duty to prove Cherokees fully equal to their white classmates in intelligence and accomplishment.

One might describe Ross's strategy as "mimicry," or "beating the whites at their own game." Certainly his early experiences and those of the Cherokees stretching back to the colonial era suggested the bankruptcy of more warlike strategies. John Ross was born in the same year as the official organization of the territory south of the Ohio River that later became Tennessee. Every year thousands of Tennesseans intruded onto the land guaranteed the Cherokees by the Treaty of Hopewell (1785) and the Treaty of Holston (1791). These treaties promised government protection of Cherokee borders and the tribe's right to govern its own affairs inside those borders. Yet conflict and intrusion continued almost unabated.

British forces and militia destroyed more than fifteen towns between 1759 and 1761. In 1775 an illegal purchase of most of the Nation's Tennessee and Kentucky hunting grounds added to the Cherokees' irritation. Continuing trespass led to Cherokee attacks on offending white settlements. In retaliation, thousands of militiamen from North Carolina, South Carolina, and Virginia laid waste to about fifty out of more than sixty towns. John Ross was four when the mutual destruction of towns, stations, and people concluded. With their newly created towns on the lower Tennessee River destroyed by white militia, the Cherokees' allies defeated at Fallen Timbers in Ohio, and the Spanish too busy in Europe to court Indians in Appalachia, the Nation chose to make peace.

As an adult and tribal leader, John Ross understood why the United States still wanted Cherokee land. But rather than seize it forcefully as had been done in the late seventeenth and early eighteenth centuries, the government and its agents wanted to acquire it legally, through a treaty. Whatever tactics of bribery or deception treaties might entail, they suggested that naked force did not appeal to the national government any more than violent resistance did to Ross. For his part, the young leader supposed that he dealt with a self-described Christian commonwealth and a republic committed to the rule of law. Therefore overcoming bribery, deception, and racism should be possible. One of his techniques was an old Cherokee stratagem: if you do not like the subject or the sponsors of a meeting, do not attend. Having the meeting at the place of your choice made you more powerful. Furthermore, among civilized countries, a sovereign nation deserves to determine in its own country where and with whom its authorities should deal. Thanks to Ross's strategy of avoidance, many conferences at which the United States planned to buy land in the Cherokee Nation never took place.

Ross also sought friends and allies among influential whites. Shortly after his niece married into that sphere, Ross joined the Methodist church, which he thought less inclined to carp and boss than the Presbyterian. He nonetheless helped the Presbyterian mission when he could and accepted its help in finding both litigants and lawyers to support cases asserting Cherokee rights. For much of his career, Ross's closest assistant was the Welsh-born Baptist minister Evan Jones. Jones was a teacher and preacher who had gone to school using a language not his own and who had the rare good sense when asked what would be good for the Cherokees to ask what the Cherokees wanted. When Democratic executives disappointed Ross, he looked to congressional Whigs to help. He also found white allies in courts, even in Georgia.

U.S. counterstrategies to Cherokee opposition to white encroachment followed two main trajectories. Separately and together, they aimed to undermine both Cherokee sovereignty and Ross's leadership. To that end, Congress passed the Indian Removal Act of May 1830. The act appropriated half a million dollars for negotiations with eastern tribes to get them to exchange their current homes for lands beyond the Mississippi.[3] The Jackson administration used the money to undermine the sovereignty and the unity of the Cherokees and others tribes. For example, in 1830 the U.S. government chose the Cherokee agent, a Georgia planter in full agreement with the removal policy of his state. In an early example of "block-busting," it also chose "emigration agents" who tried to buy individual improvements in the Cherokee Nation, enlist the sellers for emigration, and sell the improvements to eager intruders.

The United States used army units, where available, not to enforce laws and treaty guarantees against trespass but to hunt down Cherokee "criminals," even though tribesmen were legally liable to arrest and punishment only by Native authorities. The government refused to permit Cherokees to try whites for crimes committed within the Cherokee Nation, though white juries outside its borders would never convict them. Then without irony Washington authorities complained that Cherokee leaders could not keep order. When John Ross refused to follow the government's orders or comply with its subversive program, the Jackson administration did its best to discredit him and deny his recognition by national authorities, state governments, and his own people.

Ultimately the government's line of attack was to create and foster differences among Cherokees and then to support those tribe members who opposed the party in power and supported the government's agenda. In response to this divisive policy, Cherokees formally forbade any but the Nation's leaders to cede land because of the tendency of both individuals and regions to succumb to federal bribes. In spite of that decree, after leaders of the towns along the lower Tennessee River left for Arkansas, Tennesseans like John Ross's youngest brother, Andrew, tried to sell Tennessee, or perhaps Tennessee and Alabama, so that they could get a good price and relocate to the relatively unsettled West. As John Ross and his friends consolidated their hold on Cherokee policy and as the state of Georgia put increasing pressure on both the tribe and their guardians in Washington, the national government sent western Cherokees to encourage eastern Cherokees to migrate. More to the point, it secretly sent agents east to seek out and cultivate an opposition to John Ross.

They finally found a pliant and able candidate among the Nation's brightest young men. John Ridge was the son of a mixed-blood mother and Major Ridge, Ross's friend, neighbor, and political ally and a Cherokee major in Jackson's campaign against the Creek Indians in 1813–14. At seven, speaking no English, John went to a Moravian school. Within a year, he was fluent in the language. His father then sought an academy equal to his talents both in Nashville and at the American Board school at Brainerd. Finding none, he reluctantly sent the young teenager to the recently established American Board school at Cornwall, Connecticut. There, John would study classical languages, theology, and equally self-improving secular subjects. John's young cousin Buck Watie, now renamed in honor of the philanthropist Elias Boudinot, went with him. Both did well in their studies and in their social relations with the daughters of an official and of an agent of the school. When they both eventually married white women, the local paper fulminated, and one bride's brother lit a match to burn a picture of his sister and her betrothed on the town square. In the mid-1820s the Cornwall trustees repudiated intermarriage and closed their school.

Major Ridge, Elias Boudinot, and several missionaries might have been disappointed in these Yankee trustees. But each of them knew from the course of events unfolding back home that Georgians were unabashedly racist. When in 1816 Secretary of War William H. Crawford had proposed intermarriage as a way to civilization, Georgia newspapers responded with barely printable disgust. Similarly, a treaty signed in 1819 guaranteed individual fee simple reserves, which could be willed or sold to heirs, to people like John Ross, who had been left an island in the ceded territory by his great-uncle Will Shorey. It also provided 640 acres in life estate, which belonged to proprietors only during their lifetimes, for anyone who would become a U.S. citizen and live among whites. Incensed Georgian intruders, surveyors, lottery managers, and courts competed with their counterparts in Alabama, Tennessee, and North Carolina to dispossess the Cherokees and make the federal government pay for it. All the while, William McMinn, governor of Tennessee, went about the Nation buying and selling improvements and trying to enroll the whole tribe for emigration. When the Cherokee agent Return J. Meigs died, the government appointed McMinn to replace him. Those Cherokees who preferred a tribal selection of an agent less inimical to their interests protested in vain.

If that failed experiment in promoting citizenship did not prove conclusively the impossibility of integration, Georgia's denial of voting and jury privileges to members of the tribe and its delight in flooding the Cherokee Nation with intruders and whiskey should have removed all doubt. Lawyers hired by the Nation had defended two missionaries (one of them named Samuel Worcester) who challenged a state law requiring any U.S. citizen desiring to enter the Cherokee territory to obtain the permission of the governor. The Supreme Court invalidated the law, ruling that Georgia could not rule the Cherokees. Neither President Jackson nor Georgia recognized the missionary case, *Worcester* v. *Georgia*. Two missionaries remained in jail in Milledgeville until they apologized. Still John Ross's confidence in the legal system remained unshaken. He hired local lawyers to defend individual titles against divestment by the state of Georgia. A judge actually ruled the state's methods unconstitutional. Nonetheless, the state legislature overruled the judges, and John Ross's plantation became part of the city of Rome.

The bright young Cherokee men with Connecticut wives, looking on these unfolding scenes in Georgia and Washington, considered the advice of a sympathetic Supreme Court justice, concerned congressmen, and the recently released Worcester. The two decided that the Nation had better discuss its alternatives. Elias Boudinot, who now edited the Cherokee national newspaper *Phoenix*, wanted to use it to discuss the Nation's real choices.[4] John Ridge, a member of the council, desired a public discussion in that forum of all their alternatives, unpleasant and otherwise. Ross refused to permit discussion on the ground that it would impair the unity that enabled the Cherokee government to keep the Nation together. At the strong suggestion of their critics, Ridge and Boudinot observed traditional Cherokee decorum by leaving their respective jobs and ceasing to attend and participate in councils they could not agree with.

Nonetheless, Ridge and Boudinot increasingly feared that John Ross was giving his people overly optimistic accounts of their chances to ward off the encroachments of the people and the state of Georgia. Accordingly, they formed the Treaty Party, and in 1834 and 1835 sent their own delegations to Washington to negotiate for removal. The second one made a tentative treaty on the basis of a $5 million offer from the Senate. Inasmuch as gold had been discovered in Georgia in 1829, John Ross thought $20 million a more reasonable offer. Gold mines were already making rich the lottery winners who had won tracts of Cherokee land. They might do the same for Cherokees or their lessees, should a future administration take the Supreme Court's defense of the Nation's property rights more seriously. With $20 million the Cherokees might even take refuge in Mexico. But Jackson rejected that higher price, and Ross promised to take the Senate's lesser offer to the people.

He took it, however, accompanied by the Rev. John F. Schermerhorn, a peculiarly obnoxious Utican whose Christian method for negotiating a treaty included trying to persuade Tennessee and North Carolina to make life as hard for the Cherokees as Georgia had. The Ross partisans and the Treaty Party compromised on a delegation of twenty from both groups who would finalize an arrangement with the United States. By December, however, both Ridge and Boudinot had become convinced that the only arrangement Ross sought involved fee simple allotments and equal state citizenship. The Cherokees would remain in the state. John Ridge was even lighter skinned than John Ross, but he knew what kind of equality the Cherokees could expect from Georgia.

They also believed that if no treaty was signed at the time and place Schermerhorn specified—New Echota, December 1835—revengeful and irate Georgians would forcefully dispossess the Cherokees of their land. Ross, however, planned to boycott Schermerhorn's meeting and return to Washington. It was irrelevant to Ridge and Boudinot whether Ross was pursuing his usual and increasingly hazardous strategy of postpone-ment or indulging in an equally dangerous illusion of integration with egalitarian Georgians. Both promised disaster. Hence, in late December at the Cherokee capital of New Echota, seventy-nine Treaty Party mem-bers led by Ridge and Boudinot—none formally elected by members of the Nation—voted for a treaty on the basis of the $5 million offer. They took it to Washington.

Because after 1831 Cherokees were barred from holding elections in Georgia, Ross and his council could not keep themselves in power through regularly scheduled contests. They did so through a vote in 1832 at a council at Red Clay, a Cherokee capital in Tennessee that was safer to govern from than in Georgia. Thus strictly speaking, Ross and his allies, though clearly they were much more numerous, were no more constitutional than the Treaty Party. Therefore, John Ridge was free to believe that an 1832 election would have made him Principal Chief and that he and his party had saved the tribe endless expense and trouble.

By its terms the Treaty of New Echota set up an alternative govern-ment to that of Ross's. It established a committee to determine two types of claims: those made by Cherokees who migrated west, for im-provements on land they were forced to leave, and those that issued from trespass, theft, and damage to property done by Georgians. The Treaty Party offered Ross and his followers positions on this committee.

Because they did not recognize the treaty as legitimate, Ross and his allies refused. Initially, Jackson had welcomed Ross and his elected committee of twenty to Washington. When, however, the president discovered that the pact signed by the Treaty Party was soon to arrive in the capital from New Echota, he ceased to recognize Ross as leader of the Cherokee Nation.

Reasoning, as did Ridge and Boudinot, that its real choice lay between removal under an irregularly ratified but exceptionally generous treaty, on the one hand, and violent expulsion of Cherokees by Georgians on the other, the Senate ratified the New Echota agreement on May 23, 1836. The government immediately began to assemble an army of occupation—state militia under U.S. command—to prepare roads and stockades and effect Cherokee willingness for removal, which was to be complete in two years. Approximately two thousand Cherokees took advantage of this two-year window of opportunity. Unlike the later Trail of Tears migration, their journey west, despite usual problems with drought and measles, proved comparatively comfortable.

Ross's approximately thirteen thousand followers refused to take their claims awarded by the committee under the treaty. Rather, they enlarged and cultivated their fields and awaited news from their delegation in Washington. Although Jackson and his successor, Martin Van Buren, did not formally recognize Ross, to keep the peace they did keep him talking. Consequently, Ross's letters remained optimistic. Back in Georgia, however, the government's military leaders in the Cherokee Nation assured Ross's followers that the soldiers would be coming on May 23, 1838. At the same time in the U.S. capital, Secretary of War Joel Poinsett assured Ross that he could have an extra two years to move if the state governors would agree. Although North Carolina agreed, Governor George Gilmer of Georgia threatened that when Georgians themselves took over Cherokee property on May 25, blood would flow.

General Winfield Scott went to work rapidly in Georgia, telling his four thousand troops that the civilized Cherokees deserved every kindness consistent with their capture and expulsion. He also made sure that none of the one hundred militia companies within Georgia's Cherokee counties who had volunteered to assist in removal were able to participate in the capture. Several thousand Georgia Cherokees now pent up in stockades marched to Ross's Landing in Chattanooga, Tennessee, with little but the clothes on their backs. Nearly three thousand went off by steamboat before Scott, following orders from Washington, called a halt and put John Ross's government in charge of the removal. He and officials in Washington realized that Ross was the only leader whom the remaining Cherokees would follow.

Scott then made an extraordinarily generous contract to finance the emigration. Lewis Ross, John Ross's wealthy younger brother who had become and remained a merchant, made the contracts for the tribe. Scott and Lewis Ross estimated an eighty-day trip that was to start in September, after the rains had begun and the people and stock could be watered. Before they left, Christian Cherokees and other Ross partisans gathered at Rattlesnake Springs, Tennessee, to declare that as the Cherokee Nation was an eternal gift of the Great Spirit, the Cherokee Nation East was an intact government wherever it was located. Cherokee removal west was delayed until fall. The river was too low to take them all the way, there was not enough water to provide for the stock if they should go by wagon, and the fever season in the West was especially threatening. Scott agreed to let the Cherokees stay in and around the stockades until rain fell. The rains began in October. As a result, Cherokee detachments averaging one thousand each headed west and froze in the mountains and beside the icebound Mississippi. They took, on average, nearly half again as long to arrive in the Cherokee Nation West as they had expected. Along the way, they buried hundreds in disease-ridden camps on the Tennessee, more hundreds along the trail, and other hundreds in the Nation West during the feverish season after their arrival.

On arrival in Indian Territory, John Ross accepted a friendly invitation from the three chiefs of the Cherokee Nation West to meet on June 3, 1839, at Takatoka about four miles northwest of present-day Tahlequah, Oklahoma. Ross, hoping to unite the Cherokee Nation again, proposed that they agree on a set of laws. The Old Settler chiefs were angry at having their population quintupled without pay and at the thought of letting their eastern brethren settle their river valleys. Allowing the new settlers to remake the government was asking too much. The commander of Fort Gibson, Colonel Matthew Arbuckle, sided consistently with the Old Settlers in their opposition to Ross's proposal.

Originally the commissioner of Indian affairs supported majority rule (Ross emigrants outnumbered Old Settlers and treaty emigrants by roughly four to one). However, Washington officials learned that John Ridge, Major Ridge, and Elias Boudinot had been outlawed and assassinated in accordance with an 1829 Cherokee law, which prohibited cession without the council's approval. As a result, the secretary of war opted to avoid any more such tyranny by the majority and reversed the commissioner's position. In practice this reversal meant another several years of two or three delegations (Ross, Old Settler, Treaty Party) representing the Nation in Washington. Periodically administration officials refused to recognize Ross as an official of his government, all the while insisting that he exercise his governmental responsibilities to punish the murderers who had carried out the 1829 Cherokee law.

While the situation in Washington remained shifting and uncertain, in the Cherokee Nation West, despite the customary boycotting of one another's councils, the great majority from all parties agreed on an Act of Union. They also supported the drafting of a new constitution similar in most respects to the old one that structured the government in the Cherokee Nation East. The most notable difference was that the Principal Chief and his assistants were to be elected the modern way— by the people rather than by the committee and council. They further agreed to combine the traditional Cherokee practice of "oblivion" for murders with the Christian demand that Treaty Party sinners admit their guilt and apologize. Later, they would even drop the insistence on apology. This concession might have restored peace within the Nation had the U.S. government proved less anxious to empower Ross's enemies.

Collecting the money owed under the New Echota treaty proved difficult, because Ross and his council refused to have any of their unexpectedly high expenses entailed by removal deducted from the $5 million. Treaty Party people snidely pointed out that the expenses, damages, and suffering would have been considerably less if others (read: Ross) had followed their good judgment in emigrating as the treaty specified. They charged that John and Lewis Ross had more than profited from the removal; they had profiteered. Treaty Party dissidents concluded that the brothers Ross had thereby deprived the Cherokee poor of the large per capita distribution under the treaty they might otherwise have enjoyed. For their part, the Old Settlers thought themselves due their share of that capital distribution. They also complained bitterly that not just their government but their salt mines had been taken from them and given to Ross partisans.

After half a dozen years of murder, theft, and panicky flight that may have been related to a perversion of the clan revenge motif so prominent before the Cherokees took up written law, the Old Settlers and the Treaty Party demanded division of the Nation. President James K. Polk was about to grant it when the outbreak of war with Mexico led him to seek a safer southwestern frontier. The Cherokee Treaty of 1846 paid all parties what they thought their due. The final payment of the allocated monies enabled Cherokee families and their government to pay their debts. Merchants like Lewis Ross rejoiced.

Governmental generosity and Cherokee initiative rendered the 1840s and early 1850s the golden years of Cherokee institution building. Cherokees created a public school system, male and female academies, a two-story brick courthouse, and a Masonic Temple. These were years of transition for Ross as well. His first wife, Quatie, had died of pneumonia during the emigration. Ross remarried in 1844. Both his relatives from their eastern prep schools and his wife Mary Stapler's white Quaker family attended their Philadelphia wedding. Mary's relatives objected not to Ross's color but to his Methodism. Whereas Elias Boudinot's wife's brother had helped burn an effigy of them, Mary Stapler's brother John joined John Ross in business at Tahlequah. At their Park Hill plantation home, Rose Cottage, with its shade trees, its rose-bordered drive, and its mahogany furniture, John and Mary offered both Cherokee modesty and Cherokee hospitality.

Despite a promising beginning in a new home in Indian Territory, by the late 1850s, the Cherokees, like other border slave states, were riven by controversy about slavery. Full-bloods had made clear their cultural and class antagonisms with slaveholders, most of whom were members of the Treaty Party. Ironically, full-bloods were also the strongest supporters of John Ross, one of the Nation's wealthiest slaveholders. Acting upon advice from the abolitionist Evan Jones, full-bloods organized Kituwha society to achieve influence in government councils. Stand Watie, brother of the late Elias Boudinot, organized the proslavery Knights of the Golden Circle. Whereas Ross, the Nation's Principal Chief, regularly vetoed bills that would have expelled abolitionists from the Nation. Southern Democrats who staffed Indian Office agencies sympathized with the Knights.

Once the Civil War erupted, the United States left John Ross without federal protection. Stand Watie volunteered to lead several hundred Cherokees for the Confederacy. By war's end, he had become the elected Principal Chief of the Confederate Cherokees as well as a Confederate brigadier general. Conversely, Ross preferred Cherokee neutrality. But to protect his exposed political flank from Watie at a time when Confederates were courting the Nation and the U.S. government was notable for its absence, he reluctantly consented to a treaty with the Confederacy. Consequently, hundreds of Cherokees deserted the Cherokee Confederacy for the Union. Ross was extricated from this difficult situation when he allowed himself to be "captured" and taken to Washington. In

1863 Ross's followers not only revoked the nation's Confederate allegiance but made the Cherokee Nation the first former Confederate state to abolish slavery.

For years, Treaty Party members, with the support of the U.S. government, had sought a division of the Cherokee Nation among themselves, the Old Settlers, and the Ross party. In negotiations at Fort Smith and in Washington following the Confederacy's surrender, they tried again. Commissioner of Indian Affairs Dennis Cooley was hostile enough to John Ross. Yet in the wake of the Civil War, which had threatened to divide the United States, Cooley and other government officials decided not to break up the Cherokee Nation. Working from his bed, Ross spent the final months of his life trying to prevent the United States from assimilating the Cherokee and other Civilized Nations into a territory governed by whites.

From the beginning of John Ross's life to his death, the United States had done its best to degrade Cherokee sovereignty. It denied them the right to choose their own agent or to try crimes committed by non-Cherokees within their borders. The U.S. government marched soldiers in and out of the Nation to investigate or arrest without Cherokee permission. It withheld payments owed the tribe, formally and legally contracted by treaties, until the Cherokee government behaved as the United States prescribed. The government permitted everyone from the president to the commander at Fort Gibson to decide whom the Cherokees would recognize as their chief.

Still, thirty-eight years of trying to get rid of John Ross left him in place as Principal Chief. Even more decades of degradation of Cherokee sovereignty left the Cherokees, at his death in 1866, a self-governing nation that had successfully converted Christianity, republicanism, technological innovation, and business enterprise into the pattern of a syncretic culture still unique among America's peoples. The ability to survive and adapt, so characteristic of John Ross, provides the vital link between this man and his Nation. His destiny was theirs.

Notes

1. This adult name designated a rare white bird who might expect, like Bryant's waterfowl, the Great Spirit to "guide through the boundless sky" his "certain flight."

2. In traditional Cherokee law, killing a clan member was no murder, and the fetus or newborn was of the mother's clan.

3. The "Five Civilized Tribes"—Cherokee, Creek, Seminole, Chickasaw, and Choctaw—were the targets of this legislation.

4. Ironically, Ross had welcomed the council's decision in the mid-1820s to establish a national newspaper. The *Phoenix* was published in both English and Sequoyan, the syllabary perfected in 1821 by a mixed-blood, non-English-speaking silversmith who was called alternatively Sequoyah and George Guess. The national newspaper was to demonstrate Cherokee progress and civilization. It disseminated correct interpretations of the Cherokees' relations with those individuals and government agencies outside the Nation.

Suggested Readings

Agnew, Brad. *Fort Gibson: Terminal on the Trail of Tears*. Norman, OK, 1980.

Anderson, William L., ed. *Cherokee Removal: Before and After*. Athens, GA, 1991.

Boudinot, Elias. *Cherokee Editor: The Writings of Elias Boudinot*. Edited with an introduction by Theda Perdue. Knoxville, TN, 1983.

Carter, Samuel C., III. *Cherokee Sunset: A Nation Betrayed: A Narrative of Travail and Triumph, Persecution and Exile*. Garden City, NY, 1976.

Conser, Walter H., Jr. "John Ross and the Cherokee Resistance Campaign, 1833–1838." *Journal of Southern History* 44 (1978): 191–212.

Corkran, David H. *The Cherokee Frontier, 1740–1762*. Norman, OK, 1962.

Franks, Kenny A. *Stand Watie and the Agony of the Cherokee Nation*. Memphis, TN, 1979.

Gabriel, Ralph Henry. *Elias Boudinot, Cherokee*. Norman, OK, 1941.

Halliburton, Rudi, Jr. *Red over Black*. Westport, CT, 1977.

Hatley, Tom. *The Dividing Paths: Cherokees and South Carolinians through the Era of Revolution*. New York, 1993.

Hoig, Stanley. *Cherokees and Their Chiefs in the Wake of Empire*. Fayetteville, AR, 1998.

King, Duane, ed. *The Cherokee Indian Nation: A Troubled History*. Knoxville, TN, 1979.

Littlefield, Daniel F., Jr. *The Cherokee Freedmen*. Westport, CT, 1978.

Malone, Henry T. *Cherokees of the Old South*. Athens, GA, 1956.

McLoughlin, William G. *After the Trail of Tears: The Cherokees' Struggle for Sovereignty, 1839–1866*. Chapel Hill, NC, 1993.

———. *Champions of the Cherokees: Evan and John B. Jones*. Princeton, NJ, 1990.

———. *Cherokee Renascence in the New Republic*. Princeton, NJ, 1986.

———. *Cherokees and Missionaries, 1789–1839*. New Haven, CT, 1984.

———. *The Cherokees and Christianity, 1794–1840: Essays on Acculturation and Cultural Persistence*. Edited by Walter H. Conser Jr. Athens, GA, 1994.

McLoughlin, William G., Walter H. Conser Jr., and Virginia Duffy McLoughlin. *The Cherokee Ghost Dance: Essays on the Southeastern Indians, 1789–1861*. Macon, GA, 1984.

Mooney, James. *Historical Sketch of the Cherokee*. Chicago, 1975.

Moulton, Gary E. *John Ross, Cherokee Chief*. Athens, GA, 1978.

————, ed. *The Papers of John Ross.* Vol. 1, *1807–1839.* Vol. 2, *1840–1866.* Norman, OK, 1985.

Perdue, Theda. *Cherokee Women: Gender and Culture Change, 1700–1835.* Lincoln, NE, 1998.

————. "The Conflict Within: The Cherokee Power Structure and Removal." *Georgia Historical Quarterly* 73 (1989): 467–91.

————. *Slavery and the Evolution of Cherokee Society, 1540–1866.* Knoxville, TN, 1979.

Royce, Charles C. *The Cherokee Nation of Indians.* Reprint. Chicago, 1975.

Wilkins, Thurman. *Cherokee Tragedy: The Ridge Family and the Decimation of a People.* 1970. Revised edition, Norman, OK, 1986.

Young, Mary E. "The Cherokee Nation: Mirror of the Republic." *American Quarterly* 33 (1981): 502–24.

————. "Conflict Resolution on the Indian Frontier." *Journal of the Early Republic* 16 (1996): 1–19.

————. "The Exercise of Sovereignty in Cherokee Georgia." *Journal of the Early Republic* 10 (1990): 43–64.

————. "Racism in Red and Black: Indians and Other Free People of Color in Georgia Law, Politics, and Removal Policy." *Georgia Historical Quarterly* 73 (1989): 492–518.

————. *Redskins, Ruffleshirts, and Rednecks: Indian Allotments in Alabama and Mississippi, 1830–1860.* Norman, OK, 1961.

9

Peter P. Pitchlynn
Race and Identity in Nineteenth-Century America

Donna L. Akers

Peter P. Pitchlynn, like John Ross, was an opponent and victim of removal. To that end, he, too, supported tribal unity and was equally unsuccessful in realizing that goal. As an individual of mixed heritage, Pitchlynn laid claim to two worlds that increasingly were at war with one another: that of the Choctaw and that of the Euro-American. Nonetheless, Pitchlynn was unable to bridge the divide or mediate that conflict. He and others of mixed heritage occupied a unique position in American society. Although highly literate and articulate, Pitchlynn was considered inferior by Euro-Americans. Yet he, like most white Americans in the Age of Jackson, valued his individuality and pursued wealth. Pitchlynn's life, not surprisingly, was fraught with conflict and contradiction. Although he was bicultural, he was never accepted by, or felt fully part of, Choctaw or Euro-American society. Successful at moving between these two worlds, he never considered himself wanted in either. An ardent opponent of removal, he finally acquiesced in its inevitability and successfully led two parties to Indian Territory. The victim of racism, Pitchlynn owned slaves and spent the better part of his postremoval life in Washington, DC. Pitchlynn's life vividly illustrates the immense difficulties that people of mixed heritage faced, and how they negotiated their way through the terrains of white and Indian culture.

Donna L. Akers, a member of the Choctaw Nation of Oklahoma, teaches Native American history at Purdue University, West Lafayette, Indiana. She is the author of "Removing the Heart of the Choctaw People: Indian Removal from a Native Perspective," *American Indian Culture and Research Journal* 23 (1999): 63–76; and "Removing the Heart of the Choctaw People: Indian 'Removal' in Its Spiritual Context," in Clifford E. Trafzer, ed., *An Anthology of American Indian History* (forthcoming). She is currently finishing a book on the Choctaw people of the nineteenth century.

In 1806, in a crude cabin in the backwoods of what would one day be Mississippi, in the midst of the Choctaw Nation, a baby was born. His father, John Pitchlynn, paced the boards of the porch outside. He was a white trader who had come to the Choctaw Nation before the

131

American Revolution and spent his entire adult life among the Choctaw. Inside, female relatives who were members of the large and influential Choctaw clan assisted the baby's mother. Safely delivered, the baby began to squall. His first cries would come to be echoed throughout the whole of Choctaw lands.

The boy was called Ha-tchoc-tuck-nee (Snapping Turtle), but he had a white name, too: Peter P. Pitchlynn. Therein lay one of the defining elements of his life. Peter Pitchlynn had claims to two very different worlds: that of the Choctaws and that of Euro-Americans. Most Choctaws accepted him as one of them, despite his white father. Choctaw society was based upon matrilineal kinship, a system of clans in which the mother's lineage defines the children's identity. Maternal relatives were considered one's only close kin, so fathers and all other Choctaws were members of other clans and were not considered close relatives. Therefore, that Peter had a white father was largely irrelevant to the Choctaws. Peter and other children of these mixed Choctaw-white unions were, in fact, Choctaw to these Native American people.

Conversely, most Euro-Americans did not accept Pitchlynn and others of mixed heritage as equal members of their society. Even though as an adult Pitchlynn spoke English well and could appear and behave as a white man and, indeed, was the son of one, he nonetheless was a "half-breed" or "mixed blood" to Euro-Americans. Over his lifetime, he successfully functioned in both worlds. But his life among whites was always circumscribed by their racial attitudes.

Pitchlynn and other people of mixed Native American and Euro-American heritage occupied a strange and unique position within American society and thought. Among Euro-Americans, they were categorized as nonwhite and inferior. In the system of racism that developed in the United States during the eighteenth and nineteenth centuries, Indians initially were relegated to a level somewhere between that of whites and blacks. Because "mixed bloods" often had lighter skin than did "full bloods," they occupied a special niche in the racial order—closest to whites of all the people of color.

Pitchlynn's life reflected a syncretic identity—although he was bicultural, while he was in either society he was still a part of the other. In Washington, he never forgot that he was Choctaw. And in the Choctaw Nation, he continued to be aware of the lure of power in the halls of Congress. Mindful, too, of the lack of education of the Choctaw people, Pitchlynn was infected with the materialism and individualism of Euro-American society. Though he continued to assert his identity as "Choctaw" throughout his life, his identity was not that of the traditional people of the Choctaw Nation. He blended ideas from both worlds, creating in the process a new identity.

Like other people of mixed heritage, Pitchlynn tried to prove himself in two very different worlds. He was adept biculturally—that is, he was able to function well among whites in Washington society as well as among his native people in the Choctaw Nation. His agility in successfully navigating through both white and native worlds came with a price, however. At times he felt unwanted in either world. To some Choctaws, his ability to understand the white worldview made him suspect. That he spoke English, was educated and literate, and was accepted in white society caused some Choctaws to reject him. Euro-Americans also saw him as tainted—able to function and pass as one of them, but not truly one of them. People of mixed heritage in race-conscious America indeed traveled a difficult path. At times, they were excluded from the inner councils of both sides. But, for the most part, people like Pitchlynn combined and blended their cultural heritage into an identity from which they found comfort and belonging. From his experiences, perhaps we can gain a better understanding of the people of mixed heritage in nineteenth-century America.

The Choctaw peoples' ancient homelands consisted of some twenty-three million acres in what later became the states of Mississippi and Alabama. Unlike the accepted stereotype, Choctaws and most other southeastern native peoples were not nomadic; American Indians were sedentary agriculturists, who lived in towns dispersed throughout a defined territory. They raised corn, squash, beans, and other crops for their own use, occasionally trading any surplus to native groups living nearby.

In the first two decades of the nineteenth century, the U.S. government obtained millions of acres of Choctaw lands through a treaty process. These transfers were not what they seemed: an exchange of Indian lands for money through a course of action in which both parties were equally powerful. Instead, most of the large land cessions were obtained through fraud, intimidation, and threats of force on the part of the government and its representatives. By the 1820s, the Choctaws had been forced to cede more than twelve million acres of land, and still the whites wanted more.

At the same time that U.S. political leaders aggressively sought more and more Choctaw land, they also engaged in aggression of a different nature. The U.S. government sought to transform and civilize Indians into whites through education. Of course, by the lights of their own culture, Native American people already were civilized. Yet whites believed passionately that Euro-American culture and religions were superior to all others—certainly to those of American Indians. Euro-Americans believed that all peoples progressed through different stages, beginning with a state of savagery, and moved through a series of conditions until they achieved civilization. Having themselves reached this stage, Euro-Americans considered all peoples of color to be primitive.

This philosophy was both complex and convincing. Pitchlynn and other Native American people who attended white schools or were exposed to white culture were inculcated with these beliefs. During the first quarter of the nineteenth century, the great southeastern Nations of native people were particular targets of white propaganda. Their societies were not closed. They offered built-in mechanisms for dealing with change and incorporating new ideas or behaviors from external sources. For centuries they had absorbed alien societies into their confederations, tolerating a degree of dissimilar beliefs in exchange for political or economic fealty. Eventually, some alien beliefs found their way into the main culture.

The Choctaws, Cherokees, Muscogees, Chickasaws, and others of the Southeast selectively imported and integrated ideas, behaviors, technologies, and material items from Euro-Americans and their societies. Peter Pitchlynn and others of mixed parentage successfully encouraged the Nations to incorporate some of these changes. For example, the Choctaws came particularly to value education and literacy. They asked white missionaries to set up schools within the Nation in 1818 and eventually erected their own education system that was the envy of many whites in backwoods areas.

Choctaw leaders turned to people of mixed heritage to institute new mechanisms within traditional forms to deal with a changing world. For that reason Pitchlynn's biculturalism made him useful in dealing with the changing cultural circumstances of the Choctaws during this period. For instance, alcohol was disrupting and destroying the foundation of Choctaw society. Government officials used it in treaty negotiations and did little to halt its illegal importation into Indian Nations. Choctaw leaders had to invent new mechanisms to deal with this external threat. Pitchlynn's maternal uncle, Mingo Mushulatubbee, was chief of the district and as such had a great deal of power. When Pitchlynn was only eighteen, Mushulatubbee appointed him captain of the Lighthorse, a new institution within the Choctaw Nation. The Lighthorse was an internal police force whose sole mission was to halt the illegal importation of alcohol by whites into the Nation. Pitchlynn's appointment not only demonstrated his uncle's confidence in him but also Peter's ability to lead Choctaws and deal with whites.

During the first two decades of the century, Americans shared a fairly broad consensus favoring eventual Indian assimilation into white society. But after 1820, the price of cotton rose sharply on the world market, making the rich southern lands of the Choctaws extremely attractive to white land seekers. Demands for Indian "removal" became the universal cry in the backwoods, and state and federal politicians changed U.S. policy to reflect the new goal.

In 1828, Andrew Jackson, the leading proponent of Indian dispossession, was elected to the presidency. For years, he had been calling for the repudiation of the treaty agreements in which the United States recognized the rights of Native Americans to possess their lands; now he had the power to implement these ideas. When Jackson became president, Georgia and Mississippi, anxious to obtain the rich farmlands of the native people within their borders, passed legislation that would unconstitutionally extend state laws over native Nations. This legislation made it criminal for a Native American chief or captain to lead his people. Peaceful assemblies of native people were outlawed. Anyone professing to be a Choctaw leader or following Choctaw law was subject to arrest and imprisonment. Indians were not allowed to defend themselves in the state court system, so any white who brought suit against them automatically won. White Mississippians invaded the homes and farms of the Choctaws and took them by force—expelling Choctaw families into the swamps. If Choctaws resisted, they were arrested for assault.

President Jackson sent negotiators to the Choctaws demanding that they sign a treaty giving up the remainder of their lands in Mississippi and Alabama in exchange for undeveloped lands west of the Mississippi River. Jackson sent word that the federal government did not intend to uphold its treaty obligations to the Choctaws, nor would it stop the state governments from illegally extending their laws over them. Pitchlynn and other Choctaw leaders were outraged by the prospect of dispossession. Yet they saw that the Nation had only two choices: stay and fight or agree to a removal treaty. No longer a military threat to the United States, they would lose any prolonged armed confrontation. Leaving their homeland was also not an option; it was a death warrant. Pitchlynn and others struggled futilely to craft a third alternative, but the government left them none.

As this realization dawned, many Choctaws grew dispirited. Pitchlynn traveled from town to town, giving speeches, trying to ward off complete despair. Nonetheless, with white encroachment on their lands, crops could not be planted, tended, or harvested. Invading whites stole cattle and other Choctaw livestock. The men feared leaving the women and children to go hunting. The people's ability to procure food was completely disrupted. Whiskey poured through the Nation, and many dispirited Choctaws welcomed the relief of a drunken stupor. Many towns descended into confusion and chaos. Despite Pitchlynn's efforts, Choctaw society virtually stopped functioning.

Despite pressure from the national government and white encroachments, almost all members of the Nation stood fast. In October 1830, Choctaw representatives gathered at the treaty grounds refused to sell their land. Tribal tradition recounts that clan Mothers—the leaders who controlled all the Nation's lands—refused to allow the sale of another foot of Choctaw land. At an impasse, Americans declared that negotiations were over, and most tribesmen left the treaty grounds and returned to their homes. Unknown to them, however, a handful of Choctaws remained behind. Bribed by the Americans, they signed the "Treaty of Dancing Rabbit Creek." Although negotiators later told Congress that the Choctaw National Council approved the sale, fewer than twenty-five Choctaws signed this document.

Pitchlynn fought vigorously against the ratification of the treaty. He expressed outrage and shock that the Americans would break all their former treaty agreements and dispossess the Choctaws of their birthright through fraud. Choctaws and their white allies sent dozens of protests, documenting that the Choctaw signers were not authorized to sell any of the land. Despite their remonstrations, the Senate ratified the treaty on February 25, 1831. Peter Pitchlynn immediately called for the ousting of the three district chiefs, who, he said, cooperated "with the intruding enemies of our country in their plans and schemes to swindle us of the little store of wealth which we possessed." These "enemies" had corrupted the old chiefs and led them astray. With their help, the United States had procured a treaty "without the consent or knowledge of the people of the Nation."[1]

Indian removal was more than a policy; it was a human tragedy, a spiritual and physical disaster. To Choctaws, their land was not a commodity, something to be bought or sold, or traded for a similar stretch of land. Their land was held communally by all the Choctaw people. The land was assigned to the care of the clans. Any member of the Nation could use the land for hunting, farming, fishing, or other activities, but no one person actually "owned" any of it. More importantly, it was also sacred ground, given to them by the Great Spirit. Land was the essence of their identity, the Mother, the life-giver of the Choctaw people. Choctaw spiritual life and traditions centered on the Great Mother, a sacred mound that the Nation revered, called Nanih Waiya. Most importantly, Choctaw spiritual beliefs and traditions informed them that if they left the bones of their ancestors, the hunters would find no more meat, disease would come, and the Nation would die.

The U.S. government gave the Choctaw people only three years to move the entire nation out of their homelands. Federal agents were to make the arrangements for this massive endeavor, and preparations for "removal" were begun immediately. Under the strain the Choctaw Nation again sank into chaos. Factions formed and reformed, anarchy reigned, and no one could bring sense out of the madness. White observers reported that the cries of the women and children echoed night and day throughout towns and villages. The Nation literally went into mourning.

Rejecting the leadership of those who sold the Nation's lands and sold out the Nation, the people of his district asked Peter Pitchlynn to lead them west. Pitchlynn led two parties. Through his able leadership and administrative skills, most of his charges escaped the worst. His old uncle Mingo Mushalutubbbee and his hundreds of followers were not so lucky. Cholera repeatedly struck their party. Exceptionally bad winter weather—largely unknown in the region in which they traveled—snowed under the defenseless travelers, delaying them at one point for two weeks in a storm without tents or blankets. Dozens of his party died. Another group of Choctaws got separated from their main party and became lost in a huge swamp when a vicious winter snowstorm struck. When they were finally rescued several days later, one American described seeing hundreds of the Choctaws' horses standing in the swamp water up to their chests, frozen in place.

From the moment of its hasty inception to its grim conclusion, removal was an unmitigated disaster for the Choctaw people. They died in the thousands as a result of government neglect and bureaucratic ineptitude. American merchants and entrepreneurs preyed upon the Choctaws at every opportunity, providing them with rotten and underweight provisions. Owing to a lack of proper supplies, such as tents, blankets, and clothing, exposure killed many of the babies and the old ones. By the time the Choctaws reached their destination, over twenty percent of the Nation had died. Finally, a majority of the surviving Choctaws arrived in their place of exile. It consisted of what is today the southern half of the state of Oklahoma. Pitchlynn began to build a cabin and clear fields. Unfortunately, his choice of locations posed the danger of malaria and fevers from the low-lying riverbed nearby. That year, the Arkansas River flooded in a massive, extraordinary flood unlike any known before. Pitchlynn and many other Choctaws lost what little they had left. Many other Choctaws were, like Pitchlynn, trying desperately to get on their feet and provide themselves with a subsistence existence in this unfamiliar land. Pitchlynn assisted several members of his clan to relocate near him, even carving out claims for them before they arrived from Mississippi.

Pitchlynn's now elderly father, John, wrote that his mother refused to leave the spirits of her dead children. The Choctaws believed that people had two spirits—one that traveled west to the Land of the Dead and one that remained where death had occurred. The spirits of the dead watched over their remains and became offended if they were not treated with respect. They wrought terrible calamities on the descendants who neglected their sacred duty to the dead. Peter's mother therefore refused to leave the spirits of her dead children behind. John remained with her. Peter's father, however, frequently expressed his hope that before he died, all of his children would be together in the new land, "with their own people."[2]

Although once an enthusiast and supporter of assimilation, Peter began to look at Euro-American society in a different light after these experiences. Dispossession and exile convinced Pitchlynn that no matter how "white" Indians became, they would never be accepted fully by Americans. Their political and economic rights would always be a subset of, and vulnerable to, those enjoyed by people of the dominant majority. The racial hierarchy that permeated every facet of American life demanded the subordination of all people of color. Pitchlynn and many of the Native people of Indian Territory turned their faces from the whites and concentrated on rebuilding a new Choctaw society.

In 1836, Pitchlynn was instrumental in drawing up a new Choctaw Constitution. Ironically, it was modeled after those of the United States and its various states. Nevertheless, many Choctaw traditions and societal norms were also incorporated. In December 1841, Choctaw chiefs asked Pitchlynn to travel to Washington on tribal business. He left the following month. There he represented the Nation on matters of education, claims by Choctaws against the government, land rights, and representation for the Indian Territory in Congress. He returned to the Nation the following spring, and that summer Pitchlynn ran unsuccessfully for a seat on his district's council. He returned to Washington again in 1847 to represent the Nation to Congress. In 1853 the Choctaw council appointed Pitchlynn and three others as delegates to settle by treaty "all and every claim and interest of the Choctaw people against the United States."[3]

Because the Choctaws and other Indian Nations in the Territory were isolated and far away from the centers of U.S. power on the East Coast, the Choctaws and their Indian neighbors entered progressively into an illusion of independence and sovereignty, a false sense of security that Americans would not come after their lands again. From the 1830s until 1860, Americans rapidly settled the lands all around Indian Territory to the west. Pitchlynn, who was in Washington much of this time, along with other representatives from the Indian Nations, fought off repeated attempts to force a territorial government on Indian Territory, a necessary prelude to confiscation of the Indians' communal lands.

After his appointment in 1853, Pitchlynn continued to live primarily in Washington, with occasional visits back to his farm and family in the Choctaw Nation. In his absence his brother, his sons, a son-in-law, and his slaves ran his farm for periods of time. The Choctaw form of slavery was quite different from the institution in the antebellum South. Slavery among the Choctaws grew out of a long tradition. From time immemorial, captives taken in war had become slaves for a period of time. Eventually, most were adopted by a clan, at which point they became Choctaw. After that point, no differences could be discerned in their acceptance by the Choctaws. By contrast, American slavery was hereditary and permanent.

Pitchlynn's slaves were treated more like servants. They were free to move about, pursue economic engagements, and keep any earned income for themselves. Often Pitchlynn would leave a leader of the slaves, Solomon, to run the farm, and he would write to Pitchlynn in Washington about the conditions on the farm, the crops, the weather, and his own private financial endeavors. After the Civil War, Pitchlynn's former slaves remained on his farm as tenants or share croppers, continuing to live in the small communities they had built on his land during the antebellum era.

During the 1850s, while Pitchlynn was in Washington, life began to deteriorate in the Choctaw Nation. Disorder among the Choctaws and gangs of white outlaws who fled to Indian Territory to escape U.S. justice contributed to the chaos. All of it centered on the ambiguous legal relationship of the Nation to the United States. The Choctaw Nation had exclusive legal jurisdiction over crimes committed in Indian Territory involving only Choctaw people. If a white person was involved, the United States had jurisdiction. The nearest federal court, however, was outside Indian Territory—at Fort Smith, Arkansas. For people living in remote areas of Indian Territory, travel to Arkansas was expensive and difficult. Leaders of the Choctaw Nation and the other Indian Nations in Indian Territory complained frequently and with increasing urgency about the remote site of the court, the ambiguity of conflicting jurisdictions, the intrusion of white law enforcement personnel, and the outlaw intruders living in the Choctaw Nation—to no avail.

Once again, Peter Pitchlynn stood at the crossroads of this cultural conflict. In 1856, two of Pitchlynn's sons were arrested and charged with assault with intent to kill a white man. Two traveling white men had come to the Pitchlynn homestead with whiskey, obviously feeling the effects of it. Leonidas Pitchlynn came out and saw that one of the men's horses was near death. He requested that the white man take his horse and move on before it died, since Pitchlynn did not want to have to "hunt up oxen" to haul it away if it died on his property. The white man replied, insultingly, "You are too saucy for a damned Indian," and he refused to comply with Pitchlynn's request to move on. A fistfight ensued. Pushmataha Pitchlynn, another of Peter's sons, rushed out of the house with a gun and, in order to break up the fight, fired his gun over the heads of the two struggling men. Just as he shot, however, the white man threw one of his hands up and the bullet took off one of his fingers. The grand jury issued an indictment based solely on the word of the white men, and the Pitchlynns were arrested.

After the Pitchlynns made bail, one of the white men offered not to appear at their trial for a certain sum of money. They refused and were subsequently convicted of assault with intent to kill. Had Peter Pitchlynn not had connections in Washington, his sons would have gone to the penitentiary for three years. The boys' maternal uncles wrote an appeal for their pardon to President James Buchanan. One of the justifications was that "The two young Pitchlynns are themselves *almost white men*— had no prejudices or ill feeling toward white men, and they, as well as

their Father, were proverbially hospitable and kind to citizens of the
United States who traveled through the Choctaw Nation."[4]

The appeal thus in part hinged on the assertion of near-whiteness.
As their uncles had it, these were not a couple of dark-skinned, ignorant savages, but rather men who were close to the level of whiteness—
and civilization—of the men with whom they scuffled. The unwritten
assumption was that the president, like most Americans of the day, would
assess the Pitchlynns' worthiness of a pardon based at least in part on
the color of their skin. The boys' uncles, in their appeal to the president, knew that "race" would play an important role in the president's
decision.

The wording of the request for the pardon casts new light on the
experience of nonwhite peoples who became subject to the jurisdiction
of the U.S. system of justice in antebellum America. What becomes
obvious is that a system of racism informed the administration of justice in the United States. The grand jury and the federal court had taken
the word of the white men who were themselves directly involved, with
no other witnesses present. The appeal that the boys were "almost white
men" goes to the very core of the problem created by the system of
racism institutionalized in America in the nineteenth century. It also
reveals how far removed Choctaws remained from being tolerated by,
much less assimilated into, American society in the 1850s.

Although with the boys' uncles' help Peter Pitchlynn successfully
obtained a pardon for his sons, the experience was a bitter one. From
this point on, he steadfastly railed against and opposed the operation of
U.S. society and its legal system. "What can be more unjust than that
we should be dragged to distant points for trial, far beyond the reach
for witnesses and friends, for every alleged infraction of the white man's
rights," Pitchlynn complained, "and placed in the power of a Judge, as
my children were, where every prejudice is against us, and every sympathy in favor of the whites—let them never be so degraded?" But in an
ironic twist he hoped that in the future, white allies of the Indians would
see that U.S. law would be extended to Native American people. In that
case, whites who had invaded Indian Territory and were living there
illegally would "be no longer free to rob, despoil, and trample upon us
and then laugh in our faces."[5]

Unhappily for Pitchlynn's family and the Choctaws, lawlessness came
to typify their experience in Indian Territory. Some of the more remote
areas became havens for vicious criminal gangs, including the notorious

Ned Christie, Belle Starr, and the Quantrill gang. Dozens of other outlaws and renegades also lived in the Indian Territory, terrorizing Indian and white alike. But whites were not the only renegades during this era. Choctaw young men no longer had warfare and traditional male rituals with which to prove their manhood, so they often turned to alcohol and violence. Time and again fighting broke out even among friends during drinking bouts, and many personal disputes were settled with gunfire. A Choctaw Lighthorse killed Pitchlynn's youngest son, Lee, for attempting to evade arrest for the murder of another Choctaw. Pitchlynn's grandson was killed in broad daylight by two white outlaws with whom he had had a dispute. Violence became part of the warp and weft of the Nation's life in their new homeland.

As the Choctaw people struggled to find solutions to this seemingly unending circle of violence, the Civil War intervened. The war that challenged the perpetuity of the Union presented an opportunity for the Choctaws. It served both as an outlet of aggression for the young men and provided a diversion that forced the attention of everyone in the Nation to focus on the survival of the United States. Although Pitchlynn was a slaveholder, he was opposed to the Confederacy and believed that the Choctaws should remain loyal to the Union. But the Choctaws were not allowed the luxury of choice. They came to discover that they would not have the option of remaining neutral as Pitchlynn and many others favored.

The dilemma of the Indian nations of Indian Territory during the Civil War could not have been greater. On the one hand, although some Choctaws owned slaves and practiced a style of slavery seen on southern plantations, especially along the Red River, they were a tiny minority of the Nation. The Choctaw economy did not depend on slavery, and the ruin of all those who held slaves would have had very little, if any, impact upon most Choctaw people. On the other hand, the geographical location of the Choctaw Nation placed it just across the Red River from Texas, a state whose involvement with, and dependence on, plantation slavery was paramount. During the years leading up to the Civil War, Texans and Arkansans often crossed into the Choctaw Nation to "persuade" Choctaws that their interests lay with the South, often through acts of violence and intimidation. The Choctaw decision to side with the Confederacy came as a result of the withdrawal of all federal troops from Indian Territory. The troops left to fight to preserve the Union. Their departure, however, left the Choctaws and other Native people vulnerable to raids and assaults by Texans, Arkansans, and southern partisans in Kansas, who terrorized those Indian people whom they thought were pro-Union.

Taking a different, less violent tack, the Confederate government sent agents to try to entice the Choctaws into an alliance with and incorporation into the Confederacy. They promised full legal representation in the Confederate legislature, guaranteed to honor all treaty agreements between the United States and the Choctaws, and promised the Indians that they would have full political rights in the Confederate States of America. Despite their many misgivings, Choctaws declared the Nation free and independent of the United States and joined the Confederacy. They remained loyal to the South throughout the Civil War.

Ironically the Choctaw people turned to Pitchlynn, who had returned to Indian Territory to oppose an alliance with the South, for leadership during the Civil War. He was elected Principal Chief and served the Nation until the end of the conflict. Pitchlynn's astute leadership of the Nation during and after the war kept the impact of the conflict and its aftermath at a minimum. Most of the Indian Territory and its Nations were devastated during the conflict. The territory served as the stage for another civil war among the pro-Union and pro-Confederacy factions of the Cherokee and Muscogee Nations. Damage to the Choctaw Nation was not nearly so severe. Even so, the Choctaws never recovered from the devastation of the war. Worse yet, the U.S. government forced the Choctaws to give up half their lands in Indian Territory as punishment for siding with the South.

In the years after the Civil War, Pitchlynn continued to represent the Choctaw Nation in Washington. His main activity was trying to secure a resolution to Choctaw claims resulting from the treaty of 1830. Pitchlynn died on January 17, 1881, without having succeeded in persuading Congress to honor the agreement. Yet a month after his death, the House of Representatives passed legislation to implement the agreement. Five years later, the Supreme Court awarded the Choctaw Nation over three million dollars. It took fifty years and continuous negotiations and lobbying for the United States to fulfill its obligations under the Treaty of Dancing Rabbit Creek of 1830.[6]

The experience of Peter Pitchlynn and other Native Americans of mixed heritage allows us a glimpse into the complexity of their lives and how they negotiated difficult paths in both the white and Indian worlds. In Pitchlynn's case, he never forgot or tried to deny his Choctaw identity. Nonetheless, Peter probably would not have been able to do so, even if he had so desired. The United States had embarked on a disastrous course of racism that no one individual could overcome. The experience of Native American people, African Americans, Mexicans, and other people of color illustrates the enormous effects of racism on American history.

Seen from a non-Eurocentric perspective—seen from Peter Pitchlynn's point of view—the story of the United States turns into a story that is less unique than universal, and far more believable than mythic. We find a place and time in which the skin color of individuals and groups limited their rights and hedged their opportunities. We can experience and perhaps understand the rage and frustration of people excluded unjustly from the possibilities of American life. We gain an understanding of the behavior and motives of both oppressors and oppressed. American history is sometimes not a very pretty or admirable tale. Instead, it is a human story, with which we can empathize, and from which we can learn. Indian people know the past is always with us. It is never over. The story of America is the story of all of us.

Notes

1. Peter P. Pitchlynn, transcript of speech to the Nation, 1830, Cyrus Kingsbury Collection (Thomas Gilcrease Museum, Tulsa, OK).

2. John Pitchlynn to Peter P. Pitchlynn, November 23, 1832, and John Pitchlynn to Peter P. Pitchlynn, April 5, 1835, Peter P. Pitchlynn Collection (Western History Collection, University of Oklahoma, Norman). John also wrote with great anger and disgust of the invading hordes of shiftless white folks who invaded and claimed the old Choctaw lands. He charged them with stealing everything he had and cheating the few remaining Choctaws out of their land. He averred that he could no longer stand any white man—that they were all out to get land or wealth no matter what the cost to their souls. He was infuriated and astonished at the lengths to which intruding whites went to cheat the Choctaws and to take advantage of their great distress.

3. Annie Hanie, interview with author, May 1992, notes in possession of author; W. David Baird, *Peter Pitchlynn: Chief of the Choctaws* (Norman, OK, 1972), 61–63, 67–69, 97 (quotation). A skillful amalgamation of Choctaw and Euro-American ideals was blended in some of the legislation adopted by the Choctaws. For example, the Choctaw passed a law barring the murder of witches and wizards without a fair trial before the chiefs or four captains. But if any person found the entrails of a witch "going from or returning to the body," the body could be put to death, cut open "by a proper person," and examined "to see whether it has in it any entrails." The framers of the law complied with Euro-American ideas of due process but also accommodated and recognized the beliefs of traditional Choctaws that witches were a very serious threat to the people and should be killed when discovered among them. Angie Debo, *The Rise and Fall of the Choctaw Republic* (Norman, OK, 1934), 46–47.

4 . Sampson Folsom and James Gamble to James Buchanan, President of the United States, June 29, 1857, Peter P. Pitchlynn Collection.

5. Peter P. Pitchlynn, Washington City, to Messrs. Walker and Green, Van Buren, October, 1857, ibid.

6. Shortly following Peter Pitchlynn's death, the United States gave in to demands of whites for the lands of the Native American peoples in Indian Territory. Despite all its treaty promises guaranteeing that no state or territory would ever be allowed to assert its sovereignty over the Native American peoples of Indian Territory and that their landholdings would be guaranteed forever, the United States passed the Dawes Act and other legislation in the 1880s and 1890s and seized the lands of native Nations in Indian Territory. The United States dissolved their governments over the vociferous protests of the tribes.

Suggested Readings

Catlin, George. *North American Indians.* Edited and with an introduction by Peter Matthiessen. New York, 1989.

DeRosier, Arthur H., Jr. *The Removal of the Choctaw Indians.* New York, 1970.

Jennings, Francis. *The Invasion of America: Indians, Colonialism, and the Cant of Conquest.* New York, 1976.

Martin, Joel W. *Sacred Revolt: The Muskogees' Struggle for a New World.* Boston, 1991.

Rogin, Michael Paul. *Fathers and Children: Andrew Jackson and the Subjugation of the American Indian.* New Brunswick, Canada, 1995.

Stannard, David E. *American Holocaust: The Conquest of the New World.* New York, 1992.

Swanton, John R. *Source Material for the Social and Ceremonial Life of the Choctaw Indians.* Birmingham, AL, 1993.

10

Hosea Easton
Forgotten Abolitionist "Giant"

George R. Price

One of the great and tragic ironies of the Jacksonian era is that while white males were increasingly asserting their equality with one another and participating in ever larger numbers in the political arena, they did so by pushing other groups to the margins of American society. Native Americans were one such group; African Americans were another. In the early republic, although racism was prevalent and segregation increased throughout the North, African Americans, relying on self-help and uplift to lay claim to respectability with whites, contested the "color line." Hosea Easton's experiences and writings suggest, however, that by the 1830s modern racial essentialism was becoming all-pervasive. Skin color, not talent or respectability, became the fault line in American society. Easton's life bridged both of those eras and embraced the central assumptions of African American thought characteristic of each. The son of a mixed-heritage activist, Easton championed black solidarity and self-improvement in the late 1820s. After a series of riots destroyed black churches and schools throughout the Northeast and lower Midwest, Easton became convinced that the oppressors— not African Americans—had to be transformed and that whites shouldered the burden of promoting equality. His activism and uncompromising moral critique of white society would anticipate and echo throughout the civil rights movement of the 1950s and 1960s.

George R. Price is adjunct instructor in the Departments of Native American Studies and African American Studies at the University of Montana, Missoula. He is the coauthor, with James Brewer Stewart, of *To Heal the Scourge of Prejudice: The Life and Writings of Hosea Easton* (1999).

The sit-ins of the 1960s civil rights movement were not the first such protests in American history. One hundred and sixty years earlier, a Revolutionary War veteran of black-Indian heritage, James Easton, his wife, Sarah, and their seven children, used the sit-in tactic as a protest against segregated seating arrangements in two different Massachusetts churches in 1800. After they purchased a pew in the whites-only section of one of those churches, the congregation plastered their pew with tar. The family returned to the church the following Sunday, hauling their own benches in their wagon, to replace the tarred pew. When the irate white church members threw their benches out the door, the Eastons took their seats on the bare floor. Eastons repeated such protests on at least six different occasions between 1800 and 1827.[1]

Around the year 1812, Easton and his older sons established their own iron works and foundry in North Bridgewater, Massachusetts, where they manufactured various tools and the frameworks for some major construction projects. They also created a school within their factory to provide both industrial skills and an academic education to young men of color. This school was one of the first of its type in the United States, established about ten years before the manual labor education movement began nationwide. After nearly sixteen years of struggle against substantial racist opposition to their existence, both the factory and school were forced to close. James Easton died soon after in 1830. Like other leading free men of color of his generation such as James Forten and Prince Hall, Easton would not—could not—be content with anything less than equal opportunities and rights for all colored citizens of the nation that they had fought for and helped to build with their labor.[2]

Hosea Easton, the youngest child of James and Sarah, was born into this conflicted social environment of hope and struggle. By the late 1820s he had become prominent as a leader in the fight for human rights and liberty in the United States. With a family background rich in inspiration and courage upon which to draw, Hosea worked passionately and incessantly throughout the course of his brief life for the cause and against the world that he had inherited.

In March 1828, Hosea Easton was called upon to chair "a large and respectable meeting of the people of Colour" held in Boston at the Colored Methodist Episcopal Church. The purpose of that meeting was to reaffirm a commitment among the people of the community to support *Freedom's Journal*, the nation's only newspaper published by African Americans. One of the speakers at that meeting was David Walker, who published his inspirational and controversial *Appeal to the Coloured Citizens of the World* the following year. In June 1828, Easton's first published work, *An Appeal to the Christian Public, in Behalf of the Methodist Episcopal Church*, appeared.[3]

Shortly thereafter, on November 27, 1828, Easton delivered a powerful and revealing Thanksgiving Day address to the "coloured population" of Providence, Rhode Island. He had not intended to publish the lengthy speech, but, as he recalls in the introduction, "by the ardent request of a Committee chosen for that purpose, by the Coloured Population of Providence, he was influenced to yield to their solicitation." The *Address* articulated the grief and pain of discrimination, as well as the liberating hope of equality through "uplift"—self-improvement efforts by the victims of racism. Because the occasion of this speech probably coincided with the agonizing closure of the Easton family business, in which Hosea Easton had been deeply involved, Easton's words reveal how widespread racism deeply wounded and exasperated him.[4]

The speech began with a patriotic giving of thanks for the greatness and prosperity of America. But this tone soon took an ironic, almost sarcastic turn, as Easton described how some American citizens were excluded systematically from the benefits of liberty and prosperity. He fervently declared his belief that only in a state of true liberty can the human mind and spirit develop their full potential. "The voice of Liberty calls the energies of the human soul to emerge out of nature's darkness, and to explore divine spiritual principles," Easton declared. "How admirable it is, that the higher the soul arises by being expanded by intelligent perception, the more it breathes forth praise and thanksgiving to God." To him, the ultimate crime issuing from slavery and discrimination was that an entire segment of the community effectively was robbed of the experience to develop and manifest its full humanity.[5]

In the course of this address, Easton also described the violent atrocities committed within the institution of slavery; the day-to-day realities of segregation, racism, and lack of true liberty for "free" people of color in the North; the "diabolical" evil—as he saw it—of the colonization movement; and, finally, the hope of victory through "uplift" combined as it was with divine intervention.[6] This latter aspect of Easton's thought, with its emphasis on the responsibility of the victims of racism to transform their limiting circumstances, would develop in a radically different direction during the next decade of his life.

Soon after the closing of James Easton and Son's factory and school, Hosea Easton moved to Boston and became a leader in one of the most significant developments of the abolitionist movement of the 1830s: the National Convention of Free People of Color. Several years before William Lloyd Garrison established his antislavery newspaper *The Liberator* in 1831 (which is often given as the beginning of the abolitionist movement), leaders of free, colored communities in the urban areas of the North had been coming together with increasing frequency and in growing numbers to take up the causes that were in the common interests of their people. These issues included the abolition of slavery; opposition to the American Colonization Society; the education and advancement of free people of color; the organization of their own churches; the promotion of *Freedom's Journal*; and, generally, the search for other ways to oppose effectively segregation and racism. The National Convention of Free People of Color was, therefore, both a result and culmination of the growing need for such leaders to unite to achieve their common goals and fight their common enemies.[7]

The first National Convention of Free People of Color was held in Philadelphia in June 1831, and "Rev." Hosea Easton was selected as one of the four delegates from Boston. The agenda for the convention included such issues as healing divisions and strengthening the ties between the people of color, the feasibility of emigration to Canada, and how to defeat the work of the American Colonization Society. The issue of emigration to Canada surfaced as a reaction to the white race riots in Cincinnati in 1829, when hundreds of African Americans were driven out of the city and many fled to Canada. Now other people of color were contemplating a similar emigration as a means of escaping white American racial hostility.[8]

Delegates to the convention denounced the American Colonization Society because it promoted a plan that would rid the United States of free African Americans by shipping them to Africa, thereby removing the most significant indigenous threat to the institution of slavery. The mere presence of the thousands of free blacks in the South was an inspiration to slaves to seek freedom. In the North, free people of color were spearheading the abolitionist movement. The audacity of the society to promote its plan either under the guise of benevolence or even as an antislavery program proved offensive to the African American community.[9]

Perhaps the most exciting issue raised at this first convention for Hosea Easton was a proposal put forth by three radical white abolitionists—William Lloyd Garrison, Arthur Tappan, and Simeon Jocelyn—who had recently resigned in protest from the colonization society. They submitted a proposal "that a College be established at New Haven, Connecticut . . . for the liberal education of Young Men of Colour, on the Manual Labour System." This resolution raised the possibility of reviving the work begun by Easton's father some twenty years earlier but on a much grander scale. The project would require $20,000 to complete. A "benevolent individual" (most likely Arthur Tappan) had already donated the first $1,000; convention delegates were responsible for raising the remainder. The proposed college, which had the potential to be a powerful tool for the cause of "uplift," was reason for hope. So, too, was the inclusion of white allies—however small in numbers—in the movement for liberty and equality. These allies could bring more white influence and resources to the overwhelming task of eradicating racism.[10]

White abolitionists, however, were and would remain an extremely small minority in antebellum America. Society in the Age of the Common Man was becoming ever more racist and its climate less tolerant of any dissent from the ideology of white supremacy. As the nation expanded west and south, it encountered more Indians and brought more Africans—enslaved and free—into newly opened lands. White Americans collectively came to the conclusion that lines had to be drawn regarding who could participate in, and reap the economic benefits of, territorial and industrial expansion. This consensus demanded that white social domination should remain the first priority when considering issues of social inclusion. People of color, therefore, would only be included in American society where they would serve the needs and interests of the white majority. That way of thinking was the impetus for both the movement to colonize free African Americans to Africa and the Indian Removal Act of 1830. The momentum of this social development of exclusion would negate attempts at uplift, social elevation, and equal inclusion for nonwhites—even when initiated or promoted by whites.[11]

Clearly, there was no room for a "Manual Labor College for Young Men of Colour" in such a society. Reports of the proposed college reached New Haven late in the summer of 1831. A town meeting was held in September, during which delegates made many speeches against the establishment of a "colored college." Several speakers claimed to be against slavery and for the "improvement" and education of blacks, but, nevertheless, they would not allow such a school to be built in their town. The request to permit the college to be built was defeated, 4 to 700, effectively ending the possibility of the school coming into existence. It, however, did not restore New Haven citizens' sense of well-being, security, or civility. A series of inflammatory newspaper editorials followed, each criticizing the city's "unwholesome colored population." By early October, white mobs were rioting in the black section of town and pelting Arthur Tappan's home with garbage. This and similar violent reactions to black attempts at uplift, education, and any other form of self-help throughout urban areas in the North during the 1830s had a profound effect on Hosea Easton.[12]

Easton continued to participate in the annual National Convention of Free People of Color through 1834, both as chaplain, often leading prayers, and as a delegate proposing and seconding various resolutions. Between conventions, Easton worked fervently to develop antislavery sentiments, lecturing at churches and halls all over New England. Apparently, Easton was called away from the convention of 1833, since his name does not appear in the minutes after the first day. His mother, Sarah, died a couple of weeks after that convention, so he may have left to spend time with her. Sometime later in 1833, Hosea, his wife Louisa, and their two children moved to Hartford, Connecticut, where he pastored two churches and resided for the rest of his brief life.[13] Easton's first ministry was the Talcott St. Congregational Church, which had been established as a primarily African American congregation in 1819. Easton's position was not unique. After the turn of the nineteenth century, more and more free colored Christians in New England chose to start their own churches rather than suffer the demeaning experience of being forced to sit in the segregated "negro pews" and balconies in the white churches.[14]

African American churches also became meeting places for the growing number of uplift-related societies and organizations. Not long after Easton's arrival in Hartford, he joined with several local black leaders to form the Hartford Literary and Religious Institution. In January 1834, Easton was appointed the institution's "general agent." He traveled throughout New England to raise funds by speaking to churches and to sympathetic abolitionists. Unfortunately, at this same time another wave of racist-inspired mob violence spread throughout the urban Northeast, leading the members of the institution to "call him home." White race riots broke out in Boston, New York City, Utica (New York), Pittsburgh, and Hartford during the years 1834 to 1836. Easton was no longer safe to travel—especially for the cause that he was espousing.[15]

According to Edward Abdy, an English gentleman traveler and writer, Hartford in the 1830s was particularly racist. "Throughout the Union," he claimed, "there is, perhaps, no city, containing the same amount of population, where the blacks meet with more contumely and unkindness than at this place. Some of them told me it was hardly safe for them to be in the streets alone at night. . . . To pelt them with stones, and cry out nigger! nigger! as they pass, seems to be the pastime of the place."[16] Riots in Hartford in 1834 and 1835 hit Hosea close to home. In 1834 a group of white youths attacked one of the parishoners of Easton's church as the man left the building one evening. A black neighbor, Jack Blackson, defended the victim by firing a round of buckshot that hit four of the youths. White mobs responded by brawling in Easton's neighborhood for three consecutive nights, during which time they tore down Blackson's house and several other homes of free people of color.[17]

A similar event occurred in June 1835. A gang of whites again gathered outside the Talcott St. Church, shouting taunts and epithets at the congregation while they were holding a religious service. When the service was over, the mob attacked the congregation as it left the building. Although the ensuing riot lasted only two days, even the local press expressed outrage at the rioters' behavior, especially at how the incident started. In 1836, Easton founded and began to pastor a second church in Hartford, the Colored Methodist Episcopal Zion Church. It was burned to the ground that same year.[18]

During these years of racial discord and at great personal risk, Easton resumed traveling and pleading for the abolition of slavery and of discrimination. After the fire, Easton had added to his speeches a plea for funds to rebuild the church. But an even more significant change occurred. Instead of speaking of and for the uplift and self-improvement of African Americans to mixed audiences, Easton began to preach increasingly and aggressively to predominantly white audiences. He exhorted them to renounce their racism and bring a healing to American society, as he was now certain that only their actions could bring such a reconciliation. The events of the mid-1830s had convinced Easton that not only did black attempts at uplift fail to bring the desired social change, they apparently provoked an almost unimaginable Afrophobic hysteria. At the time he wrote his *Address* in 1828, Easton had only sensed the futility of African American self-improvement and uplift. Nine years later, he fully realized it. The defenders of slavery and racism needed to change, not the victims. Still a man of profound Christian faith, the Reverend Easton was now convinced that the ultimate hope for colored Americans lay in God's power to lead white racists to repentance and transformation. He saw himself playing the role as one of God's agents working in the vineyards to realize that vision.[19]

Easton's *A Treatise on the Intellectual Character, and Civil and Political Condition of the Colored People of the U. States; and the Prejudice Exercised Towards Them*, published four months before his death in 1837, was the crowning achievement of his brief life. It was his supreme and final attempt to reach white Americans with a message that he now believed they needed to hear. Within its fifty-four pages, the *Treatise* unfolds as a philosophical and theological discourse on the subject of race and racism. As such, it is arguably of greater scope and depth of analysis than anything else previously written on this topic by an American—white or black.[20]

Easton began his treatise in a manner appropriate for a Christian minister writing on the topic of race. He argued for the original oneness of humanity and coupled it to a biblical and historical account of the loss of that original God-ordained oneness. The first sentence of Easton's introduction offered a powerful counterpoint to all of the conflict and disharmony that he described throughout the remainder of the *Treatise.* "One great truth is acknowledged by all Christendom," he wrote, "viz.—God hath made of one blood all nations of men for to dwell on all the face of the earth." Easton then went on to give an environmental, though paradoxically Christian, explanation for the physical variety within the human species. That was followed by a biblical-historical account of the divergent paths taken by the descendants of Noah's sons who populated Africa and Europe, and thereby he provided an explanation for variety in cultural and intellectual development among different human groups.

At this point, the *Treatise* takes on an Afrocentric focus that is more apparent than real. Although not the first to do so, Easton extolled the glories of ancient African civilization by repeatedly making references to the glories of Egypt. In contrast, Easton described how the descendants of Noah, who eventually settled in Europe, became brutal and cruel barbarians. Easton attributed Europe's eventual ascendancy in technology and domination over Africa and the rest of the world to a combination of brute force and the adaptation of African cultural refinement. Yet the point of Easton's historical survey was not to make any sort of argument for innate African cultural, spiritual, or intellectual superiority over Europeans. Rather, Easton was attempting to reveal an environmental, cause-and-effect relationship between worldwide historical events and the degradation of all of humanity, which eventually and inevitably shaped the abysmal state of interracial relations in antebellum America.[21]

The final four chapters of the *Treatise* deal with the damage done to the victims of slavery; the nature of racial "prejudice" and the means by which it is passed on from generation to generation; the effects of racism on the so-called free people of color in the North; the failure of the U.S. government to extend its promise of life, liberty, and the pursuit of happiness to all of its citizens (including colored veterans of two of the nation's wars); and, Easton's very biblical, radically Christian solution to these problems.

Several slights that Easton himself suffered growing up in Massachusetts, as well as experiences in his adult life traveling throughout New England, clearly influenced the chapter that details the ways in which racism is taught and passed through generations. Based on his own life, Easton was able to provide a number of firsthand examples of racist instruction. He related stories and common sayings told to children. Easton noted the frequent use of the terms "negro" and "nigger" as slurs. He recalled to his readers visual reminders of black degradation that took the form of public posters insulting blacks. Finally, Easton noted the negative but instructive effect of segregated public facilities, including, of course, the "negro pews" in the churches.[22]

Easton also made a claim for the economic motivation that perpetuated racism in the North and that correspondingly supported slavery in the South. "Cotton, rice, indigo, tobacco, and sugar, are great blessings to the world, say they, and [the enslaved Africans] may as well be made to make them as not," he observed. "But to come at the truth, the whole system is founded in avarice. I believe the premises to be the production of modern philosophy, bearing date with European slavery; and it has been the almost sole cause of the present prevailing public sentiment in regard to the colored population." One of the profound strengths of the *Treatise* is Easton's consistent effort to tie the viability of the institution of slavery in the South to the "prevailing public sentiment" of racism in the North. Throughout his treatise, he clearly demonstrated how both sections of the country profited from slavery and the perpetuation of racism. Neither antislavery colonizationists nor even some sincere abolitionists escaped his condemnation.[23]

Easton was similarly critical of the Christian clergy for its complicity in the perpetuation of racism. "It becomes the interest of all parties, not excepting the clergy, to sanction the premises [of racism], and draw the conclusions, and hence, to teach the rising generation," he declared. "'The love of money is the root of all evil'; it will induce its votaries to teach lessons to their little babes, which only fits them for destroyers of their species in this world, and for the torments of hell in the world to come. When clergymen, even, are so blinded by the god of this world, as to witness the practice of the most heinous blasphemy in the house, said to be dedicated to God . . . without raising their warning voice to the wicked, it would not be at all surprising if they were to teach their children . . . that a negro is not like a white man, instead of teaching them his catechism."[24]

His parents' resistance to segregated seating in the church gave meaning to Easton's phrase "most heinous blasphemy." Though he certainly was attempting to appeal to the conscience, he by no means tried to appease whites' sensibilities. Rather, he was serving as God's prophetic voice, warning a people doomed for eternity if they did not repent.[25] He even envisioned the form that their repentance should take, and he found it in the biblical example of the Good Samaritan. "New York emancipated her slaves, after beating them several hundred years, left them, half dead, without proscribing any healing remedy for the bruises and wounds received by their maltreatment," Easton scorned. "But the good Samaritan had quite a different view of the subject." Easton then elaborated on what it meant to be a Good Samaritan in the early nineteenth-century United States, calling for affirmative, remedial action on the part of white Americans to heal the wounds of people injured by their avarice: "Emancipation embraces the idea that the emancipated must be placed back where slavery found them, and restore to them all that slavery has taken away from them. Merely to cease beating the colored people, and leave them in their gore, and call it emancipation, is nonsense. Nothing short of an entire reversal of the slave system in theory and practice—in general and in particular—will ever accomplish the work of redeeming the colored people of this country from their present condition."[26]

Of course, when Easton, a staunch anticolonizationist, observed that those emancipated must be placed back where slavery found them, he was not referring to Africa. He was alluding to the restoration of an elevated human condition—what, in Easton's perception, the captive Africans had once been.[27]

Easton considered slavery to be the root cause of the physical and psychological damage of African Americans. It was also the source of the oppressive social circumstances—North and South—in which they were forced to live. At several points in the *Treatise*, Easton emphasized not only the devastation wrought by slavery on human life but how its cumulative effects carried over from generation to generation to create an ever-worsening human condition. Its effect upon whites who supported the institution was no less significant. Easton described it as primarily spiritual, manifesting itself in a degradation of their moral character and thus endangering their eternal souls. For blacks, to the contrary, the effects were physical, mental, moral, and psychological. They increased in severity in direct proportion to the amount of time that individuals and their ancestors spent under slavery's degrading power. Easton asserted that slaves who had come more recently from Africa and freedmen or escapees who were born in Africa (and had spent relatively little time under slavery) were in a more "elevated" state. By making this point of comparison, Easton hoped to persuade his audience that the effects of the institution and white prejudice—not inherited traits—shaped and defined their perceptions and characterizations of the negative personal characteristics and faults that they claimed to find in nearly all of the colored population.[28]

Easton also argued that the human damage inflicted by the institution was so severe that slaves and ex-slaves could not be rehabilitated through their own efforts. Therefore, whites bore the primary responsibility for their recovery and restoration. In making this argument, Easton employed several illustrations that, taken out of their carefully constructed context, could easily be found offensive. Descriptions of actual and alleged African American physical characteristics, which whites had claimed were all examples of personal and racial defects, were repeated by Easton. To his credit, he attempted to sort out those characteristics that were the result of slavery and those that were part of God's intended "variety in nature." In neither case were they inherent shortcomings.

Combined with his descriptions of the psychological damage done to African Americans by slavery, Easton portrayed an image of slave degradation and helplessness that must have been particularly unsettling at best, and offensive at worst, to those who had recently escaped from slavery. By preaching white responsibility and the need for the oppressors to encourage and promote racial healing and redemptive thought and action throughout American society, Easton ran the real risk of offending both whites and blacks, including some key figures within the abolitionist movement. It was a risk Easton was willing to take; nonetheless, his critique had a direct effect on how he and his work were remembered or, rather, forgotten, by those who came after him.

Two key reasons explain why later abolitionists ignored and neglected Hosea Easton and his *Treatise*. The first involves the changes in personnel and tactics within the movement that began shortly after his death. In the early 1840s the colored leadership in the movement shifted from primarily free people of color, such as the Eastons who had been free for generations, to men and women who until recently had been slaves themselves. Besides Easton, the former group included such figures as William C. Nell, John T. Hilton, and Samuel Cornish. The latter group comprised better-known activists such as Frederick Douglass, Henry H. Garnett, Martin Delany, and William Wells Brown. With Frederick Douglass's advent on the abolitionist speaking circuit in 1841, abolitionist leaders like William Lloyd Garrison and Wendell Phillips decided that an effective tactic would be to promote dignified former slaves skilled in oratory, such as Douglass and Brown. This strategy would have the effect of making the institution of slavery appear even more dreadful for limiting the potential and abusing the talents of such nonstereotypical African Americans. Although some whites within the antislavery movement preferred and referred to the image of the helpless, debilitated slave, many gladly welcomed this shift in tactics. It kept the focus squarely on slavery in the South instead of on the unpleasant, uncomfortable, and troubling topic of racism in the North, which Easton had tried to force them to address.

Subsequent to this tactical shift and related to it, slave narrative autobiographies, which had been infrequently published before this time, soon became a profusion. How, then, could passages from the *Treatise* that argue that slavery had a completely debilitating and dehumanizing effect upon the slaves either aid the new abolitionist tactical approach, or be received as anything but an affront to the dignity and pride of people like Douglass, Brown, Harriet Tubman, and Sojourner Truth? Easton believed that the slave was metamorphosed into a machine and thus "lost all the innate principles of a freeman." When slavery ceased to act upon the slave, Easton concluded, "he is left a mere out-of-use wreck of machinery." Ultimately, the freedman would be left alone and exposed to "the withering influence of the pelting rain of wickedness." Douglass, Brown, Tubman, and Truth gave lie to that belief.[29]

Although Garrison and others often had quoted from Easton's *Thanksgiving Day Address* and several of his speeches and convention resolutions, the *Treatise* received little notice after 1840. Most notably, the name of Hosea Easton was omitted from several histories of the African American movement for freedom and equality written by members of this new black abolitionist leadership. Such works as Martin Delany's *The Condition, Elevation, Emigration, and Destiny of the Colored People of the United States* (1852), which even omits Easton from a list of the founding members of the National Convention of Free People of Color, and William Wells Brown's *The Black Man: His Antecedents, His Genius, and His Achievements* (1869), which also contains many minibiographies of colored American leaders and accomplished persons, make no mention of Easton.

The second reason for Easton's neglect is simply and prosaically timing. He died of an unnamed brief illness in July 1837, just four months after the publication of the *Treatise*. Therefore, he was not alive to debate or defend its tenets, much less to publish a modified version. Had Easton lived to revise slightly another edition of his *Treatise*, he might have left out the more excessive descriptions of slave degradation. Conversely, he might have included the experiences of some of the former slaves whom he knew personally to be individuals of high ability and noble character. In that case, he would probably have been much better remembered. As it was, Easton probably believed that it was necessary to magnify the helplessness of the enslaved population for the purpose of convincing his primary intended audience—potentially sympathetic whites—that the needed redemptive, restorative work could not be done without their help.[30]

Despite the controversial and potentially inflammatory content of the *Treatise* and its author's negligible legacy, Easton did not offend all, and neither did all forget him. The Reverend Amos G. Beman, a well-known black abolitionist whom Easton mentored at the Talcott St. Church, asserted in 1859, "We have had the instruction of some of the best minds of our race which the country has produced. Dr. Hosea Easton, a giant in his day, as many remember, lectured and wrote much." After the Civil War, he proclaimed, "Long will the name of Rev. Hosea Easton, whose powerful mind knew no superior among the colored people of the country, be remembered."[31] Evidently, twenty to thirty years after Easton's death, Beman still knew many people, such as the accomplished black abolitionist William C. Nell, who remembered and thought well of Easton.[32]

As a result of the neglect of Easton and his work, an important and articulate voice of opposition to racism and a significant piece of African American writing was nearly lost. Neither the man nor his work had the impact on antebellum race relations—particularly, on white American social and theological thought—it possibly might have. Yet, considering its eloquent, uncompromising, moral critique of white American society both North and South, its Afrocentric account of world history, and, finally, its prophetic call for racist Christians to repent, it most likely would not have found much popular interest. Just a glance at the full title of the *Treatise* would have offended most Americans. By 1837, a majority of Americans in the free states had made up their minds about the "intellectual character, and . . . condition of the colored people." The history of these decades too clearly proves that they did not want to hear anything about "the prejudice exercised toward them"— certainly not from any "Rev. H. Easton, a colored man."

Notes

1. William C. Nell, *Colored Patriots of the American Revolution* (Boston, 1855), 33–34; Barbara M. Van Amburg Delorey, ed., *A Copying Out of ye Olde Recordes, Beginning with ye 4th Church of Christ in Bridgewater—1740* (Brockton, MA, 1980), 418–19, 459, 572, 662; Bradford Kingman, *History of North Bridgewater, Plymouth County, Massachusetts, from its first settlement to the present time* (Boston, 1866), 95, 96. The only twentieth-century historians to mention James Easton and his church-seating protests are James Oliver Horton and Lois E. Horton, *Black Bostonians: Family Life and Community Struggle in the Antebellum North* (New York, 1979), 39; and George R. Price and James Brewer Stewart, eds., *To Heal the Scourge of Prejudice: The Life and Writings of Hosea Easton* (Amherst, MA, 1999), 3–6.

2. Nell, *Colored Patriots*, 34; Hosea Easton, *A Treatise on the Intellectual Character, and the Civil and Political Condition of the Colored People of the U. States; and the Prejudice Exercised Towards Them* (Boston, 1837), reprinted in Price and Stewart, *To Heal the Scourge of Prejudice*, 110, 111; Benjamin F. Roberts, "Our Progress in the Old Bay State," *The New Era* 31 (1870); Kingman, *History of North Bridgewater*, 379.

3. *Freedom's Journal*, April 25, 1828; David Walker, *Appeal . . . to the Coloured Citizens of the World*, ed. Charles Wiltse (1830; reprint ed., New York, 1965); Hosea Easton, *An Appeal to the Christian Public in Behalf of the Methodist Episcopal Church* (Boston, 1828).

4. Hosea Easton, *An Address: Delivered Before the Coloured Population of Providence, Rhode Island, on Thanksgiving Day, November 27, 1828, by Hosea Easton of North Bridgewater, Mass.* (Boston, 1828).

5. Ibid., 3–5.

6. Ibid., 7. Even though Easton concludes with a lengthy exortation on the importance of uplift, there is a hint in an earlier section of the speech that uplift and efforts at self-improvement may not be enough. In one instance, while dealing with the problem of lack of opportunity for higher means of employment, Easton describes the futility experienced by young people of color, like the students from the Easton's school, when they tried to apply their skills in the job market only to find closed doors. "When they have obtained their education," he observed, "they know only to feel sensible of their misery. Their minds being expanded, their perception brightened, their zeal ardent for promotion; they look around for business, they find that custom cuts them off from all advantages."

7. *The Anglo-African*, quoted in Howard Holman Bell, ed., *Minutes of the Proceedings of the National Negro Conventions, 1830–1864* (New York, 1969), 5, 6.

8. Ibid.; Richard H. Wade, "The Negro in Cincinnati, 1800–1830," *Journal of Negro History* 39 (1954): 49–51; John M. Werner, "Race Riots in the United States in the Age of Jackson, 1824–1849" (Ph.D. diss., University of Indiana, 1973). This was the second time on record in which Easton was referred to by the title of "Reverend," but there is no record of him pastoring a church until two years later, in Hartford.

9. Easton had described this ploy very accurately in a section of his *Address*: "Our ancestors were stolen property, and property which belonged to God. This is well known by our religious community; and they find that the owner is about to detect them. Now if they can slip away those stolen goods, by smuggling all those out of the country, which God would be likely to make an instrument of, in bringing them to justice, and keep the rest in ignorance; by such means, things would go on well with them, and they would appease their consciences by telling what great things they are doing for the coloured population and God's cause. But we understand better how it is. . . . They will steal the sons of Africa, bring them to America, keep them and their posterity in bondage for centuries . . . then transport them back to Africa; by which means America gets all her drudgery done at little expense. . . ." Easton, *Address*, 9–10. Garrison and other abolitionists repeated the charge. William Lloyd Garrison, *Thoughts on African Colonization* (1832; reprint ed., New York, 1968), part 2, 63–64.

10. Bell, *Minutes*, 6–7.

11. Ronald Takaki, *Iron Cages: Race and Culture in 19th-Century America* (New York, 1990) 103, 80–144; Russell Thornton, *American Indian Holocaust and Survival: A Population History since 1492* (Norman, OK, 1987), 113–18; Angie Debo, *A History of the Indians of the United States* (Norman, OK, 1970), 117–49.

12. Robert A. Warner, *New Haven Negroes: A Social History* (New Haven, CT, 1940), 50–55; Michael Kuczkowski, "One Blood: The Lost Legacy of a Radical Black Activist Who Was Ahead of His Time," *Hartford Advocate*, February 5, 1998.

13. Bell, *Minutes*; Kingman, *History of North Bridgewater*, 498; Carter G. Woodson, *Free Negro Heads of Families in the United States in 1830* (Washington, DC, 1925), 72.

14. Rev. King T. Hayes, "A Historical Profile of Fifteen Black Churches of Hartford, Connecticut" (unpublished and undated in Special Collections of the Hartford Public Library, Hartford, CT), 2–5; *Sesquicentennial Celebration of Metropolitan A. M. E. Zion Church, Hartford, Connecticut* (Hartford, CT, 1983), 3–5; Ellsworth and Marion Grant, *The City of Hartford, 1784–1984* (Hartford, CT, 1984), 60.

15. *The Emancipator*, February 17, 1835.

16. Edward Abdy, *Journal of a Residence and Tour in the United States of North America, April, 1833–October, 1834*, 3 vols. (London, UK, 1835), 3: 206–207.

17. John W. Steadman, *Scrapbooks on Hartford, Connecticut History*, 4 vols. (Collections of the Connecticut Historical Society, Hartford, CT).

18. *Hartford Courant*, June 15, 1835. No report on the fire could be found in the local papers, and the brief mentions by Easton and *The Liberator* do not state the fire's cause.

19. Easton, *A Treatise*, in Price and Stewart, *To Heal the Scourge of Prejudice*, 122, 123; *The Concord New Hampshire Observer*, reprinted in *The Liberator*, April 14, 1837; Jennie F. Copeland, "Mansfield in Other Days," *Mansfield News* (Massachusetts), March 27, 1937.

20. For a more thorough analysis of Easton's *Treatise*, see Price and Stewart, *To Heal the Scourge of Prejudice*. This book includes reprints of both the *Treatise* and Easton's 1828 *Address* as well as a biographical introduction with analysis by the editors.

21. Easton, *A Treatise*, in Price and Stewart, *To Heal the Scourge of Prejudice*, 67–82.

22. Ibid., 104–7.

23. Ibid., 107–8.

24. Ibid., 108.

25. Ibid.

26. Ibid., 119.

27. Ibid., 118–20.

28. Ibid., 83–89, 111–12, 118–20.

29. Ibid., 118; James Brewer Stewart, *Holy Warriors: The Abolitionists and American Slavery* (New York, 1996), 41–42; Charles T. Davis and Henry Louis Gates Jr., *The Slave's Narrative* (New York, 1985), xv–xvii, 319–27; David W. Blight, ed., *Narrative of the Life of Frederick Douglass, an American Slave, Written by Himself* (Boston, 1993), 2–20.

30. Easton's obituary appeared in *The Liberator*, July 14, 1837, written by the Rev. Jehiel C. Beman, an "old guard" leader from Connecticut, and father of the Rev. Amos G. Beman. For more on the Rev. Henry Drayton and the Vesey conspiracy, see Peter P. Hinks, *To Awaken My Afflicted Brethren: David Walker and the Problem of Antebellum Slave Resistance* (University Park, PA, 1997), 26–27, 38, 63, 97, 104. Ironically, Easton wrote an obituary for Henry Drayton in *Zion's Watchman*, June 2, 1837, just a little over a month before his own death. On the Easton family's emancipation, see Easton, *A Treatise*, 26; and Price and Stewart, *To Heal the Scourge*, 3, 4, 40n.

31. Amos G. Beman Scrapbooks (Beinecke Library, Yale University, New Haven, CT), vol. 2.

32. Nell, *Colored Patriots*, 34, 333–36. Several lengthy passages from Easton's *Treatise* are quoted in Nell's book. Significantly, none of the passages that Nell cites dealt with slave degradation; rather, they focused on issues of equal rights for American citizens of color, especially veterans, and the systemic denial of those rights due to white racism.

Suggested Readings

Curry, Leonard. *The Free Black in Urban America, 1800–1860.* Chicago, 1981.

Davis, David Brion. *The Problem of Slavery in the Age of Revolution, 1770–1823.* New York, 1975.

Fredrickson, George. *The Black Image in the White Mind: The Debate on Afro-American Character and Destiny, 1817–1914.* New York, 1971.

Hinks, Peter P. *To Awaken My Afflicted Brethren: David Walker and the Problem of Antebellum Slave Resistance.* University Park, PA, 1996.

Hodges, Graham R. *Slavery and Freedom in the Rural North: African Americans in Monmouth County, New Jersey, 1665–1865.* Madison, WI, 1997.

Horton, James Oliver, and Lois E. Horton. *Black Bostonians: Family Life and Community Struggle in the Antebellum North.* New York, 1979.

———. *In the Hope of Liberty: Community and Protest among Northern Free Blacks, 1700–1860.* New York, 1997.

Melish, Joanne Pope. *Disowning Slavery: Gradual Emancipation and "Race" in New England, 1780–1860.* Ithaca, NY, 1998.

Nash, Gary B. *Forging Freedom: The Formation of Philadelphia's Black Community, 1720–1840.* Cambridge, MA, 1988.

Nash, Gary B., and Jean Soderlund. *Freedom by Degrees: Emancipation in Pennsylvania and Its Aftermath.* New York, 1991.

Price, George R., and James Brewer Stewart, eds. *To Heal the Scourge of Prejudice: The Life and Writings of Hosea Easton.* Amherst, MA, 1999.

Saxton, Alexander. *The Rise and Fall of the White Republic: Class Politics and Mass Culture in Nineteenth-Century America.* London, 1990.

Takaki, Ronald. *Iron Cages: Race and Culture in 19th-Century America.* New York, 1990.

White, Shane. *Somewhat More Independent: The End of Slavery in New York City, 1770–1810.* Athens, GA, 1991.

Winch, Julie. *Philadelphia's Black Elite: Activism, Accommodation, and the Struggle for Autonomy, 1787–1848.* Philadelphia, 1988.

11

Laura Wirt Randall
A Woman's Life, 1803–1833

Anya Jabour

Women, like African and Native Americans, insisted that white Americans accept fully the political principles of liberty and egalitarianism. Yet they too suffered from restrictions—political, social, and cultural—that barred their full participation in a male-dominated society. Moreover, at roughly the same time that Indian removal and discrimination against African Americans increasingly marginalized and segregated these nonwhite groups in the late 1820s and early 1830s, white women similarly faced new, additional barriers to their claims to equality. As the family became the focal unit of American society, women were expected to devote their time and energy to the private sphere of the home, not the public arena of politics and business. Laura Wirt Randall's troubled marriage proves that freedom of choice in selecting a mate (in that open market) and the supposedly elevated status of motherhood did not necessarily translate into individual happiness. Laura's unconventional education, which was encouraged by her father, embraced a wide range of intellectual pursuits and spoke to the possibility that women might liberate themselves from a "woman's proper sphere." Unhappily, her parents also pressured Laura into a conventional and ultimately hollow marriage that more accurately reflected the "proper" role that women were to play. Her conflicted life embraced the outer limits to, and ultimate constrictions on, a woman's personal freedom in this Age of the Common Man.

Anya Jabour is an associate professor of history at the University of Montana, Missoula, where she teaches courses in U.S. women's history and the history of the American South. She is the author of *Marriage in the Early Republic: Elizabeth and William Wirt and the Companionate Ideal* (1998) and is currently at work on a study of women's coming-of-age experiences in the nineteenth-century South.

"You can be equal to any girl in . . . the United States, if you choose to be so: and why should you not strive to be so," wrote William Wirt to his daughter, Laura, when she was ten years old.[1] When Laura read these words in the early nineteenth century, she was encouraged to expand her intellectual horizons and to strive for constant self-improvement and public achievement. Only later did Laura become aware of the contradictions in her father's words. As an adult, Laura would learn that while she might strive for personal success and fulfillment, her opportunities would continue to be limited by her gender. Despite William's enthusiasm for his daughter's ability to "be equal to any girl in the United States," her life would provide an answer to his rhetorical question, why she "should not strive to be so": she was a woman in the early nineteenth-century United States.

The compelling life story of Laura Wirt Randall sheds light on the experiences of women in the early republic. Her life and writings spanned the exciting first three decades of the nineteenth century, from 1803 to 1833. In this formative era new ideas about women's education, relationships between men and women, and women's rights flourished. Women's lives and work were shaped by the rise of industrialization in the North and the entrenchment of slavery in the South. Laura, the daughter of Virginia slaveholders who lived in border cities along the Mason-Dixon Line, witnessed these changes from a unique vantage point. She felt both the new sense of possibility that northern women gained in the new nation and the stifling restrictions that southern women continued to experience in the Old South. Laura Wirt Randall's life serves to demonstrate the limited possibilities open even to a well-educated and talented woman in the new American nation.

Laura Henrietta Wirt was born in Richmond, Virginia, on September 3, 1803, the first child of Elizabeth and William Wirt. The Wirts were prominent, well-to-do members of southern society. Elizabeth was the oldest daughter of a respected Richmond merchant, Robert Gamble; William, the orphaned son of immigrant tavern-keepers, earned wealth and renown as a lawyer and author. Although comfortably well off, the Wirts were not members of the planter class; they derived the bulk of their income from William's professional work and business investments. Elizabeth supplemented the family's income by supervising the Wirts' slaves—a work force that ranged from five to ten adults—in domestic work and household production.

Like most southern parents, Elizabeth and William lavished love on their newborn. Elizabeth breast-fed Laura, and William implored his wife to send him lengthy descriptions of Laura's first words when business called him away from home. For Laura and her parents, love between parents and children was not only an end in itself but also a source of discipline. Like other parents of their generation, the Wirts expected that earning her parents' love would be Laura's chief motivation to meet their expectations. "Jewels and diamonds cannot make you happy,"

William reminded Laura when she was six years old, "but the love of your parents can always do it."[2]

One of the most important ways that the Wirts expected Laura to earn their love was by applying herself to her studies. Shortly after Laura's birth, William resolved to give his firstborn extraordinary advantages in education, informing his friend Dabney Carr that "if . . . her mind fulfills the promise of her face, I will spare no pains" in raising her. William was as good as his word. Like many other Americans in the new nation, Laura's father believed that educating women would enable them to participate in the democratic republic indirectly, as wise counselors to their husbands and as capable teachers of their sons. With this goal in mind, William designed an ambitious plan of education for Laura, refusing to limit his hopes because she was a girl. "I have a notion of making my daughter a classical scholar," he decided. William's plan for Laura included Latin, French, Italian, Spanish, and English grammar and composition, and he urged her to excel in all of them. William succeeded in spurring his oldest daughter to academic achievement. By the time she was six, Laura, with her mother's help, was writing letters to William assuring him that "I will try to learn very fast to please my dear Father."[3]

As she grew older, William continued to urge his daughter to earn his love by dedicating herself to intellectual improvement. "I hope to hear from your mother that you are a fine, sweet girl and are very industrious in your studies," he reminded Laura shortly before her seventh birthday, because such attention to duty "is the only way to make your parents happy and to make them love you dearly. . . ." At the same time that William urged his daughter to be "very industrious" at her lessons, he confided to his friends that despite the classical curriculum he planned for Laura—the same offered to boys who were expected to enter the professions or politics—her education was different because she was a girl. Eventually, he remarked to Carr, Laura would "enter the world"— that is, make her debut and begin a search for a suitable husband.[4]

In accordance with his assumption that Laura would enter society and marry, William made some modifications to his plan to make her a "classical scholar." He included traditional feminine accomplishments such as dancing, painting, and piano in the list of subjects he designed for Laura. He also occasionally reminded his daughter that she should avoid unfeminine pride in her intellectual accomplishments. Most importantly, William set a date for Laura to finish her studies. "Laura ought to have her education by the time she is sixteen," he reminded Elizabeth when their oldest daughter was only six; "that is little enough for all the acquirements I wish her to possess."[5] Although he was willing to postpone Laura's debut, William assumed that at seventeen Laura would leave the schoolroom to "enter the world," and that by the time she was twenty she would marry and devote herself to her husband and children. Her education would not prepare her for an alternative to marriage but would make her a better wife and mother.

The most consistent message Laura received from her parents between ages six and sixteen, however, was to strive for higher and higher levels of intellectual cultivation. William even suggested that Laura might aspire to fame as an author. He assured her that her intellectual growth would bring her the approval not only of her parents but of all she met. "Go on writing in this way, and pursue all the studies, to which you are directed, with persevering spirit," he advised, "and when you grow up, you will be the pride and ornament of your parents, and a blessing to society—and if you add to your studies, the fear and love of Heaven, you will be an ornament to the church and a blessing to the world."[6]

When Laura was fourteen, William accepted President James Monroe's invitation to serve as U.S. Attorney General, and the family moved from Richmond to Washington. As she entered her teens, Laura remained eager to continue her studies. "I am determined to study very hard after I get to Washington," she promised her father. Laura continued her schooling, including Latin, first at one of the female academies that were then appearing in cities and towns across the nation and later at home under the direction of her father and private tutors. After a bout of scarlet fever when she was sixteen, Laura went to the Virginia plantation of her aunt, Elizabeth's sister Nancy, for the summer of 1819. Nancy's husband, William H. Cabell, promised to "keep her to her books following the course [her father] shall prescribe" alongside her cousin, Louisa Elizabeth Cabell.[7]

Laura and Louisa already were well acquainted with each other due to the Wirts' habit of spending summers at the Cabell plantation. The cousins' friendship intensified during the months they spent together completing their formal schooling. Nineteenth-century women commonly formed close relationships with other women while away at school in their teens. At a time when many Americans perceived men and women as being endowed with wholly different personal qualities that suited them for their different "spheres"—the private world of the home for women and the public world of work for men—it was natural for young women to look for understanding and affection from members of their own sex. "To you, Louisa, I have always spoken my whole heart," Laura once confided to her cousin, and *"you know me."*[8]

Despite the romantic and even erotic overtones that characterized female friendships in nineteenth-century America, most women found that what historians call homosocial relationships served as preparation for, rather than alternatives to, heterosexual relationships. Particularly in the South, where such friendships tended to overlap with kinship, scholars have found little evidence that female friendship offered women alternatives to conventional marriage. Nonetheless, relationships between women could pose an obstacle to marriage because these intense attachments taught women to look for more understanding and equality than was typical of nineteenth-century marriages.

It was difficult for men and women to attain the candid self-revelation and mutual affection that characterized Laura and Louisa's friendship. Despite a new ideal of love and respect within "companionate marriage," conjugal mutuality was difficult to achieve in the nineteenth-century United States. Women married at the cost of their legal identity; under common law, husbands took possession of the money their wives earned or inherited. In addition, men's experience of the world, education, wage-earning ability, and physical strength usually exceeded that of their wives. These limitations on true companionship characterized the whole nation. Southern women additionally had to contend with exaggerated age differences and the continuing popularity of the patriarchal image of the family in which a man ruled over his dependents—wife, children, and slaves. Small wonder that after parting from Louisa, Laura wrote many letters to her cousin detailing "how much I feel the want of a companion—of such a companion as you. . . . O! my dear Louisa, you cannot conceive how much I miss you!"[9]

Laura and Louisa made a solemn promise to each other to remain single. The two friends planned to found an "Old Maid's Hall" where, together with other like-minded women, they would "live and die in single blessedness." Laura vowed her own eager anticipation of life in this "Charming happy society." "Oh! Louisa, does not your heart dance at the thought of the pleasures which await our *honourable body*? Who so happy as we shall be! at our charming 'Retreat' at View Hill."[10]

Quite possibly Laura and Louisa were acquainted with literature of the time that encouraged a positive reassessment of single life for women. Whereas previous generations had considered single women to be objects of scorn, or at best pity, the postrevolutionary generations, who learned to value companionate marriage so highly, began to advance the idea that marriages that did not measure up to the exacting standards of companionate marriage—mutuality rather than male dominance—should be actively avoided. Instead of making a loveless match, antebellum writers advised, women should embrace the potential happiness and fulfillment of the single life, devoting themselves to their own intellectual or creative growth, to service to their family or community, and to reform. Laura and Louisa followed the advice of such authors when they vowed to share a life of "single blessedness" that they would devote to music making and other "refined delights," such as literature and self-improvement, and to "promot[ing] the happiness" of others.[11]

Laura was soon left to search for a life of single blessedness on her own when in 1820 Louisa decided to marry. While Laura assisted Louisa in wedding preparations, her parents made their own preparations for Laura to follow in her friend's footsteps. Although Laura planned to return quickly to Washington "because I could not spare so much time from my studies," her mother had other plans. It was time, she wrote, for Laura to "*turn in*" and acquaint herself with "the *minutia* of housekeeping." William, too, made it clear that despite Laura's education, it was time for her to learn specifically female accomplishments. "To make yourself pleasing," he admonished his daughter, was "the sweetest charm" of "your sex." An intelligent woman "may be admired," admitted William, "but she will never be beloved."[12] Laura's formal education was at an end.

Laura, who had enjoyed her studies and hoped to continue her intellectual pursuits as an adult, lamented the new responsibilities that interfered with academic work. In 1823, she complained that "the empty frivolities of the Beau Monde" made intellectual improvement impossible. Washington's season of balls and parties was antithetical to intellectual seriousness, she grumbled. Responding to her brother Robert's "uncivil observation" on her comments on literature, Laura indignantly informed him "that women have sometimes some faint glimmerings of intellect, & often a taste more nice & discriminating that that [that is, than that] of your own lordly sex . . . tho', Lord keep them! They are obliged, of necessity, to confound their wee bit of native sense with such an imbroglio of ribbons, laces, gauze tassels, &c &c &c as wd. strike Newton himself 'all of a heap.' "[13]

Laura was no more pleased with the housewifery skills that her mother attempted to teach her. When she was fifteen, Laura admitted to her grandmother that despite "Mama's insisting upon it yesterday that I must learn to ply my needle with more industry," she undertook the task "very reluctantly" and found many excuses to interrupt her progress. The next year, Laura moaned to Louisa that "I kept house today and am to do so for this week, besides mending and making my clothes!—darning stockings, and all the other disagreeable occupations that you can imagine." Elizabeth identified the source of her daughter's discontent when she described keeping house as "the necessary, tho *un*intellectual, duties of domestic life."[14]

By the winter of 1820–21, seventeen-year-old Laura was ready for a full-fledged debut, which involved attending formal teas, balls, and parties during the capital city's winter "season." "I had no notion that Laura had in reality and bona fide *turned out*," her brother Robert wrote in February 1821. "But I see it is the case and wish her success with all my heart:—admonishing her at the same time to be ambitious, and not to be contented with any thing less than a member of congress, or—a soldier."[15]

Robert's 1821 comments made it clear that from that point on, Laura's considerable ambitions were to be trained on a specific and limited goal: finding a good husband. William had pushed his precocious daughter to become "a classical scholar," attaining a level of education that would have prepared her, had she been a boy, to enter the professions. But as a woman in the early nineteenth-century South, there was little Laura Wirt could do with her excellent education. Although increasing numbers of women in the urban Northeast were delaying or avoiding marriage and embarking on new careers as writers and reformers, marriage was the usual destiny of women throughout the United States, and especially in the South, where the ratio of men to women was high and the defense of slavery forestalled efforts at reform.

Laura spent the next six years struggling with the conflict generated by her superior education and her limited opportunities. Trained from her childhood to exercise her mind to its fullest extent and to seek the applause of everybody she knew, Laura discovered that as a woman, the only way she could become, as her father had urged her, "the pride and ornament of your parents, and a blessing to society," was to marry and devote her life to domestic duties.[16]

Laura hesitated for six years before relinquishing her single status and her studies in favor of marriage and domestic duties. Between 1823 and 1824, she rejected three suitors: Thomas Randall, a lawyer and former army captain; Henry Middleton, a neighbor; and Mr. Lear, a family friend. On the eve of her twenty-first birthday, Laura had been out in society for nearly five years without making a match. She had many reasons to avoid marriage. The companionate ideal urged women to find true love or not to marry, and Laura had not yet met a "companion" to replace Louisa. "What put it into your head that I was in love? I assure you I am not," she wrote to Louisa in July 1824. "I do not fall in love," she maintained.[17]

Furthermore, Laura may well have had misgivings about the institution of marriage itself. Marriage in the early-nineteenth-century United States was a nearly irrevocable step that deprived women of a legal identity of their own, subjecting them to the whims of their husbands. Even women with model husbands spent most of their married lives bearing and caring for children and managing a household—activities Laura had disparaged earlier as "disagreeable occupations."

Laura also feared the dangers of childbirth and the burden of caring for sickly children as the inevitable aftermath of marriage. Heavily burdened by the onerous duties of childcare on a secluded plantation, Louisa warned Laura not to marry in 1822, causing Laura to demand "the real opinions of my friends, *pro and con*, as the lawyers say." Soon thereafter Laura had a vivid reminder of some of the possible negative consequences of marriage and childbearing when her recently married friend Ann Middleton was struck by a terminal illness just after bearing her first child. When Ann finally died, Laura was both fascinated and repulsed by the ravages the long illness had wrought on her friend. "Oh, Louisa, how fearfully was she changed by disease and death!" cried Laura. "She looked like an old woman of sixty. . . . Her once tender and snowy skin was now stretched like yellow parchment tightly over the bones, and her cheek, once brilliant with health, sunken, hollow and livid. . . . Poor, poor Ann!"[18] Knowledge of the dangers marriage and childbirth posed to women's health and happiness reinforced Laura's schoolgirl resolve to avoid marriage.

Laura's activities while she resisted her suitors' pressure for an engagement also indicated that she had not surrendered her dreams of single blessedness. In 1823, as she approached her twentieth birthday, Laura announced to Louisa that she was making it her special project to become "an exemplary domestic character." Laura's purpose was not to prepare for marriage but to investigate a possible route to respectable independence as the author of a textbook on household management. "I have made a great many discoveries in the culinary art," she boasted in July 1824, "and intend some time hence to put forth a Book on the subject."[19]

Not surprisingly, considering Laura's previous negative judgments on housekeeping, her interest soon waned. Her next project, teaching her younger sisters, seemed more promising. Laura exhibited "a great deal of enthusiasm . . . and most surprising perseverance" for her latest project, which offered both intellectual stimulation and a respite from the pressure to marry.[20]

Soon, however, Elizabeth and William Wirt became concerned about their daughter's disposition to "rusticate at home." Considering twenty-two-year-old Laura's "time of life," they worried in 1825 that they were not doing "our duty as parents in relation to our daughter"—that is, the duty to assist her in finding a husband. With eight other living children, William was anxious to ensure his children a secure future. Because there were few opportunities for respectable and remunerative employment for women, William believed that his daughter would need a "natural protector"—a husband.[21] Correctly perceiving Laura's activities as schoolmistress as an obstacle to her marriage, the Wirts began to lay plans to reenter their reluctant daughter into society.

While Laura traveled with her father and her cousin Emma to the Virginia Springs in August and September, Elizabeth took steps to ensure that her oldest daughter would not return to her previous occupation as spinster schoolmistress. Over Laura's protests, she enrolled all the younger girls at a local school. Although she placated Laura by assuring her they could be withdrawn on Laura's return, they never were. She also urged Thomas Randall—now called Colonel Randall after a year's appointment as Special Minister to the West Indies—to resume his attentions to Laura upon her return to Washington. William also encouraged the relationship, even suggesting that Elizabeth hint to Randall "that Laura without knowing it, herself, is partial to him." "The truth is," William felt, "that if she does not love him she loves no body."[22]

William may have been correct in his assessment of his daughter's feelings for Randall. By the spring of 1826, Laura was corresponding with him regularly during a stay with her grandmother in Richmond. But when she returned to Washington in June and Randall proposed a second time, after "a long and painful" conversation Laura rejected him and requested him to cease his visits for the time being, apparently giving as her reason Randall's lack of a secure income. She revealed other motives in a letter to her friend Louisa immediately after rejecting Randall. Her own character, Laura stated, was not suited to the demanding but tedious role of housewife. "Monotony kills me as dead as a door nail," she pronounced. "It will never do for me to be married."[23]

Despite her rejection of his proposal, after a while Laura requested Randall to call on her, which he did almost daily. Laura's contradictory behavior suggests that she had at last fallen in love but that her misgivings about marriage persisted. Apparently Laura never told her parents she did not wish to marry, and they grew impatient with their "coquet[t]ish" and "fickle" daughter's inability to "be sure of her affections and of her own fixed resolve" in the affair.[24]

Meanwhile, Randall continued to visit every evening, until by late June the whole town was buzzing with the rumor that Laura was engaged. Under these circumstances, her parents' anxiety and impatience grew still more. "I told her to day that she was sealing her own doom, beyond her own control," Elizabeth worried to her husband, "and whether for better or for worse she would be obliged to marry the man that she thus palpably encouraged[.]" If it was not already too late for "retreat," Elizabeth admonished Laura, she must either cease seeing Randall immediately, or else "marry at once and take all the consequences." Concerned with the danger posed to their own and their daughter's reputation by the increasingly unfriendly gossip about Laura's conduct, Elizabeth and William pressured their daughter to make an engagement. "I am strongly inclined to doubt whether it wd. not be better for her to marry at once—than to go on as she is going," concluded William.[25]

For Laura, who had been raised to value her parents' approval and social acceptance so highly, the pressure to marry must have been agonizing. She searched desperately for convincing explanations for her "coquettish" behavior and for an escape from social and parental pressure to marry Randall. In late July and August, Laura accompanied her father and two of her sisters to the Virginia Springs. She told her father that she was unwilling to make a decision about Randall until she had news of his success or failure in his bid for a clerkship at the Supreme Court. Privately, Laura told her mother that she hoped that her sojourn in Virginia would imply to the Washington gossip mill that she herself wished to marry Randall but was forbidden by her parents. Such a rumor would have had the double advantage of placing the censure for a late rejection on Laura's parents, rather than herself, as well as offering her a socially acceptable reason for refusing any future suitors and retiring into confirmed singlehood.

Recognizing Laura's plan as detrimental to their own reputations, Elizabeth and William responded with still more displeasure with their wayward daughter. Because of the difficulty of achieving economic or social security as a single woman, Laura would have needed the support of fellow single women or her family, or both, to realize her dreams of single blessedness. But Laura's closest female friend had married, and Laura's own parents, with the best of intentions, frustrated their daughter's attempt to find a niche as a spinster teacher in their home. They withdrew the rewards of parental approval that had been so effective in directing Laura toward academic achievement, and they refused to aid her in her final attempt to find a socially sanctioned reason to refuse Randall. Marriage was now the only way for Laura to win her parents' favor and society's blessing. With her own feelings and her parents' obvious preferences both pushing her toward Randall, Laura was soon exchanging messages with him through her sister Catharine.

Although no record exists of another formal proposal, by mid-August the entire family, including Laura, assumed that an engagement had taken place. William was soon consulting Elizabeth on how best to ensure their daughter's financial security in her marriage to a poorly paid lawyer. He proposed to Elizabeth that they assist the newlyweds by giving them land and slaves to begin a plantation in the newly opened Florida territory, as well as to use his influence to obtain a position for Randall as one of the three judges of the Florida supreme court. "I have never said a word to Laura upon the subject—and dont know how she wd. take it," he added as an afterthought.[26]

Laura reacted to the news with dread, fearing that the move would mean that she would never again see her friend Louisa or the rest of her family. "I cannot endure the thought! The very prospect breaks my heart!" she exclaimed in early October. "My Uncles John and Robert [Gamble] contemplate a removal thither very soon; and they, as well as Father . . . are of opinion that it would be the best thing Col. Randall could do, at present, to remove thither also, and acquire that wealth which there seems to be no hope of in this part of the world—and without which they have taken up a notion that there is no existing for me. If it is so, they must know me better than I know myself. I think I could be very happy without it."[27]

Laura found that her own preferences had little weight against her male relatives' eagerness to achieve the fabled wealth of the frontier, and she allowed new love to blur the harsh outlines of this inequity of power.

The compulsion of love that had earlier pushed Laura to achieve now dictated surrender of her hopes to her husband's wishes. "It would go very hard with me to be transplanted to this new country," she confided to Louisa, "and there is but one man under the moon for whose sake I would consent to it. I should be glad, however, that he would not make so cruel a proof of my affection." Laura concluded, however, with the thought that her love for her husband demanded the sacrifice. "If it is so much for his interest as it is thought, I ought to consent, I suppose, without murmering [*sic*]."[28]

The following fall, on August 21, 1827, Laura Wirt and Thomas Randall said their wedding vows before a group of their relatives. Laura's sister Catharine described the wedding as a happy and lavish affair, with six bridesmaids and six groomsmen in attendance. Laura's uncle, Robert Gamble, made a more sobering remark. "The Judge is obliged to hold court at Tallahassee in October on the first Monday," he observed, "which will compel him to set out early next month—Laura goes with him[.]" By the fall of 1827, it was clear that Laura's new husband would indeed "make so cruel a proof of [her] affection." Despite her resolve to submit to her husband's wishes "without murmuring," Laura could not help confiding her trials to Louisa. With her husband ill upon arrival in their new home, where Laura found "a destitution of everything like comfort," she admitted, "I am disappointed in everything."[29]

One of Laura's disappointments was her relationship with Thomas Randall, whom she still referred to as "my husband" or "Colonel Randall," indicating she had not achieved the intimacy she had hoped for with her husband, who had "lost" the "charms" he had displayed while courting Laura. "I never was less happy in my life than the two first months of my marriage," Laura admitted to Louisa. Rather than attribute her unhappiness to the circumstances of nineteenth-century marriage or to her husband's refusal to exhibit the proper spirit of mutuality, Laura concluded that her hopes of wedded bliss had been mere "charming illusions." She would "learn to be happy under the change of circumstances," she told Louisa, by lowering her expectations and devoting herself to her duties as a wife and mother.[30]

Disappointed in her hopes of a marriage in which romantic love would overcome all the obstacles to true companionship between husbands and wives, Laura also found that her earlier fears that marriage would mean a limited and arduous life of housekeeping and childcare were correct. The "regular and unvarying routine" of housekeeping was interspersed only with illness and childbirth. In 1827 or 1828, Laura

Wirt Randall suffered a miscarriage. Still weak from that miscarriage, Laura bore her first child, Elizabeth, in the summer of 1828; the next summer, in "*perilously delicate*" health, she took opium to avoid a second miscarriage while she awaited the birth of her second child, Kate. By 1831, Laura had borne yet a third child, named Agnes. Laura's letters to Louisa after her marriage suggested that she was both physically exhausted and emotionally despondent. "The cares of maternity, and of housekeeping fall very heavily upon your humble servant, and truth to say I am almost as tired of one as of the other. Three babies in less than three years are enough to make one tired of babies, I think: at least, so I generally say when my feeble health makes me feel the toil of nursing and the loss of rest with peculiar heaviness."[31]

Despite her weariness, Laura took joy in her children as well. She wrote enthusiastically of her three daughters' "striking" beauty and early signs of "intellectual" capacity. Yet she concluded with the thought that her children's demands were greater than she could meet: "I am blessed in . . . my children, poor little *picanines.* Tho' they *are* so troublesome, and I feel as if I were ungrateful in repining at the only thing really hard in my lot. The rapid increase of their number. If I could only enjoy health and strength proportioned to the demands they make on me, I should have no right to complain even of that. But they decline, as is usually the case, in an inverse ratio to the increase of my family," Laura lamented.[32]

Laura's comments on motherhood suggested the limited gains that nineteenth-century women made in controlling their fertility. Although white women's birthrates nationwide dropped dramatically in the nineteenth century, contraception methods were unreliable. Consequently, women could control their childbearing only with their husbands' cooperation. Thomas Randall apparently was unwilling to suspend sexual activity in order to preserve his wife's increasingly fragile health.

It was an uphill struggle for Laura to maintain her marriage as well as to cope with housekeeping and mothering. "I am now," remarked Laura in 1831, "as my husband declares 'the most miserable, poor, good-for-nothing woman he ever saw,' which compliment comes with an ill grace from him at all events." In the face of her own poor health and her husband's lack of appreciation for her efforts to meet the demands of housekeeping and motherhood, Laura struggled for optimism. "I am blessed in my husband and children," she insisted.[33] Laura did not write to Louisa again. She died on December 17, 1833, after giving birth to yet a fourth child, another daughter, who died soon afterward.

Laura Wirt Randall's brief life illustrates the limited nature of women's gains under the conditions of legal and economic inequality that prevailed in the early American republic. Laura's life was shaped by contradictions. Trained by her father to constantly expand her intellectual horizons in classical study, she devoted her adult years to childbearing and to what her mother called "the unintellectual duties of domestic life." Marrying at a time when romantic love and "companionate marriage" was the ideal, she found herself in a relationship characterized by emotional distance. Although as a child Laura strove to be "equal to any girl in the United States," as an adult, she learned that all her efforts could only succeed in making her a "miserable, poor, good-for-nothing woman." Thus, Laura's life suggests both the changes and the continuities in American women's lives in the early American republic.

Notes

1. William Wirt to Laura Wirt, October 28, 1813, William Wirt Papers, Maryland Historical Society, Baltimore, MD.
2. William Wirt to Laura Wirt, July 14, 1810, ibid.
3. William Wirt to Dabney Carr, June 8, 1804, William Wirt Letters to Dabney Carr, 1803–1831, Library of Virginia, Richmond, VA; William Wirt to Dabney Carr, December 21, 1809, William Wirt Papers; Laura Wirt to William Wirt, June 15, 1810, ibid.
4. William Wirt to Laura Wirt, July 14, 1810, William Wirt Papers; William Wirt to Dabney Carr, December 21, 1809, ibid.
5. William Wirt to Elizabeth Wirt, September 11, 1809, ibid.
6. William Wirt to Laura Wirt, October 21, 1813, ibid.
7. Laura Wirt to William Wirt, November 24, 1817, ibid.; William Wirt to Elizabeth Wirt, ca. April/May 1819, ibid.; Laura Wirt Randall Papers, preface, Virginia Historical Society, Richmond, VA.
8. Laura Wirt Randall to Louisa Cabell Carrington, March 26, 1828, Laura Wirt Randall Papers.
9. Laura Wirt to Louisa Cabell Carrington, September 12, 1822, ibid.
10. Laura Wirt to Louisa Cabell, November 4, 1819, ibid.
11. Ibid.
12. Laura Wirt to Elizabeth Wirt, April 29, 1820, ibid.; Elizabeth Wirt to Laura Wirt, May 26, 1820, William Wirt Papers; William Wirt to Laura Wirt, May 23, 1820, ibid.
13. Laura Wirt to Robert Wirt, January 20, 1823, ibid.; Laura Wirt to Robert Wirt, January 12, 1823, ibid.
14. Laura Wirt to Catharine Gamble, May 24, 1818, ibid.; Laura Wirt to Louisa Cabell, May 3, 1819, Laura Wirt Randall Papers; Elizabeth Wirt to William Wirt, November 22, 1824, William Wirt Papers.
15. Robert Wirt to Elizabeth Wirt, February 26, 1821, William Wirt Papers.

16. William Wirt to Laura Wirt, October 21, 1813, ibid.; Elizabeth Wirt to William Wirt, November 22, 1824, ibid.

17. Laura Wirt to Louisa Cabell Carrington, July 10, 1824, Laura Wirt Randall Papers.

18. Laura Wirt to Louisa Cabell Carrington, April 27, 1822, ibid.; Laura Wirt to Louisa Cabell Carrington, November 27, 1822, ibid.

19. Laura Wirt to Louisa Cabell Carrington, February 14, 1823, ibid.; Laura Wirt to Louisa Cabell Carrington, July 10, 1824, ibid.

20. Elizabeth Wirt to William Wirt, May 6, 1825, William Wirt Papers.

21. William Wirt to Elizabeth Wirt, May 20, 1825, ibid.; William Wirt to Dabney Carr, November 17, 1828, William Wirt Letters to Dabney Carr.

22. William Wirt to Elizabeth Wirt, August 12, 1825, William Wirt Papers.

23. Elizabeth Wirt to William Wirt, June 11, 12, 13, 1826, ibid.; Laura Wirt to Louisa Cabell Carrington, June 13, 1826, Laura Wirt Randall Papers. On the couple's correspondence, which has not been preserved, see Elizabeth Wirt to William Wirt, May 23, 1826, Catharine Wirt's postscript to Rosa Wirt to William Wirt, [May 1826], all in William Wirt Papers.

24. William Wirt to Elizabeth Wirt, June 13, 1826, William Wirt Papers; Elizabeth Wirt to William Wirt, June 14, 1826, ibid.

25. Elizabeth Wirt to William Wirt, June 24, 1826, ibid.; William Wirt to Elizabeth Wirt, June 30, 1826, ibid.

26. William Wirt to Elizabeth Wirt, August 31–September 1, 1826, ibid.

27. Laura Wirt to Louisa Cabell Carrington, October 8, 1826, Laura Wirt Randall Papers.

28. Ibid.

29. Catharine Wirt to Emma Cabell, September 8, 1827, Carrington Family Papers, Virginia Historical Society; Robert Gamble (1781–1867) to James Breckinridge, August 16, 1827, Breckinridge Family Papers, Virginia Historical Society; Laura Wirt Randall to Louisa Cabell Carrington, n.d., ca. 1827–1828, Laura Wirt Randall Papers.

30. Laura Wirt Randall to Louisa Cabell Carrington, March 6, 1828, Laura Wirt Randall Papers.

31. Laura Wirt Randall to Louisa Cabell Carrington, March 6, 1828, ibid.; Laura Wirt Randall to Louisa Cabell Carrington, May 27, 1829, ibid.; Laura Wirt Randall to Louisa Cabell Carrington, May 23, 1831, ibid.

32. Laura Wirt Randall to Louisa Cabell Carrington, May 23, 1831, ibid.

33. Ibid.

Suggested Readings

Bleser, Carol, ed. *In Joy and in Sorrow: Women, Family, and Marriage in the Victorian South, 1830–1900.* New York and Oxford, 1991.

Cashin, Joan E. *A Family Venture: Men and Women on the Southern Frontier.* New York, Oxford, 1991.

———. " 'Decidedly Opposed to the Union': Women's Culture, Marriage, and Politics in Antebellum South Carolina." *Georgia Historical Quarterly* 78 (1994): 735–59.

Censer, Jane Turner. *North Carolina Planters and Their Children, 1800–1860*. Baton Rouge, LA, 1984.

Chambers-Schiller, Lee Virginia. *Liberty, a Better Husband: Single Women in America: The Generations of 1780–1840*. New Haven, CT, 1984.

Clinton, Catherine. *The Plantation Mistress: Woman's World in the Old South*. New York, 1982.

Cott, Nancy F. *The Bonds of Womanhood: "Woman's Sphere" in New England, 1780–1835*. New Haven, CT, 1977.

Farnham, Christie Anne. *The Education of the Southern Belle: Higher Education and Student Socialization in the Antebellum South*. New York, 1994.

Fox-Genovese, Elizabeth. *Within the Plantation Household: Black and White Women in the Old South*. Chapel Hill, NC, 1988.

Jabour, Anya. *Marriage in the Early Republic: Elizabeth and William Wirt and the Companionate Ideal*. Baltimore, MD, 1998.

Kerber, Linda K. *Women of the Republic: Intellect and Ideology in Revolutionary America*. Chapel Hill, NC, 1980.

Lebsock, Suzanne D. *The Free Women of Petersburg: Status and Culture in a Southern Town, 1784–1860*. New York, 1984.

Lewis, Jan. *The Pursuit of Happiness: Family and Values in Jefferson's Virginia*. Cambridge, MA, 1983.

Lewis, Jan, and Kenneth Lockridge, " 'Sally Has Been Sick': Pregnancy and Family Limitation among Virginia Gentry Women, 1780–1830." *Journal of Social History* 22 (1988): 5–19.

McMillen, Sally G. *Motherhood in the Old South: Pregnancy, Childbirth, and Infant Rearing*. Baton Rouge, LA, 1990.

Norton, Mary Beth. *Liberty's Daughters: The Revolutionary Experience of American Women, 1750–1800*. Boston, 1980.

O'Brien, Michael, ed. *An Evening When Alone: Four Journals of Single Women in the South, 1827–67*. Charlottesville, VA, 1993.

Scott, Anne Firor. *The Southern Lady: From Pedestal to Politics, 1830–1930*. Chicago, 1970.

Smith, Daniel Scott. "Family Limitation, Sexual Control, and Domestic Feminism in Victorian America." In *A Heritage of Her Own: Toward a New Social History of American Women*, edited by Nancy F. Cott and Elizabeth H. Pleck, 222–45. New York, 1979.

Smith-Rosenberg, Carroll. "The Female World of Love and Ritual: Relations between Women in Nineteenth-Century America." In Carroll Smith-Rosenberg, *Disorderly Conduct: Visions of Gender in Victorian America*, 53–76. New York, 1985.

Stowe, Steven M. "Intimacy in the Planter Class Culture." *Psychohistory Review* 10 (1982): 141–64.

———. " 'The *Thing*, Not Its Vision': A Woman's Courtship and Her Sphere in the Southern Planter Class." *Feminist Studies* 9 (1983): 113–30.

Wishy, Bernard. *The Child and the Republic: The Dawn of American Child Nurture*. Philadelphia, 1968.

12

Rebecca Reed
Anti-Catholic Agitator

Daniel A. Cohen

The 1830s and 1840s witnessed not just the rise of class, race, and gender conflict but also ethnic and sectarian discord. Discrimination against recently arrived immigrant groups, especially but not exclusively the Irish, rose in these years, and an organization to oppose immigration, the Native American Association, was formed in 1837. Central to this rise in nativism was hostility to Catholicism. Protestants especially feared that Irish Catholics would come to control urban politics and fretted that the Church of Rome was coming to influence, and to their minds subvert, American government. Rebecca Reed's flirtation with, and subsequent alienation from, the Catholic Church brings together the conflicted and conflicting issues of class, gender, and sectarianism. Reed, born into humble circumstances, viewed religion, specifically her conversion to Catholicism and entry into the Ursuline Convent, as a means of upward mobility. Like thousands of men in this era, she, too, was in pursuit of the main chance. Reed, however, became disillusioned with the institution and left the convent. When a Protestant mob sacked and torched the Ursuline Convent, she became embroiled in a public battle over her role in instigating that riot. The subsequent struggle for the soul and reputation of Rebecca Reed reflected and helped to exacerbate the cultural rivalry between Protestants and Catholics that would crest in the 1850s with the emergence of the Know Nothing movement.

Daniel A. Cohen is associate professor of history at Florida International University in Miami. His publications include *Pillars of Salt, Monuments of Grace: New England Crime Literature and the Origins of American Popular Culture, 1674–1860* (1993); and *The Female Marine and Related Works: Narratives of Cross-Dressing and Urban Vice in America's Early Republic* (1997). He is currently working on a book about Rebecca Reed and the burning of the Charlestown convent.

R ebecca Reed has long figured as one of the more disreputable villains in the annals of American religious intolerance. The daughter of a poor Protestant farmer from Charlestown, Massachusetts, she converted to Catholicism in June 1831, at the age of nineteen, and entered the Ursuline Convent in her hometown later that year as either a postulant or a student. But she became unhappy after only a few months, left the institution in January 1832, and began telling friends and neighbors about various abuses that allegedly occurred there. When a Protestant working-class mob ransacked and burned the convent in August 1834, Catholics and their sympathizers accused Reed of having instigated the riot with her false rumors concerning the establishment. The young woman responded in March 1835 by publishing a best-selling exposé of the Ursuline community entitled *Six Months in a Convent* (alleging that various uncouth penances and cruel austerities were imposed on the nuns) and became engaged in a bitter public controversy with the Ursuline superior, who quickly issued a vitriolic *Answer* to Reed's charges. After several months of intense public attention, Reed slipped back into obscurity and died of consumption just a few years later, at the age of twenty-six, in February 1838. The Charlestown convent controversy marked a key turning point in the history of American nativism, launching the first of several successive waves of anti-Catholicism that would only crest with the enormously popular Know Nothing movement of the 1850s.[1]

Despite her pivotal role in the Charlestown convent affair, most subsequent historians of the event have refused to take Rebecca Reed seriously. For example, Ray Allen Billington, the pioneer historian of antebellum nativism, characterized her allegations as "chatter" and dismissed Reed herself as "a commonplace chit of a girl." And Robert H. Lord, one of the authors of the standard history of the Archdiocese of Boston, suggested that Reed may have suffered from "hallucinations and paranoia" and condemned her book as "scurrilous and mendacious."[2] Perhaps part of the reason for the easy dismissal of Rebecca Reed may lie in her superficial similarity to Maria Monk, another "escaped nun" who published an even more popular exposé of a Canadian convent less than a year after the appearance of Reed's book. Because Monk's book manifestly was scurrilous and fraudulent, it has been easy for scholars to assume the same about the earlier work.[3] Reed's book, however, is very different from Monk's and much evidence suggests that Reed was a rather more complex and interesting character than acknowledged by scholars like Lord and Billington. A close examination of the life of Rebecca Reed sheds light not only on an important incident in the history of American sectarian conflict but also on evolving gender norms and roles during a period of profound social transition.

Historians have long recognized the second quarter of the nineteenth century as a crucial period of economic change and class forma-

tion, particularly in the northeastern United States. Eastern Massachusetts was one of the first areas to make the shift from agriculture to
industry, and Charlestown of the 1830s was still in the midst of that
transition. Although the crowded peninsular section of the town was
already largely urban, farmers continued to live in the thinly populated
mainland portion of the community, which was also the site of the
Ursuline Convent. As a Yankee farmer who owned no land and barely
scraped by on rented property in mainland Charlestown, Reed's father
occupied unmarked and insecure ground between the emerging middle
and working classes. His daughter's status was equally ambiguous. Supporters claimed that the young woman was genteel, respectable, and
possessed of a tasteful assortment of dresses (all key indicators of middle-
class status), whereas critics dismissed her as ignorant, impoverished,
undisciplined, lacking a decent wardrobe, and unfit even for domestic
service.

As illustrated by the debate over Reed's character, one key element
in the formation of class identity during the second quarter of the nineteenth century was the emergence of a new dominant gender ideology,
variously designated by modern scholars as "domesticity," "separate
spheres," and the "cult of True Womanhood." Exponents of domesticity not only required that True Women be genteel and respectable in
their personal deportment but, more broadly, emphasized the divergent
social roles of the two sexes. The new ideology consigned men to the
competitive "public" spheres of politics and the marketplace and women
to the nurturing "private" spheres of home and family, where they were
expected to fulfill the noblest aspirations of their sex as wives and mothers. Although domesticity was never entirely accurate as a description
of social reality—for example, tens of thousands of young single women
worked in factories during the antebellum period—it did embody several powerful and popular social norms, especially for the emerging
middle class and for those who aspired to middle-class status.

One key aspect of antebellum gender ideology was its tendency to
discourage women's active participation in the public sphere; a True
Woman, or genteel lady, generally was expected to avoid open involvement in public controversies, particularly those bandied about in the
popular press. Not surprisingly, the very visible public roles of Rebecca
Reed and the Ursuline superior in the controversy that followed the
destruction of the Charlestown convent evoked considerable comment
and discomfort. More broadly, the post-riot debate was often framed in
terms of the newly ascendant gender ideology: the convent's destruction

was alternately assailed as a brutal violation of the female domestic sphere and implicitly justified as a patriotic attempt to safeguard American True Womanhood from Catholic subversion.

The early decades of the nineteenth century were not only a time of transition in economic relations and gender norms but also a period of exceptional growth and promise for the Roman Catholic Church in the United States. Although Catholics had been a tiny and despised minority throughout most of the American colonies, they began emigrating to the United States in large numbers as early as the 1820s. By 1832 an estimated 500,000 Catholics lived in the United States—and their numbers were rising rapidly. The growth was particularly dramatic in Massachusetts.

As thousands of immigrants poured into the country, Catholic leaders in New England and across the United States struggled to ensure that church institutions would keep pace with the demographic growth. Aside from the hundreds of Catholic churches that were established during the first half of the nineteenth century, perhaps the most impressive evidence of institutional development was in the field of female education: dozens of elite Catholic schools or academies for girls were established around the country. Although they frequently were operated by nuns and attached to convents, many of the students at the new Catholic schools were the daughters of wealthy or middle-class Protestants. Such institutions promised to provide not only a rigorous academic education but also training in a variety of genteel social graces and accomplishments, including painting, ornamental needlework, music, and even dancing. Further, in order to attract an elite Protestant clientele, advertisements for the schools often assured parents that no attempts would be made to influence the religious beliefs of their children.

One of the more prominent and successful of the convent schools was established in Boston, Massachusetts, in 1820, by the Ursulines, the largest of the Catholic teaching orders founded during the Counter-Reformation. During the late 1820s and early 1830s, the residential school generally enrolled between thirty and sixty girls, typically ranging in age from about six to fourteen. The great majority of those students were Protestants, many of them the daughters of prominent local merchants and professionals.[4] Although the school was first located in the city itself, the Ursulines moved in 1826 to a picturesque estate on Mount Benedict, a hill in the neighboring community of Charlestown. There they erected an impressive building to house both the school and the order of nuns. There was only one problem with the lovely new location. Surrounding the Ursuline establishment, with its beautiful gardens, were a number of brickworks that employed rough Protestant laborers from the New England backcountry, men with deeply embedded ethnocultural traditions of hostility toward Roman Catholicism.

Although local brickmakers may have eyed the new convent school with deep suspicion, at least one young Charlestown resident was impressed much more favorably by the Ursuline nuns and their genteel female students. In fact, Rebecca Reed dated her infatuation with Catholicism to the arrival of the Ursulines in her community in 1826. After discussing the new convent with a young Catholic classmate at the local town common school, Reed decided that she would like to withdraw from the world, become a nun, and join the Ursulines on Mount Benedict. A few months later she so informed her Protestant parents, who were anything but pleased. Shortly thereafter, the Reeds sent their daughter off to visit some friends or relations in New Hampshire. The trip was ostensibly undertaken as therapy for her delicate health, but perhaps her parents hoped that the excursion might also cure Rebecca of her alarming new ambition.[5]

Rebecca Theresa Reed had been born in Charlestown about fourteen years earlier, in January 1812. She was the daughter of William Crosby Reed, a respectable but down-on-his-luck local farmer. Reed and his wife had one son and seven daughters, widely spaced in age, who survived infancy. The family lived in the relatively poor Charlestown neighborhood of Milk Row, a largely rural area that combined farming with newer industrial occupations like textile bleaching. Having lost whatever land he may once have owned, Mr. Reed was eventually reduced to renting a house and garden, sometimes depending on financial assistance from his grown son.[6]

Still, during the early-to-mid-1820s, Mr. and Mrs. Reed somehow managed to scrape together enough money to send three of their daughters, including Rebecca Theresa, to a small private school in East Cambridge devoted to the genteel accomplishments of mezzotinto, shell-work, drawing, and ornamental painting. "They were all well-behaved children, and possessed a degree of refinement which was remarked as not being usually found in a farm-house," the two female proprietors of the school later recalled of the Reed girls. "They were always neat and genteel in appearance and dress, and were respected in the school." The teachers also claimed that Rebecca was "the most capable" of the sisters and had been "uniformly obedient and correct."

Though the elder Reeds may have fallen on hard times—barely clinging to respectability—they clearly hoped that their daughters would lead easier lives.[7]

But the future did not look bright for Rebecca Reed or her sisters by the late 1820s. Mrs. Reed was stricken with cancer at about the time that the Ursulines arrived in Charlestown. Over the next three years Rebecca watched helplessly as her mother suffered and slowly wasted away. Because she had to spend much of her time at home caring for her sick parent, Rebecca was forced to neglect her own education. In November 1828, at the request of her failing mother, Rebecca and two of her younger sisters went to an Episcopal church in Cambridge to be baptized. Just two months later, in January 1829, her mother finally died. According to Rebecca's own published account, Mrs. Reed's last injunction to her daughters was that "if there was a holier people than the Church of England, we had only to seek and we should find them." According to the Ursuline superior and Charlestown's parish priest, however, Reed had told them that her mother's dying request was that she become a Roman Catholic.[8]

After the death of their mother, Rebecca's younger sisters were sent off to live with older married siblings in Boston. Rebecca may have also gone to stay with kin in the city for a while; she certainly spent a good deal of time there. In July 1829 she enrolled as a student at a private school in Boston. There she studied embroidery and needlework exclusively, perhaps with a view toward acquiring skills that would allow her to support herself. By the time the federal census taker arrived at the Reed's door during the summer of 1830, however, Rebecca was back home in Charlestown. The once crowded household of William Crosby Reed had been reduced to only two occupants: one male between the ages of 70 and 80 and one female between the ages of fifteen and twenty. Bereft of the female companionship of her mother and sisters, Rebecca Reed was left alone to keep house for her elderly and impoverished father on Milk Row. She later recalled it as a period of "great trouble and grief."[9]

It was at about that time that Rebecca again became interested in Catholicism and in the Ursuline Convent school. As early as the spring of 1830, Reed confided to her Boston schoolmistresses that she wished "to enter the Convent" in order to "complete her education." Later that year she told an Episcopal clergyman in Cambridge that she intended to join the community on Mount Benedict as a nun.[10] A humble intermediary facilitated her initial entry into the social world of the Ursulines.

An unemployed Catholic servant who had formerly worked in the neighborhood came to the Reed's home in the fall of 1830 and begged Rebecca "to keep her as a domestic a little while, as she had no place." After consulting with her father, Reed allowed the woman to stay. Soon the servant introduced Rebecca to some of the mysterious devotional practices and paraphernalia of Roman Catholics: rosary beads, Hail Marys, and an *Agnus Dei*. Upon discovering that the woman was acquainted with the Ursuline superior, Rebecca asked the domestic to accompany her to Mount Benedict so that she might meet her.[11]

According to her own account, what followed was a dramatic struggle for the young woman's soul—one that engaged the highest levels of Catholic authority in New England. At their first meeting, which probably took place in December 1830, Reed explained to the superior that she wished to enter the convent school, complete her education, and become a nun. Rebecca recalled that the superior, Sister Mary Edmond St. George, "embraced" her affectionately and asked her a series of questions about her personal background and religious attitudes. At one point, after inquiring as to whether she had "ever assisted in domestic affairs," the superior allegedly took Rebecca's hand and commented: "O, it feels more like a pancake than any thing else." The implication was that Reed did not have the calloused hands of a servant but the soft or smooth palms of a genteel young lady. The superior, Rebecca's anecdote suggested, recognized her as a suitable candidate for the schoolroom or the choir but certainly not the scullery.[12]

At a subsequent meeting on Mount Benedict, the superior supposedly suggested that Reed consult with the bishop in order to determine whether she "had a vocation for a religious life." Sometime thereafter she was introduced to Benedict Fenwick, the urbane prelate of Boston. By her own account, Rebecca then became a "constant visiter" at Mount Benedict, often meeting with the superior and the bishop. She also received instruction from Patrick Byrne, the parish priest in Charlestown, and began attending the Catholic church there. Her new friends not only plied her with compliments and spiritual advice but also showered her with pious and genteel gifts. Bishop Fenwick allegedly gave her a beautiful wax figure of her namesake St. Teresa, as well as two devotional volumes with her newly adopted Catholic name, Mary Agnes Theresa Reed, stamped in gold on the front covers. She also received presents of ten dollars, a crucifix, and a pearl cross, all in return for some fancy needlework that she did for the bishop and for some other Catholic friends. Such attractive devotional gifts were certainly intended to stimulate

Reed's spiritual sensibilities but—like the superior's praise of her delicate hands—may have also served to reassure Reed that the Catholic community recognized her somewhat questionable claims to gentility.[13]

The courtship of Rebecca Reed by local Catholics coincided with a period of growing sectarian polarization in Boston. Late in 1830 the influential orthodox Congregational minister Lyman Beecher commenced a series of public lectures attacking the evils of Catholicism. Beginning in January 1831, Catholics responded with their own series of evening lectures in rebuttal, delivered alternately by Bishop Fenwick and his eloquent chief lieutenant, the Reverend Thomas J. O'Flaherty. Despite some severe winter weather, Boston's Catholic cathedral was jammed for those polemical lectures, attended mostly by curious Protestants wanting to hear the Catholics defend themselves. After both series of lectures were discontinued a few months later, each side naturally claimed victory; however, a few press reports suggested that Fenwick and O'Flaherty had got the better of the exciting exchange. Rebecca Reed attended the Catholic lectures in the cathedral and was undoubtedly caught up in the drama of the controversy as she wrestled with her own spiritual options.[14]

By the following March, Rebecca Reed had left her father's household and was estranged from other members of her own family. For a time she lived in the home of Mrs. Jane Graham, a "respectable" Scottish widow who kept house for her brother and another Scotsman on Milk Row, quite close to Mr. Reed's; all three of them worked as laborers at the nearby textile bleachery. Although her new housemates were nominally Protestants—either Presbyterians or Episcopalians—they clearly sympathized with the Catholics and eventually converted to the Roman Catholic faith. Later Reed stayed successively with the Hoynes and the Paynes, two working-class Catholic families who lived in the urban peninsular section of Charlestown, much farther away from her father's house and much closer to the town's only Catholic church.[15]

In June, Reed was upset by a confrontation with her brother on a bridge between Charlestown and Cambridge. She told Father Byrne how her enraged sibling "shook her violently by the arm, and threatened to throw her over into the water."[16] That August or September, Rebecca Reed—by then calling herself Mary Agnes Theresa Reed—was ready for her own most dramatic leap of faith. Perhaps hoping to exchange the superficials of one form of gentility for the substance of another, she gave away her few worldly baubles—two or three finger rings, a pair of earrings, a handkerchief pin, some goldfish, and a globe—and entered the convent on Mount Benedict, determined, by her own account, to become an Ursuline nun.[17]

Several years later, after the destruction of the convent, the superior and her supporters offered a very different version of Rebecca Reed's early life and entrance into the Ursuline community. By their account they had not sought out Rebecca Reed; rather she had thrust herself repeatedly upon them. They claimed that Reed was the daughter of a poor and ignorant farmer who was utterly unable to provide his children with any guidance or education. While her sisters were "employed as permanent domestics in respectable families," Rebecca herself remained footloose and undisciplined, working only sporadically as casual "help" in a number of local households. After turning to Roman Catholicism, she was evicted from her father's house, abandoned by her other friends and family members, and forced to seek refuge—as an object of charity—in a number of Catholic households. Given *that* biographical sketch, it becomes easier to understand why many supporters of the Ursulines were so contemptuous of Reed's pretensions to gentility—and why, even at the outset, the superior might have been reluctant to interest herself in the plight of such a shiftless and abandoned teenager.[18]

But in December 1830, after allegedly rebuffing her several times, the superior finally did agree to meet with Rebecca Reed. At that first and subsequent meetings, Rebecca pleaded with the superior to admit her into the convent as a servant, assuring her that "she both *could* and *would* be able to wash, iron, scrub the floors, *and do other laborious work.*" According to an unpublished account by the superior, Reed also claimed that, because of her determination to become a Catholic, "her brothers and sisters had treated her most inhumanly, and had even beat her till she was bruised in every part of her body." By that account, Reed had threatened to kill herself if not admitted to the Ursuline community. The superior was unmoved, noting that "it appeared to me, from the first time that I saw her, that she was a romantic and ignorant girl; and it was from this persuasion, that I told her I wished to have nothing to do with her." Yet the superior finally admitted Reed to Mount Benedict in September 1831. And she entered not as a servant or a postulant but, the superior insisted somewhat incongruously, as a special student who was to live with the nuns, all the while being trained to support herself as a teacher.[19]

It may never be possible to determine with any degree of certainty which account of Rebecca Reed's entrance into the convent is more accurate. In fact, neither one is entirely credible. On the one hand, it seems likely that Reed's account of her ardent courtship by the superior and the bishop was somewhat exaggerated. Although the superior acknowledged that Reed did meet with her repeatedly—if not as frequently as Rebecca implied—the timing of those meetings suggests that the superior was at least hesitant, if not reluctant, to take the Protestant girl into the Ursuline community. Both sides agreed that Reed was eager to gain entry into the convent when she first met with the superior late in 1830, and yet she was not actually admitted into the community until the following August or (more likely) September. The superior was probably telling the truth when she claimed that she deflected Reed's early request for entry into the Ursuline community and urged her instead to seek religious training from the "Catholic clergy."[20]

Thus rebuffed by the immediate object of her suit, Rebecca Reed seems to have adopted a dual strategy. First she cultivated connections with relatively humble though respectable Catholic laypeople and sympathizers like the Hoynes, the Paynes, and Mrs. Graham. Then she used those connections (as she had earlier used the Catholic domestic in her own household) to seek the patronage of two powerful authority figures within the Church hierarchy: Father Byrne of Charlestown, who had been the bishop's earliest pastoral associate in Boston, and Bishop Fenwick himself. After being introduced to those two officials by working-class intermediaries, Reed went on to study with Father Byrne for about three months before he baptized her and for another three months before he admitted her to communion. For a time, Reed actually came to the parish priest for instruction "once or twice a week, and sometimes oftener."[21]

Only after months of intensive spiritual apprenticeship was Rebecca finally admitted to the convent. And even then, the superior implied, it was only because the bishop and the priest were "moved to compassion by her [Reed's] stories" that she relented and admitted the young woman.[22] That reconstruction suggests that Reed had not been lured into the convent by powerful Catholic seducers but rather had gained entry through her own skillful manipulation of networks of patronage within the Catholic community—networks encompassing the widest possible gamut of social ranks, from a homeless Catholic servant to the urbane bishop of Boston.

If Rebecca Reed's account of her ardent courtship by the superior does not ring entirely true, neither does the superior's version of her early dealings with Rebecca Reed. According to her, Reed was an "ignorant" and impoverished young girl who had repeatedly pestered her for employment at Mount Benedict as a servant but with whom she wanted "nothing to do." Why then would the superior have admitted her at all, let alone as a student? And why would she have housed her with the nuns, rather than in the student dormitories or with the convent's other servants? The superior might have replied that she was bowing to the pressure of Bishop Fenwick and Father Byrne. Yet by all accounts, Sister Mary Edmond St. George was a strong-willed woman, not easily imposed upon. As the superior testily informed a Boston newspaper editor: "I think it would be a difficult matter for any man to control me!" In that light, it is hard to believe that the superior did not have her own reasons for overriding earlier doubts and admitting the persistent young proselyte.[23]

If neither Reed's nor the superior's account is entirely convincing, both versions probably contain important elements of truth. On the one hand, it seems clear that some members of the local Catholic community were eager to draw Rebecca Reed into the fold—and very actively sought to do so. Even the superior's supporters admitted that Reed was given books of religious instruction both by the parish priest and by local Catholic laypeople (in at least one case, acting on the instructions of the bishop himself). And shortly before her entry into the convent, Boston's only Catholic newspaper, The *Jesuit*—then operating under the direct editorial control of Bishop Fenwick and his clergy—boasted of Reed's conversion and claimed that her infuriated brother had threatened to throw her over the side of a bridge. There indeed had been a contest for the soul of Rebecca Reed, and by the summer of 1831 at least some prominent local Catholics were proud to declare victory.[24]

On the other hand, there is probably also some truth in the superior's image of Reed as an impoverished young woman trying desperately to avoid the endless drudgery of a life of domestic dependence and household service. Even her supporters admitted that Rebecca had done sewing for one family and worked briefly as a nursemaid in the household of another.[25] Unless she could come up with some alternative—and attractive vocational options were extremely limited for women during this period—her future seemed to promise only more of the same. It must have been a dreary prospect for a proud young woman still clinging to the remains of her family's threadbare gentility. Having been stripped of the female companionship of her mother and sisters, living alone with her aged father, on the edge of utter destitution, is it any wonder that Rebecca Reed wished desperately to escape from her own increasingly constricted social world and to withdraw into the mysterious and autonomous community of genteel women on Mount Benedict? Perhaps there she could find a new "mother" and "sisters" to replace the ones whom she had lost.

As it turned out, Rebecca Reed did not find the sort of congenial refuge that she sought on Mount Benedict. By her own account, she was soon disillusioned by the harsh penances and austerities of monastic life, particularly those cruelly inflicted upon a dying nun. Sometime after her arrival at the convent, she also complained that the superior did not pay enough attention to her or treat her as kindly as she had before. For whatever reason, Reed fled the convent in January 1832, less than half a year after her arrival, and quickly joined an Episcopal church. In August 1834 the Ursuline convent was burnt to the ground by a Protestant mob, probably led by local brickmakers. Defenders of the convent claimed that they had been inflamed by Rebecca Reed's defamatory stories concerning Mount Benedict. Several months later, in March 1835, Reed published her charges in an exposé, entitled *Six Months in a Convent*. Five thousand copies were reportedly sold within the first day or two of publication, ten thousand within a week, twenty-five thousand within a month, and more than fifty thousand by the end of the year. Reed's account had become antebellum America's first "great" anti-Catholic bestseller.[26]

After several months of intense public controversy, Rebecca Reed probably resumed the sort of private life appropriate to a respectable young woman with genteel pretensions, living with relatives and perhaps giving music lessons when her fragile health permitted. At least that would seem to be a reasonable inference, given the absence of any public record of her activities after 1835. But presumably the remarkable success of her book had freed her from some of the economic insecurities that dogged her earlier years. If, as reported, Reed received a royalty of 6 1/4 cents per copy for *Six Months in a Convent*, the sale of fifty thousand copies during the first nine months of publication would have yielded her a nest egg of more than $3,000, enough to have supported her in comfort for many years. But that was not to be. Just three years after the appearance of her book, at the beginning of March 1838, Boston newspapers announced an untimely death: "DIED, In this city, on Wednesday morning, of consumption, contracted while a novice in the Charlestown Nunnery, Miss Rebecca Theresa Reed, 26." Some of the papers then added a detail that may have been of interest to their Protestant readers: "The Sacrament of the Church of which she was a member, was administered to her by the worthy pastor, when her last hour was expected, and she then attested to the truth of her Narrative."[27]

Whether an exemplar of "truth" or hypocrisy, the controversial life of Rebecca Reed offers historians a valuable perspective on gender norms and roles in America's early republic. On one level, Reed's brief but remunerative venture into the realm of public controversy suggests that the line between "private" and "public" spheres, while very important as a gender ideal, was by no means an impassable barrier for respectable women; rather, it was a permeable boundary that could be traversed cautiously on religious or patriotic grounds—or even in the interests of personal vindication. On another level, Reed's experiences suggest some of the surprisingly aggressive ways in which aspiring women of low or ambiguous social status could seize upon and manipulate religious affiliation as an instrument of personal fulfillment and upward mobility. For a struggling farmer's daughter like Rebecca Reed, the genteel Ursuline establishment on Mount Benedict probably embodied fantasies of both spiritual and social elevation. Yet, as it turned out, Reed's worldly success was based less on her conversion to Roman Catholicism than on her uncanny ability to play off both sides in the sectarian rivalry to her own advantage.

In her groundbreaking study of gender relations in early national New York City, Christine Stansell described how young women were able to gain a measure of social leverage by bartering their bodies in an informal "sexual economy" that characterized courtship practices among the working classes.[28] The experiences of Rebecca Reed suggest that such young women also occasionally could improve their social options and prospects by deploying their souls in a "spiritual economy" that flourished with the expansion of denominational pluralism in America's early republic. Their leverage could be particularly powerful in settings where Roman Catholics had succeeded in establishing their faith as an attractive alternative to the various Protestant denominations. Aside from its intrinsic spiritual appeal (which should not be underestimated), one of the particular lures of Roman Catholicism to American women was a convent system that combined most of the approved social virtues of gentility, respectability, and domesticity with a degree of security, sorority, and female autonomy that was often not available to them elsewhere. That young women like Rebecca Reed became caught up in the cultural rivalry between Protestants and Catholics is not surprising: the contest offered rewards both to sincere idealists and to shrewd opportunists. Indeed, one of the frustrations of studying her life is that it is impossible to know for certain whether, in turning against her Catholic sponsors, Reed had sold her soul—or saved it.

Notes

1. Ray Allen Billington, *The Protestant Crusade, 1800–1860* (New York, 1938), 68–92; R. A. Billington, "The Burning of the Charlestown Convent," *The New England Quarterly* 10 (1937): 4–24.

2. Billington, *Protestant Crusade*, 71; Billington, "Burning," 10; Robert H. Lord, John E. Sexton, and Edward T. Harrington, *History of the Archdiocese of Boston*, 3 vols. (New York, 1944), 2:209, 226.

3. Maria Monk, *Awful Disclosures of the Hotel Dieu Nunnery of Montreal* (1836; reprint ed., Salem, NH, 1977); Billington, *Protestant Crusade*, 99–108; R. A. Billington, "Maria Monk and Her Influence," *The Catholic Historical Review* 22 (1936): 283–96.

4. Lord et al., *History of the Archdiocese of Boston*, 2:199–201; Bishop Benedict Joseph Fenwick, S.J., Bishop John Bernard Fitzpatrick, S.J., and Archbishop John Joseph Williams, S.J., *Memoranda of the Dioceses* [sic] *of Boston*, 4 vols., original and typescript located at the Archives of the Archdiocese of Boston (Brighton, MA) [all page citations from the typescript version] 1:65–237, Jan. 28, 1828–Sept. 19, 1833, passim; *Trial of John R. Buzzell* (Boston, 1834), 10; *The Charlestown Directory for the Year 1831* (Charlestown, MA, 1831), appended advertisements [1]; *Report of the Committee, Relating to the Destruction of the Ursuline Convent* (Boston, 1834), 6; Billington, *Protestant Crusade*, 68–69.

5. Rebecca T. Reed, *Six Months in a Convent* (Boston, 1835), 49–51; *Commercial Gazette* (Boston), April 6, 1835.

6. Reed, *Six Months*, 51; Baptismal Register, St. Mary's Parish, Charlestown, MA, 1828–1855, 6, Archives of the Archdiocese of Boston; Thomas W. Baldwin, comp., *Vital Records of Cambridge, Massachusetts, to the Year 1850*, 2 vols. (Boston, 1914–15), 1:588–89; Jacob Whittemore Reed, *History of the Reed Family in Europe and America* (Boston, 1861), 541–42; Thomas Bellows Wyman, *The Genealogies and Estates of Charlestown* (Boston, 1879), 804; The Committee of Publication, *Supplement to "Six Months in a Convent"* (Boston, 1835), 157; Mary Anne Ursula Moffatt, *An Answer to Six Months in a Convent* (Boston, 1835), xv; "Documents Relating to the Imposture of Rebecca T. Read [sic], and the Burning of the Ursuline Convent, at Charlestown, Mass.," in Ignatius Aloysius Reynolds, ed., *The Works of the Right Rev. John England*, 5 vols. (Baltimore, 1849), 5:275.

7. Committee of Publication, *Supplement to "Six Months in a Convent,"* 231–32.

8. Ibid., 156, 157, 174, 183; Baldwin, *Vital Records*, 1:589, 2:710; Correspondence Fragment, Madam St. George to Unidentified Male, n.d., The Ursuline Convent, Charlestown, MA, Collection, The Catholic University of America Archives, Washington, DC; Moffatt, *Answer*, 58; "Documents Relating to the Imposture of Rebecca T. Read," 5:276.

9. Reed, *Six Months*, 52–53; Committee of Publication, *Supplement to "Six Months in a Convent,"* 233–36; U.S. Census, 1830, no. 19, Microfilm Roll 66, 48; but cf. J. W. Reed, *History of the Reed Family*, 541.

10. Committee of Publication, *Supplement to "Six Months in a Convent,"* 226–27, 233.

11. Reed, *Six Months,* 52–54. My characterization of the Catholic practices and paraphernalia as "mysterious" refers to Reed's own probable perception of them.

12. Ibid., 53–56; Moffatt, *Answer,* 8.

13. Reed, *Six Months,* 56–65; Committee of Publication, *Supplement to "Six Months in a Convent,"* 162–63.

14. Lord et al., *History of the Archdiocese of Boston,* 2:199–201; Fenwick, Fitzpatrick, and Williams, *Memoranda,* 1:137–41, January 9, 1831–May 1, 1831, passim; Reed, *Six Months,* 61n.

15. Reed, *Six Months,* 64, 180; Moffatt, *Answer,* xvii, xxviii, 58–59, 61.

16. *The Jesuit,* August 6, 1831; Moffatt, *Answer,* 60; Reed, *Six Months,* 39, 67–68.

17. Reed, *Six Months,* 4, 65–66, 72; Committee of Publication, *Supplement to "Six Months in a Convent,"* 188; Moffatt, *Answer,* 3, 59–60.

18. "Documents Relating to the Imposture of Rebecca T. Read," 5:275–76.

19. Moffatt, *Answer,* xv–xix, 8 (quotation), 12, 57–60; Correspondence Fragment.

20. Moffatt, *Answer,* 12.

21. Ibid., 57–60; Baptismal Register, 6.

22. Moffatt, *Answer,* 8; Correspondence Fragment.

23. Boston *Recorder,* September 26, 1834. One probable reason for admitting Reed was the superior's desperate need for an additional music teacher to help staff the community's thriving school; see Daniel A. Cohen, "Miss Reed and the Superiors: The Contradictions of Convent Life in Antebellum America," *Journal of Social History* 30 (Fall 1996): 157.

24. Moffatt, *Answer,* xxxi, 58, 60; *The Jesuit,* August 6, 1831; Reed, *Six Months,* 38–39, 67–68.

25. Committee of Publication, *Supplement to "Six Months in a Convent,"* 195n.

26. Reed, *Six Months,* 69–174, passim. The sales figures, remarkably high for the 1830s, are based on reports in a variety of contemporary newspapers and seem to have been accepted by both sides in the convent controversy.

27. *Daily Advertiser* (Boston), March 1, 1838; *American Traveller* (Boston), March 2, 1838.

28. Christine Stansell, *City of Women: Sex and Class in New York, 1789–1860* (New York, 1986), 98–99. The phrase "sexual economy" is not Stansell's; she refers to it as a system of "heterosexual exchange."

Suggested Readings

Billington, Ray Allen. *The Protestant Crusade, 1800–1860.* New York, 1938.

Binford, Henry C. *The First Suburbs: Residential Communities on the Boston Periphery, 1815–1860.* Chicago, 1985.

Bisson, Wilfred J. *Countdown to Violence: The Charlestown Convent Riot of 1834.* New York, 1989.

Blaine, James Gillespie, II. "The Birth of a Neighborhood: Nineteenth-Century Charlestown, Massachusetts." Ph.D. diss., University of Michigan, Ann Arbor, 1978.

Blumin, Stuart M. *The Emergence of the Middle Class: Social Experience in the American City, 1760–1900*. Cambridge, England, 1989.

Bushman, Richard L. *The Refinement of America: Persons, Houses, Cities*. New York, 1992.

Cohen, Daniel A. "Miss Reed and the Superiors: The Contradictions of Convent Life in Antebellum America." *Journal of Social History* 30 (1996): 149–84.

———. "The Respectability of Rebecca Reed: Genteel Womanhood and Sectarian Conflict in Antebellum America." *Journal of the Early Republic* 16 (1996): 419–61.

Cott, Nancy F. *The Bonds of Womanhood: "Woman's Sphere" in New England, 1780–1835*. New Haven, CT, 1977.

Degler, Carl N. *At Odds: Women and the Family in America from the Revolution to the Present*. New York, 1980.

Ewens, Mary. *The Role of the Nun in Nineteenth Century America*. New York, 1978.

Franchot, Jenny. *Roads to Rome: The Antebellum Protestant Encounter with Catholicism*. Berkeley, CA, 1994.

Gilje, Paul A. *Rioting in America*. Bloomington, IN, 1996.

Griffin, Susan M. "Awful Disclosures: Women's Evidence in the Escaped Nun's Tale." *Publications of the Modern Language Association* 111 (January 1996): 93–107.

Hamilton, Jeanne (O.S.U.). "The Nunnery as Menace: The Burning of the Charlestown Convent, 1834." *U.S. Catholic Historian* 14 (1996): 35–65.

Hammett, Theodore M. "Two Mobs of Jacksonian Boston: Ideology and Interest." *Journal of American History* 62 (1976): 845–68.

Handlin, Oscar. *Boston's Immigrants: A Study in Acculturation*. Cambridge, MA, 1979.

Hewitt, Nancy A. "Beyond the Search for Sisterhood: American Women's History in the 1980s." *Social History* 10 (1985): 299–321.

Isenberg, Nancy. "Second Thoughts on Gender and Women's History." *American Studies* 36 (1995): 93–103.

Kenneally, James J. "The Burning of the Ursuline Convent: A Different View," *Records of the American Catholic Historical Society of Philadelphia* 90 (1979): 15–21.

Kerber, Linda K. "Separate Spheres, Female Worlds, Woman's Place: The Rhetoric of Women's History." *Journal of American History* 75 (1988): 9–39.

Lewis, James R. " 'Mind-Forged Manacles': Anti-Catholic Convent Narratives in the Context of the American Captivity Tale Tradition." *Mid-America* 72 (October 1990): 149–67.

Lord, Robert H., John E. Sexton, and Edward T. Harrington. *History of the Archdiocese of Boston*. 3 vols. New York, 1944.

Mannard, Joseph G. "Converts in Convents: Protestant Women and the Social Appeal of Catholic Religious Life in Antebellum America." *Records of*

the American Catholic Historical Society of Philadelphia 104 (1993): 79–
90.

———. "Maternity . . . of the Spirit: Nuns and Domesticity in Antebellum
America." *U.S. Catholic Historian* 5 (Summer/Fall 1986): 305–24.

Misner, Barbara. *Highly Respectable and Accomplished Ladies: Catholic Women
Religious in America, 1790–1850.* New York, 1988.

Pease, Jane H., and William H. Pease. *Ladies, Women, & Wenches: Choice &
Constraint in Antebellum Charleston & Boston.* Chapel Hill, NC, 1990.

Ryan, Mary P. *Women in Public: Between Banners and Ballots, 1825–1880.* Baltimore, MD, 1990.

Schultz, Nancy L. "Haunted, Doomed and Parodied: Literary Representations
of the 1834 Charlestown Convent Riot." Salem State College Working
Paper, 1994.

———. *A Veil of Fear: Nineteenth-Century Convent Tales.* West Lafayette, IN,
1999.

Stewart, George C., Jr. *Marvels of Charity: History of American Sisters and Nuns.*
Huntington, IN, 1994.

Thompson, Margaret Susan. "Women, Feminism, and the New Religious His-
tory: Catholic Sisters as a Case Study." In *Belief and Behavior: Essays in the
New Religious History*, edited by Philip R. Vandermeer and Robert P.
Swierenga (New Brunswick, NJ, 1991), 136–63.

Welter, Barbara. "The Cult of True Womanhood, 1820–1860." *American Quarterly* 18 (Summer 1966): 151–75.

13

Margaret Eaton
The Politics of Gender in Jacksonian America

John F. Marszalek

The "Eaton affair," as it is known, is generally portrayed as a political conflict between President Andrew Jackson and his vice president, John C. Calhoun, over the proper etiquette that was to be accorded to the wife of the secretary of war. Its acrimonious resolution would drive a wedge between the two and elevate Martin Van Buren as Jackson's successor. The affair, though, grew out of conflicting views of class and gender in the Jacksonian period. Peggy Eaton's modest social background—she was the daughter of a boardinghouse owner—was an offense to the supposedly more cultured and socially prominent cabinet wives who sought to ostracize her from Washington society. Even more distasteful to them was Eaton's precocious behavior and her refusal to be constrained by conventional gender expectations. As a child, she related easily to and conversed with congressmen while tending her father's bar. As a teenager, she tried to elope twice. Peggy married well: that was to her credit. Yet she continued to seek out the company of men while her husband, a naval purser, was away on voyages: that was not. She was rumored to have had an affair with Jackson's friend John Eaton, and she married him soon after her husband died in 1828. The "affair," therefore, reflected more Peggy's challenge to established gender boundaries in this democratic era than the duller stuff of cabinet intrigues.

John F. Marszalek is the William L. Giles Distinguished Professor of History at Mississippi State University, Mississippi State, Mississippi. He has written or edited numerous books, including *Sherman, A Soldier's Passion for Order* (1993); and *The Petticoat Affair: Manners, Mutiny, and Sex in Andrew Jackson's White House* (1997).

The president of the United States, Andrew Jackson, was furious. He had been spending the first days of his administration investigating accusations of sexual impropriety against Margaret Eaton, the wife of his good friend, Secretary of War John Henry Eaton. The whole matter was even more upsetting because Jackson's own wife, Rachel, had suffered from similar attacks during the recent 1828 presidential election campaign and had died from a massive heart attack just as they were preparing to leave for Washington. The attacks on his wife Rachel and his friend Margaret were a plot against him, he was convinced. Margaret Eaton, whom he had known since she was a young girl, was no sexual sinner. "She is as chaste as a virgin!" he believed, and he was going to prove it.

Andrew Jackson is included routinely in any listing of the nation's great presidents. Yet he spent better than half of his first term dealing not with substantive issues but with the question of a woman's purity. He and Washington society took the matter so seriously that it resulted in the dismissal of his cabinet and was at the heart of his disagreement with his vice president. Sexual propriety and gender relations controversies buzzing around Margaret Eaton shaped the presidency of one of the most revered chief executives in American history. This sex scandal was a long and complicated story, the result of the backgrounds of the major protagonists and the accepted societal mores of the age. Politics and etiquette, the presidency and gender all became intertwined in a manner that put the nation through a crisis of the first magnitude.[1]

Andrew Jackson had a long history of defending women's honor, and much of it revolved around his beloved wife, Rachel. The two met when Jackson, a young bachelor lawyer, boarded with the family of Rachel Donelson Robards in Nashville. The young Mrs. Robards was in an unhappy marriage and was separated from her husband, who lived in Kentucky. Jackson, obviously taken with her, provided support that rumors soon insisted went beyond the legitimate. When Rachel's husband allegedly was coming to Nashville to force her to return to Kentucky, Mrs. Robards decided to flee to Natchez, Mississippi. Jackson went along as one of her escorts. This action was suspicious enough, but for the two years Rachel Robards remained in Mississippi, Andrew Jackson apparently visited her every chance he had. When word filtered down from Kentucky of Lewis Robards's divorce from Rachel, Jackson quickly married her in early 1790. Three years later, the couple learned that Robards's divorce had not become official until 1793, so they reluctantly went through another ceremony in January 1794 to make their marriage legal.[2]

From that point on, any critical comments from anyone about Rachel's virtue resulted in Jackson going to the field of honor to defend his wife's reputation with a pistol. During the presidential elections of 1824 and 1828, when his political opponents lambasted him with charges of adultery and his wife with bigamy, he became furious. Slurs that his mother had been a prostitute and his father an upstart black man only made him angrier. He never forgave those politicians who castigated him and his beloved wife. When he became president, his reaction to similar attacks on Margaret Eaton was, therefore, visceral.

Born the daughter of an Irish-American boardinghouse keeper in Washington, DC, Margaret Eaton was from early on a controversial person.[3] In those days, congressmen rarely took their wives and families with them to Washington because Congress did not remain in session year round. Consequently, legislators lived together in boardinghouses in the capital city. William O'Neale, Margaret's father, ran one of these establishments, so Margaret and her siblings grew up around political leaders.

Margaret was a precocious child, the favorite of the lonely legislators. As a young girl, she would frequently sit on congressmen's laps and listen to their political discussions. As she matured into a beautiful young lady, she began to participate in their conversations. Her beauty attracted suitors, not from among the congressmen but from young army officers in the District of Columbia. One military man threatened suicide over her, and another followed her to New York City, where her father sent Margaret to live with De Witt Clinton and to go to school. She came home after a short time and at the age of sixteen married John B. Timberlake, a purser in the United States Navy. Timberlake resigned his nautical post to start a store next to his new wife's family boardinghouse, but the business failed and he had to go off to sea again. Margaret remained at home, continuing to work in her father's boardinghouse and in the tavern he added to it.

Margaret O'Neale Timberlake's beauty, her attraction for men, her work around them in the boardinghouse and tavern, and her ability to talk politics had sparked rumors that she was not a proper woman. With her husband off to sea, she was frequently seen, both at the boardinghouse and around Washington, in the company of Tennessee senator and widower John Henry Eaton. The gossip increased, and Washington society clearly believed that Margaret was carrying on an illicit affair with Eaton, while her unknowing husband was on the ocean trying to make an honest living. In April 1828, Timberlake committed suicide, and gossips were sure that he had taken his life because of shame at his philandering wife back home. Adding to the scandal, Senator Eaton and Mrs. Timberlake married on January 1, 1829, less than a year after the suicide. The marriage even more convinced the critics that there had indeed been an affair between the senator and the purser's wife. Margaret O'Neale Timberlake Eaton was clearly no lady. When, therefore, Andrew Jackson, himself an alleged sexual reprobate, appointed John Henry Eaton to his cabinet and thus made this sinner a cabinet wife, society was aghast.

Jackson's political enemies took advantage of the situation to try to weaken his presidency at its very beginning. But there was more to the matter than politics. Even Jackson's cabinet, those at the center of his administration, condemned Margaret Eaton and refused to have anything to do with her. Washington's critical attitude toward her can only be understood if it is considered within both its political and gender parameters.

Jackson's presidency encompased years of enormous change. Commonly known as the age of the "Market Revolution," all aspects of American life appeared to be in flux.[4] It was all very exciting but also very frightening. The way people made a living, the way they traveled, the money they exchanged, the churches they attended, and the attitudes they held—all seemed to be in turmoil. Even the new president came from wilderness Tennessee, not civilized Virginia or Massachusetts. He was an Indian fighter, not a statesman. The American people were not sure what it all meant, and established leaders in society and politics were worried: How were they and others to behave toward one other in this dizzying new universe?

One way to confront a confusing world—then as now—was to search for some absolutes, and gender provided an important one. According to the conventional wisdom of the age, men were to participate in business and politics; women were to remain at home and protect morality and ensure its propagation to the next generation. A woman's task was to serve as a crucible of virtues. She was to exemplify submissiveness, piety, purity, and domesticity.[5] A woman, therefore, was to look to her father, husband, or brother for direction when it came to politics and business; the men, however, were to look to her for direction in morality. She, not they, set the standard of virtue. For her to accomplish this task successfully, she had to stay out of the public arena of business and politics, the realm where morality and virtue came under constant attack. If she became involved in man's work, she lost her ability to be the moral guardian that society expected and needed women to be.

The major determinant of a woman's ability to be a moral arbiter was her purity. Any woman who was impure was not a true woman, no matter what else she might be or might do. Antebellum society viewed women as sexually passionless, while men were seen as filled with lust. The woman's job was to tame the lustful man, to turn his energies away from sex to more productive activities, like participation in the expanding market economy. A woman who lacked purity not only sinned herself but was also unable to accomplish the task of restraining lustful men. Thus, impurity was not simply a private sin; it was a sin against society as a whole. An impure woman was not upholding morality and not insuring certitude in a rapidly and confusingly changing world.[6]

The idealized woman of these years was to be pale and thin, her very figure and appearance symbolizing virtue. She did not have the sensual hour-glass figure of women in the late nineteenth century. The woman of the early republic was to be a guardian of morality in her appearance and in her manner. She was never to speak loudly or publicly display her intelligence. Her control was to be less direct than that. She ruled by example as much as by actual statement.[7] Should her husband die, the true woman was to follow a prescribed mourning ritual. She was to wear special clothes and withdraw from society in a specifically established manner for a period of two years. Not following this proper grieving process meant that a woman was disrespectful not only of her husband's memory but also of the proper workings of society.[8]

Washington society women, influenced by this contemporary perception of woman's proper role, found Margaret Eaton shockingly lacking. She was of common birth, the daughter of a lowly Irish boardinghouse keeper at a time when to be Irish was to be viewed as rowdy and uncouth. More significantly, Margaret did not behave like a proper woman. She debated politics with men, showing interest in a topic that was to be man's concern alone. She exuded a sensuality that by its very appearance seemed to be a threat to sexual virtue. Men found her much too exciting.

Her alleged salacious activities spoke even more forcefully than her loud voice or striking appearance. She had been overly familiar with men at her father's boardinghouse for a long time, or so the story went. Then she had cheated on her husband when he was away at sea; she displayed no shame. Even her husband's death did not stop her flouting of convention, since she did not honor his memory by observing the proper mourning ritual but rushed into marriage. This action only proved that the accusations of her previous sexual sinning had been accurate. She was no proper woman and thus not worthy of inclusion in the sisterhood of morality, whose task it was to protect society's virtue. Accepting her into society would negate any claims women had to be arbiters of morality.

Washington society dealt with Margaret as it would with any other woman considered unworthy. It kept her out of its circle of virtue. In Washington, there was a formal protocol requiring a woman to pay visits on other women, in a specified order and manner. The exchange of calling cards was the concrete exemplification of this etiquette. Washington women simply refused to extend this courtesy to Margaret Eaton and thus indicated their unwillingness to accept her as a proper society woman.[9]

Soon after their wedding but before his appointment as secretary of war, John Eaton and his bride called on John C. Calhoun, the vice president of the United States, and his wife, Floride. Calhoun was absent, but Mrs. Calhoun greeted the visitors politely. The Eatons stayed only a short time, but Margaret made her point. She was fulfilling her social responsibilities like any other proper woman. Floride Calhoun, however, was not impressed. The next morning she told her husband that she would not return Margaret's visit because to do so would signal her acceptance into society. Although she had been away from Washington for three years, Floride Calhoun knew all about Margaret's reputation. Floride decided that she would not return any visits from her unless other women of Washington's upper crust did so first. She did not know personally if the accusations against Margaret were true or false, but that detail was of no significance. She decided to follow the practice of Washington society women and ostracize her.[10]

The wife of the vice president, therefore, supported what Washington women had long been doing. She too snubbed Margaret Eaton. Because she was to leave Washington for South Carolina immediately after the inauguration, Floride Calhoun did not see herself taking a leadership role, or any role for that matter, in the affair. She was simply following the lead of those who had known Margaret Eaton for a long time and had refused to include her in the society of virtuous women.

When Andrew Jackson announced in February 1829 that John Eaton was going to be his secretary of war, the news, although already rumored and the object of concern, proved shocking anyway. Nathan Towson, U.S. Army paymaster and the husband of one of Washington's leading ladies, confronted Jackson directly, warning him that including the controversial Margaret in his cabinet family was a mistake.[11] Jackson refused to listen to Towson or to any of the political delegations that came to visit him. The president would have Eaton in his cabinet, and he would not tolerate any untoward and unfair comments about Eaton's wife. Jackson's attitude did not matter to Washington society women, to cabinet wives, or even to Emily, the White House hostess and the wife of his nephew Andrew Jackson Donelson. Women snubbed Margaret Eaton during the inauguration ceremonies, the swearing-in, the White House reception, and the grand ball. They did it for social— not political—reasons.

Andrew Jackson had not realized the extent of the opposition to Margaret Eaton until he received a letter from the Reverend Ezra Stiles Ely, clerk of the General Assembly of the Presbyterian Church of the United States. The Philadelphia minister, who had been a strong supporter of Jackson during the recent election and who had just returned home from the inauguration, wrote a series of letters urging Jackson to fire Eaton and rid himself of the official's immoral wife. According to Ely, it was common knowledge in Washington that she had been involved in a number of illicit affairs before and after her marriage to John Timberlake. Among other accusations, Ely wrote that John Eaton and Margaret Timberlake had stayed together in a New York hotel. More to the point, he went on, Margaret had experienced a miscarriage a year after Timberlake had been away at sea.[12]

Jackson was outraged at such gossip. He immediately launched an investigation and discovered, to his satisfaction, that all accusations were false. When he confronted Ely with the facts, the minister backed down, admitting that everything he had told Jackson had come from a government clerk he hardly knew. Nonetheless, Margaret's ostracism continued. The most dramatic example occurred on board a ship taking Jackson, his niece Emily, Margaret, and other government officials on an excursion to Virginia. Emily was pregnant and grew light-headed during the course of the voyage. Margaret rushed forward to offer her help, but Emily preferred to faint rather than accept aid from the woman she had been avoiding. Margaret became so angry that she told Andrew Jackson Donelson that his uncle, President Jackson, should send them back to Tennessee rather than allow a continuation of such behavior.[13]

Margaret took a similar straightforward position toward the Reverend Ely. When she learned about his accusations, she hurried to Philadelphia to confront him, once more acting in a manner improper for a woman of that day. She threatened the minister with physical violence and after six hours of interrogation forced him to admit that another Presbyterian leader, Reverend John N. Campbell, the pastor of Andrew

Jackson's and the Eatons' own church, had made the charge about her miscarriage.

Margaret then rushed back to Washington to confront Campbell. She so intimidated the pastor that he hurried to the White House to explain himself to the president. After several such meetings with the minister, Jackson called a cabinet meeting to reassert Margaret's innocence. He came away satisfied that he had refuted all the charges, but the cabinet members and the Reverend Campbell were not convinced. They continued to believe she was an immoral woman. John Henry Eaton became so angry that he challenged the Reverend Campbell to a duel. Campbell refused the challenge, but his days in Washington were numbered. He took a pastorship in Albany, safe from the irate husband's wrath.[14]

However, Margaret's social isolation did not disappear. Rather, it became even more dramatic. Normally the presidents held dinners for their cabinet early in the first term in office. Yet because of the controversy over Margaret, Andrew Jackson delayed the entertainment until late November 1829. The gathering, however, was a decided failure. The evening was stiff and formal, as cabinet wives maneuvered to avoid the infamous wife of the secretary of war. Secretary of State Martin Van Buren held the next dinner because Vice President John C. Calhoun's wife was in South Carolina, and thus he could not fulfill his social duty. The cabinet wives refused to attend Van Buren's event rather than have to deal with Margaret again. Then, to make the point even clearer, they held parties of their own and refused to invite her.

The result of such social animosity was acute tension within Jackson's cabinet. Eaton began to quarrel with his colleagues; violence seemed possible. In January 1830, as matters continued to deteriorate, Jackson called on Richard M. Johnson, a Kentucky congressman and subsequent vice president of the United States, to approach the three cabinet members whom Jackson found particularly offensive toward the Eatons. Johnson told Secretary of the Navy John Branch, Attorney General John M. Berrien, and Secretary of the Treasury Samuel D. Ingham that Jackson insisted that their wives invite Margaret Eaton to their parties and exchange calling cards with her, or the president would fire them.

The three men let it be known that they would not allow the president or anyone else to dictate social matters to their families. Besides, women handled such matters; their husbands' obligation was simply to follow their spouses' plans. Jackson called the three in and told them that although he made no claims on their social obligations, the president would not tolerate any of them or their wives inciting opposition to Margaret Eaton. He would have harmony in his cabinet, or he would dissolve it. The three secretaries agreed to work toward that harmony, and the matter was defused for the moment.[15]

At first, Andrew Jackson had blamed his old political enemies, Henry Clay and John Quincy Adams, for these attacks on Margaret Eaton, but he soon came to view John C. Calhoun as the chief villain. The two men had forged a marriage of political convenience during the election of 1828, although they disagreed on major political and policy issues. In April 1830, with Jackson convinced that Calhoun was at the bottom of what he believed was an organized opposition to the Eatons—and thus to him—he and his vice president clashed publicly over the nature of the Union and South Carolina's right to nullify a federal tariff. Soon after, Jackson accused Calhoun of working, while in James Monroe's cabinet, to censure him over Jackson's 1818 activities against the Seminoles in Florida. Calhoun had led Jackson to believe he had supported him at the time in this Seminole Affair, but in reality he had indeed led the attack on him. "Et Tu Brute," Jackson wrote Calhoun and severed relations with him.[16]

At the same time that he was cutting his ties to Calhoun, Jackson was growing increasingly close to his secretary of state, Martin Van Buren. The dapper New Yorker was going out of his way to be friendly to Mrs. Eaton, and Jackson appreciated this show of support. Politicians had been sure that Calhoun would someday replace Jackson in the White House, but Van Buren now became a serious rival. Jackson's disgust with Calhoun and his friendship for Van Buren were creating a major change in the presidential landscape.

The Eaton imbroglio spread to the White House itself. Emily and Andrew Jackson Donelson continued to be prominent among those shunning Margaret Eaton. To most people the Donelsons' participation would have indicated that more than political intrigue was involved. To Andrew Jackson, however, the actions of his niece and nephew were only further proof of the vastness of the Calhoun conspiracy. When Jackson and the Donelsons returned to Nashville during the summer of 1830, personal animosities grew worse. As a result, Emily did not accompany her husband and uncle back to Washington that fall. Jackson and his nephew grew so hostile to each other that for a time they communicated only by letter while living together in the White House.

Finally, young Donelson returned to Nashville to be with his wife and refused to come back to Washington until Jackson withdrew his demand that they accept Margaret Eaton socially.

Margaret and her husband continued to battle back. Eaton grew increasingly angry over the continual affronts to his wife, and she was not averse to continuing to violate social mores by confronting men and women who dared oppose her. At one of Van Buren's parties, for example, she and the wife of an army general accidentally bumped into each other on the dance floor. Their resulting shouting match was the talk of the town. Margaret Eaton was not about to back down from anyone, once more demonstrating to her opponents that she was no lady.[17]

As early as January 1830, Jackson had threatened to dissolve his cabinet if its members and their wives did not treat Margaret Eaton sociably. Her opponents, however, remained firm in their disdain for the allegedly scarlet woman. In the spring of 1831, Van Buren took action to break the stalemate. He shocked Jackson by offering his resignation, urged the president to rid himself of all those opposed to the Eatons, and suggested that he begin anew with a fresh group of advisers. When Eaton learned of Van Buren's plan, he volunteered to resign, too, believing he, not Van Buren, was at the center of the controversy. He delayed his final decision, however, until he received Margaret's cooperation. After what must have been a tense scene, she agreed. Eaton resigned, but so did Van Buren, to make sure that Eaton's opponents in the cabinet had no excuse for not doing the same.[18]

On April 20, 1831, after a great deal more background maneuvering achieved the dissolution of the cabinet, their resignations were announced in the press. The nation was shocked, and many wondered if the country—like the cabinet—was breaking apart. When word filtered out and then poured forth that Margaret Eaton and her social acceptability were the main reason for the dissolution of the cabinet, the nation was appalled even further. As the former cabinet members began protesting in public, newspapers all around the nation picked up the story. The Eaton affair became a national sensation—not a Washington spat.

The controversy continued throughout that summer and into the fall of 1831 and became increasingly personal. The argument became particularly heated between Eaton and Secretary of the Treasury Samuel Ingham, whose wife was reputed to be the leader of the cabinet wives' opposition to Margaret Eaton. Eaton decided to challenge Ingham to a duel, encouraged by Andrew Jackson, who told him that if the treasury secretary refused to fight on the field of honor, Eaton should simply kill him. Eaton was determined to demand satisfaction from Ingham, and Margaret urged him to do so, offering to perform a function that no woman was ever supposed to carry out—second in a duel.

Early one morning in late June 1831, Eaton and several friends went out looking for Ingham, walking back and forth in front of the treasury building and before Ingham's home, daring him to show himself—so Eaton could challenge him, as his supporters said, or kill him, as Ingham and his friends insisted. Ingham wrote to Jackson protesting Eaton's stalking. Yet knowing that he could expect no help from the president, Ingham raced out of town surrounded by six armed body guards.[19]

Logically, the political crisis should now have been over. The cabinet had been dissolved, and physical distance separated many of the key protagonists. But such was not the case. The press continued its inflammatory reporting, calling Margaret such names as Czarina, Bellona, and Helen of Troy. Then, Eaton and Calhoun both wrote long essays defending their positions, and newspapers all over the nation reprinted them. In September 1831, Eaton accused those calling his wife immoral of doing so only to try to gain unfair advantage for John C. Calhoun. In October, Calhoun responded by insisting that moral women, not his political supporters, rightfully had expressed their duty to preserve the nation's morality by refusing to accept Margaret Eaton into their circle. The Eatons made no further response, and the "Petticoat Affair" faded from public view.[20]

John and Margaret Eaton returned to his hometown of Franklin, Tennessee, and in 1833, despite Jackson's support, Eaton lost in his effort to return to the United States Senate. In March 1834 the president named him to a three-year term as governor of the Florida territory. Margaret never liked the assignment, but she enjoyed the generally friendly welcome she received. In March 1836, Jackson named Eaton minister to Spain, where he had an unproductive tenure during a time of internal Spanish upheaval. Margaret was a favorite of the diplomatic community, however, and was sorry to leave the country when President Martin Van Buren recalled her husband in 1840. In anger over his recall, Eaton supported the Whig candidate William Henry Harrison in the 1840 presidential race, earning Andrew Jackson's animosity. Eaton remained in Washington and became a leading attorney, while Margaret enjoyed a full social life. The Eatons did not repair the breach with Jackson until shortly before the former president's death in 1845.

John Eaton died in September 1856, leaving Margaret to raise the children of her deceased daughter and son-in-law. At the age of fifty-nine, she married again, this time to a nineteen-year-old Italian dance instructor named Antonio Buchignani. After several years of a seemingly happy marriage, Buchignani swindled Margaret out of most of her money and then ran off with one of her granddaughters. When Margaret died in November 1879, she was destitute. She was buried next to Eaton in Washington's Oak Hill Cemetery and among some of the very people who had snubbed her during the Jacksonian presidency. Only in her final resting place did she gain the social acceptance that she had craved in the 1830s.

Margaret O'Neale Timberlake Eaton Buchignani played an important role in nineteenth-century American history. Her story, so full of twists and turns, influenced the age in which she lived in a way that few people have ever been able to do. In her life may be seen the intertwining of politics and gender that twentieth-century historians have come to realize had such an important impact on the direction of the American story. Margaret Eaton was no feminist pioneer, but in the tale of the infamous "Peggy" of the Jacksonian years, one can see the struggle of women to break free from the barriers American society established for them. Margaret did not fit the description of her era's ideal woman, so she was considered immoral and unwomanly. All too often other aggressive women have suffered a similar fate in all periods of American history.

Notes

1. The most complete studies of Margaret Eaton and the conflict that swirled around her during the Jacksonian Era are John F. Marszalek, *The Petticoat Affair: Manners, Mutiny, and Sex in Jacksonian America* (New York, 1998); John F. Marszalek, "The Eaton Affair, Society and Politics," *Tennessee Historical Quarterly* 55 (1996): 6–19; and Kirsten E. Wood, " 'One Woman So Dangerous to Public Morals': Gender and Power in the Eaton Affair," *Journal of the Early Republic* 17 (1997): 237–75. For an excellent study of the impact of early-nineteenth-century women on politics, see Catherine Allgor, "Political Parties: Society and Politics in Washington City, 1800–1832" (Ph.D. diss., Yale University, 1998).

2. Harriet Chappell Owsley, "The Marriage of Rachel Donelson," *Tennessee Historical Quarterly* 36 (1977): 479–92; Robert V. Remini, *Andrew Jackson and the Course of American Empire, 1767–1821* (New York, 1977), 57–69.

3. Margaret Eaton left no body of correspondence, but she did write a memoir that was published long after her death. Margaret Eaton, *The Autobiography of Margaret Eaton* (New York, 1932). A secondary account, which is well researched but not so

well organized or written, is Queena Pollack, *Peggy Eaton: Democracy's Mistress* (New York, 1931).

4. Charles Sellers, *The Market Revolution, Jacksonian America, 1815–1846* (New York, 1991).

5. Barbara Welter, "The Cult of True Womanhood, 1820–1860," *American Quarterly* 18 (1966): 151–74; Linda K. Kerber contends that the concept of "separate spheres" that Welter discusses is "a static model" "imposed on dynamic relationships." Linda K. Kerber, "Separate Spheres, Female Worlds, Woman's Place: The Rhetoric of Women's History," *Journal of American History* 75 (1988): 38.

6. Linda Gordon, *Woman's Body, Woman's Right: Birth Control in America*, 2d ed. (New York, 1990), 21; William Taylor and Christopher Lasch, "'Two Kindred Spirits': Sorority and Family in New England, 1839–1846," *New England Quarterly* 36 (1963): 35; Estelle Freedman, *Their Sisters' Keepers: Women's Prison Reform in America, 1830–1930* (Ann Arbor, MI, 1981), 19–21.

7. Lois W. Banner, *American Beauty* (Chicago, 1983), 5, 6, 45, 50; Thomas Hamilton, *Men and Manners in America*, 2 vols. (Edinburgh, 1834), 2:15.

8. Madame Celnart, *The Gentleman's and Lady's Book of Politeness and Propriety* . . . (Boston, 1833), 210–12; Karen Halttunen, *Confidence Men and Painted Women: A Study of Middle Class Culture in America, 1830–1870* (New Haven, 1982), 135–38.

9. Eli Field Cooley, *A Description of the Etiquette at Washington City* (Philadelphia, 1829).

10. John C. Calhoun, "Reply to John H. Eaton's Address," in *The Papers of John C. Calhoun*, 22 vols. to date, ed. E. Edwin Hemphill, Robert L. Merriwether, and Clyde Wilson (Columbia, SC, 1959–), 11:474–81.

11. "Narrative by Major William B. Lewis," October 25, 1859, in James Parton, *The Life of Andrew Jackson*, 3 vols. (New York 1861), 3:160–61.

12. Curtis Dahl, "The Clergyman, the Hussy, and Old Hickory: Ezra Stiles Ely and the Peggy Eaton Affair," *Journal of Presbyterian History* 52 (1974): 137–55. The correspondence between Jackson and Ely is found in the Andrew Jackson Papers, Library of Congress, Washington, DC.

13. Pauline Wilcox Burke, *Emily Donelson of Tennessee*, 2 vols. (Richmond, 1941), 1:202–3.

14. Eaton, *Autobiography*, 96–104.

15. Parton, *Life of Andrew Jackson*, 3:303–7; John M. Berrien to Richard M. Johnson, July 7, 1831, in *Niles Register* July 30, 1831; Memorandum in Jackson's Handwriting [January 29, 1830], in *Correspondence of Andrew Jackson*, 7 vols., ed. John Spencer Bassett (Washington, DC, 1926–1935), 4:123–24.

16. *Niles Register*, April 24, 1830; Robert V. Remini, *The Life of Andrew Jackson* (New York, 1988), 195–97; Jackson to Calhoun, May 30, 1830, in Bassett, *Correspondence of Jackson*, 4:137–41.

17. John C. Fitzpatrick, ed., *The Autobiography of Martin Van Buren* (Washington, DC, 1920), 348–50.

18. Ibid., 402–6.

19. A convenient place to study the press reaction to the controversy is the *Niles Register*, Washington *Globe*, and *United States Telegraph* for the period from late April to the fall of 1831.

20. John Henry Eaton, *Candid Appeal to the American Public* . . . (Washington, DC, 1831); Calhoun, "Reply to John H. Eaton's Address," in Hemphill, Merriwether, and Wilson, *Papers of Calhoun*, 11:474–81. The Eaton statement first appeared in the Washington *Globe*, September 15, 1831, while the Calhoun response first appeared in the *Pendleton (SC) Messenger*, October 19, 1831. Both essays were widely reprinted throughout the nation.

Suggested Readings

Cole, Donald B. *The Presidency of Andrew Jackson*. Lawrence, KS, 1993.

Dahl, Curtis. "The Clergyman, the Hussy, and Old Hickory: Ezra Stiles Ely and the Peggy Eaton Affair." *Journal of Presbyterian History* 52 (1974): 137–55.

Eaton, Margaret. *The Autobiography of Margaret Eaton*. New York, 1932.

Kerber, Linda K. "Separate Spheres, Female Worlds, Woman's Place: The Rhetoric of Women's History." *Journal of American History* 75 (1988): 19–39.

Latner, Richard B. "The Eaton Affair Reconsidered." *Tennessee Historical Quarterly* 16 (1977): 330–51.

Marszalek, John F. *The Petticoat Affair: Manners, Mutiny, and Sex in Andrew Jackson's White House*. New York, 1998.

———. "The Eaton Affair, Society and Politics." *Tennessee Historical Quarterly* 55 (1996): 6–19.

Pollack, Queena. *Peggy Eaton: Democracy's Mistress*. New York, 1931.

Remini, Robert V. *Andrew Jackson and the Course of American Freedom, 1822–1832*. New York, 1981.

Welter, Barbara. "The Cult of True Womanhood, 1820–1860." *American Quarterly* 18 (1966): 151–74.

Wood, Kristen E. " 'One Woman So Dangerous to Public Morals': Gender and Power in the Eaton Affair." *Journal of the Early Republic* 17 (1997): 237–75.

14

Benjamin Tappan
Democrat, Scientist, Iconoclast

Daniel Feller

The early national era was a time of increased possibilities for some Americans and, ironically, new restrictions on others. It was also an age of political transformation. The life and public career of Benjamin Tappan are reflections and extensions of this evolution of American society. Born three years before the revolution, he died three years before South Carolina's secession from the Union. In an era that celebrated individual achievement and uplift, by any measure he enjoyed a successful, if turbulent, career. Tappan was by turns a lawyer, jurist, politician, scientist, and promoter of educational and social reform. He lived comfortably within this age of romantic reform, seeking human improvement through communitarian societies, experimental schools, and scientific endeavors. Like Abraham Bishop, he began his career as a Jeffersonian Republican. He subsequently joined the party of Andrew Jackson. When the issue of slavery extension came to dominate and reshape the political landscape, Tappan abandoned the allegedly proslavery Democratic Party and became a Republican. Though he opposed the South's "peculiar institution," Tappan was no abolitionist. Tappan's partisan conversions, the centrality of religion to his outlook on the world, and the transformative effect of slavery on his political views illuminate the central themes of this unsettled period in American history.

Daniel Feller is professor of history at the University of New Mexico, Albuquerque. He is the author of *The Public Lands in Jacksonian Politics* (1984) and *The Jacksonian Promise: America, 1815–1840* (1995); and is the editor of Harriet Martineau's *Retrospect of Western Travel* (2000).

O n April 21, 1857, Lewis Tappan, a New York City merchant, philanthropist, and abolitionist, received a telegram relayed through his brother John: their elder brother Benjamin had died at age 83 at his home in Steubenville, Ohio. "Poor brother!" confided Lewis to his journal. "He now knows whether the opinions he had professed & held for upwards of 60 years are true or not, and whether his heart was right with God. He has been the subject of much prayer & much entreaty. What the result has been God only knows."[1]

213

The opinions that Benjamin Tappan professed in politics and religion and the choices he had taken in consequence of those opinions made him something of an outcast in his native New England and even in his own family. They also brought him renown and influence as a jurist, a promoter of science, a politician, and finally a U.S. Senator. The rapid expansion of the United States between the Revolution and the Civil War opened the way for Tappan and thousands of other Americans both to carve out new identities for themselves and to attempt to redirect their country's future. Tappan seized those opportunities in ways original and controversial. As one admirer observed, his career offered "evidence of the enlarged genius and various capacity of the American Character."[2]

Benjamin Tappan was born May 25, 1773, in Northampton, Massachusetts, the eldest son and second of ten surviving children of Benjamin and Sarah Homes Tappan. Tappan's father was a goldsmith and merchant who had apprenticed in Boston and moved to Northampton in 1768. Though the Tappans were not wealthy, they had deep New England roots. Benjamin's Massachusetts ancestry traced to 1637 and included several Puritan ministers and ties to leading families. An uncle, David Tappan, was Hollis Professor of Divinity at Harvard; Benjamin's mother was a grandniece of Benjamin Franklin. Benjamin's own upbringing was conventional, both in its patriotic politics (his father was a Revolutionary War veteran) and in its orthodox Calvinist faith.

Young Tappan prepared for Harvard at a Northampton academy but left school at fourteen to support himself. For seven years he worked at mechanical trades, acquiring a wide range of skills and in his spare time reading everything he could get his hands on. In 1794, he made a Caribbean voyage and then ended up in New York, where he engaged as a student and copyist with the renowned painter Gilbert Stuart. After his training, Tappan did a brief turn as a country portraitist and by 1796 was back home tending his father's store.[3]

At exactly what point Benjamin became a rebel remains unclear. The earliest signs came in childhood, when he spurned efforts to convert him at a Northampton revival. Still, youthful religious doubtings and an itch to see the world were hardly unusual. It was Tappan's next adventure that would confirm his apostasy in politics and religion, two subjects that in the New England of the 1790s were virtually inseparable.

In 1796, Tappan began to study law with Gideon Granger in Suffield, Connecticut, not far downriver from Northampton. Together the Federalist Party and the official, state-supported Congregational Church ruled Connecticut under the rubric of the "Standing Order," with President Timothy Dwight of Yale College at its head. Granger led the Jeffersonian opposition, in which Tappan readily enlisted. The three years of his legal apprenticeship coincided with an escalation of party feeling over foreign relations and the Alien and Sedition Acts, further inflamed in Connecticut by controversies over church and state. Tweaking the nose of the Federalist gentry, Tappan sported Democratic insignia on his person, published a satire of President John Adams's call for a national day of fasting and prayer, and even picked quarrels with Federalist judges in his father's own parlor.

Tappan emerged from these encounters a confirmed Jeffersonian Democrat and religious skeptic, identities he retained throughout his life. To match his versatile intellect and omnivorous curiosity in matters mechanical and scientific, he cultivated a contempt for orthodoxy in both politics and religion. A disciple of the rationalist Enlightenment, he dismissed the Holy Scriptures, the very staple of a proper New England upbringing, as a "knavish invention" and "all damned nonsense." Instead he read David Hume, Voltaire, and Thomas Paine. From his youthful contests with authority, Tappan also developed a pugnacious manner and an abrasive, sarcastic sense of humor, qualities that would entangle him in endless personal disputes and later hamstring his political career. Though some who penetrated his caustic exterior found him fascinating, Tappan was not an easy person to like. He thought most men fools or scoundrels and poured his scorn freely on both.[4]

By 1799, when he was admitted to the Connecticut bar, Tappan had alienated many of the lawyers and judges with whom he would have to practice. He had also strained relations with his mother, who feared he would corrupt his youngest brother Lewis, fifteen years Benjamin's junior and already his closest companion. Providentially, an opportunity offered itself at this moment by which Tappan could escape his confining environment while enhancing his own prospects and without severing family ties. Benjamin's father had invested in the Connecticut Land Company, which held title to the vast Western Reserve district of northeastern Ohio. In 1798 the company distributed its holdings among the shareholders. Tappan's portion, costing $8,392, came to more than thirteen thousand acres.[5]

It was a risky venture. Benjamin's father had bought his shares on credit, at a price far beyond his normal means. To avoid default and ruin, he now needed to realize an income from raw, remote frontier lands while competing in a market glutted by other shareholders in similar straits. Clearly the family needed someone enterprising and trustworthy to manage the property. Benjamin, who had urged his father to make the purchase, volunteered. In April 1799, at age twenty-five, he left Northampton on horseback with a team of oxen, a cow, and a wagonload of farm tools.

The journey to Ohio by land and water took more than a month and involved much peril. Crossing the Niagara River, Tappan's boat got caught in the current and was nearly swept over the falls. Reaching the future site of Cleveland, Tappan cut a trail south to his family's main holding in Ravenna township and began to clear land. He was the second white settler in what later became Portage County.

Tappan was one of many scions of New England families who filtered out to pioneer on the Western Reserve. Most were young men, intrepid, versatile, and ambitious. Though they brought New England customs and institutions to midwestern soil, many, like Tappan, had also been dissenters back home in religion or politics who came west to breathe freer air. On the Ohio frontier, they found adventure, hardship—and opportunity.

For a decade, Tappan struggled to turn a profit on the family lands. But because of the Connecticut Land Company's peculiar distribution procedures his properties were widely scattered, and the core holding in Ravenna was off the main path of settlement. To populate the area, Tappan had to offer easy terms and take what buyers he could get. With little money coming in, Tappan's father back in Northampton was barely able to make his payments and avoid bankruptcy. Over the years the continuing anxiety and distress soured family relations, producing sharp words and even a threat of lawsuits between Tappan and his father and brothers.

Meanwhile, however, Tappan was finding success in other spheres. If the Western Reserve had no shortage of raw lands for sale, it did have a shortage of skilled lawyers. In 1800, Tappan gained public notice by winning an acquittal in an important capital murder case. That winter, he returned to New England for business and a family visit, and while there renewed an acquaintance with Nancy Wright of Berlin, Connecticut. In the spring they married.

By this time, agitation for Ohio statehood was building, fueled by resentment of the autocratic regime of territorial governor Arthur St. Clair. The statehood struggle replicated the party division back East of Federalists and Jeffersonians, and Tappan of course threw in with the latter. In an Independence Day oration at the village of Hudson in 1801, he proclaimed his democratic creed. With its banners of freedom waving, America stood "in the vanguard of the world" as the herald of universal liberty. Yet the threat of despotism was everywhere—in European and American opposition to the French revolution; in the national Federalist policies of standing armies, exorbitant debt, profligate expenditures, and civil repression; and in the "illegal extortions" of St. Clair's territorial administration. Tappan further spiced this inflamed party speech with what one horrified auditor described as "many grossly illiberal remarks against Christians and Christianity."[6]

In 1803, Ohio became a state, and soon after Tappan won a special election to fill a vacancy in the state senate—the only popular elective office he would ever hold. In the legislature, he at once assumed a commanding role, introducing militia, taxation, judiciary, and county government bills. Governor Edward Tiffin, in urging a federal appointment for Tappan, called him "a man of correct politics & as firm as a rock." But he also offended both voters and fellow legislators (whom he privately deemed a "damnable sett of blockheads") with his bluntness and irascibility. After a year in the senate, he was defeated for reelection.[7]

In the next few years, Tappan and his wife grew increasingly restive in their backwater location at Ravenna. They even thought of going back to Connecticut, but instead Tappan decided to move where he could get more legal business. After platting a town at Ravenna and securing its future as a county seat, he turned over his land business to his younger brother William (the family ne'er-do-well, who soon turned to drink). In 1809, Benjamin and Nancy moved south off the Western Reserve to Steubenville, just up the Ohio River from Wheeling, Virginia.

Here they would live the rest of their lives. Steubenville was a thriving community with good prospects. River port, Jefferson County seat, and nascent manufacturing center, it was briefly Ohio's second largest city behind Cincinnati. Within two years, Tappan was its leading lawyer and town president. Gradually he and Nancy built a network of personal and business associates. They included her brother John Crafts Wright, who came out to read law with Benjamin in 1810 and later became a congressman and judge; Bezaleel Wells, founder of Steubenville and owner of its woolens factory, in which Benjamin purchased a partnership in 1819; and newspaperman James Wilson (grandfather of President Woodrow Wilson), whom Benjamin helped bring from Philadelphia to edit the Steubenville *Western Herald* in 1815. Together these men headed the town's civic affairs and worked to advance its fortunes by establishing industries, roads, banks, and schools.

Tappan also continued to be active in Ohio politics, where he would occupy a unique role through the 1830s. Legal business often took him to the state capitol during sessions of the legislature. There he wielded great influence behind the scenes, drafting bills and resolutions, devising political strategy, manipulating the press, and advising on appointments, especially to the state judiciary. Admired for his acumen and wide-ranging intellect, yet hated and feared for his irreverence and acid tongue, Tappan was, as one critic said, "the most unpopular, the ugliest and smartest" Democrat in eastern Ohio. Indeed, despite his Jeffersonian principles, Tappan never acquired the common touch. He sought elective office repeatedly but never successfully. His penchant for making enemies also scuttled his chances for a series of appointive positions, both state and federal.[8]

As a major in the Ohio militia, Tappan rallied to the colors upon the declaration of war against Britain in 1812 and led troops to the front for the first year's campaign on the northern frontier. But he did not see combat and resigned after a year, complaining of General William Henry Harrison's incompetence and the Madison administration's mismanagement of the war. After the peace, Tappan in 1816 was appointed chief judge for the new Fifth Circuit Court of Common Pleas, comprising Jefferson and seven surrounding counties. He took notes on his cases and in 1818–19 published *Tappan's Reports*, Ohio's first volume of recorded judicial decisions. In a new society where many legal points were still unsettled and most lawyers and judges were only haphazardly trained, such volumes were especially useful. They established precedents, clarified the law, and thus ensured consistency in its application. Tappan's publication won him much reputation, but it also helped embroil him in the most unseemly feud of his career.

His antagonist was John Milton Goodenow, another brother-in-law (his wife was a sister of Nancy Tappan and John C. Wright) and Steubenville attorney-politician. Goodenow noisily attacked Tappan's ruling in one case that a man could be convicted in Ohio under the common law of crimes, a system of law derived from British tradition rather than specific legislation. Goodenow wrote a treatise excoriating Tappan's verdict as arbitrary and despotic. He and another attorney also brought impeachment charges against Tappan, alleging several counts of "corrupt and flagrant abuse of power" on the bench. Despite a general dislike of Tappan as being "very aristocratic and overbearing," impeachment failed in the state legislature. Undeterred, Goodenow sued Tappan for slander for calling him, among other things, a "d——d rascal," "an immoral and base man," "a disgrace to his profession," and a fugitive from justice. In 1822 the Ohio supreme court heard the case and found for Goodenow, awarding an impressive six hundred dollars in damages. The next year Tappan's seven-year judicial term expired, and the legislature did not reappoint him.[9]

Meanwhile, the close of the 1810s had brought a provisional political peace to Ohio, as leaders of both camps joined to promote the state's econonic development and its interests in national affairs. Together, old Federalists and Jeffersonians demanded federal subsidies for transportation and tariff protection for manufactures, resisted financial constraints imposed by the Bank of the United States, and opposed the extension of slavery in Missouri. Tappan shared in all these efforts. In 1820, he offered an Independence Day toast damning any proslavery northerner as a "*dough faced traitor*."[10] He also pushed for a state canal network to link the Ohio River with Lake Erie, thus completing the chain of internal navigation begun by New York's Erie Canal. In 1822 the Ohio legislature appointed Tappan to a seven-man commission to survey possible routes. Three years later it authorized construction of a canal system and again put Tappan on the commission in charge of building and operating it, where he served until 1836.

The presidential elections of 1824 and 1828 reawakened partisan antagonisms in Ohio and in doing so broke apart Tappan's Steubenville circle. In 1824, Tappan fixed his hopes at first on De Witt Clinton of New York, a northern man and a friend of internal improvements and domestic manufactures. But Clinton had no more popularity than Tappan himself. The contest in Ohio soon narrowed to three men: Henry Clay of Kentucky, who was favored by most of Tappan's friends; John Quincy Adams of Massachusetts, son of Federalist president John Adams; and an upstart candidate with surprising popular appeal, Andrew Jackson of Tennessee. Tappan declared no preference, but he warned his friends in Congress, including brother-in-law John C. Wright, "not to commit yourselves against the sovereign will."[11]

They disregarded the warning. When no candidate received an electoral majority and the choice fell to the U.S. House of Representatives, Wright and the Ohio delegation followed Henry Clay's lead and threw their vote to Adams, helping to make him president. Adams had run a poor third in Ohio, and his election by the aid of Ohio congressmen aroused voters' discontent. For Tappan, this thwarting of democracy revived old political memories and thus fixed his new allegiance. Branding the Clay-Adams alliance as Federalism reborn, he became a Jackson man. So, oddly enough, did his archenemy Goodenow, who challenged and defeated his brother-in-law Wright for Congress in 1828.

In the 1828 presidential rematch between Adams and Jackson, Tappan campaigned for Old Hickory. At the Ohio Jackson convention, Tappan gave the main oration, hailing the Tennessean as a friend of domestic manufactures and denouncing Adams as a "usurper."[12] With Jackson's sweeping triumph, Tappan's own influence rose rapidly. When Ohio Jacksonians, now calling themselves Democrats, convened again to support their hero's reelection in 1832, it was Tappan who called them to order, wrote their state platform, and in the fall headed their victorious ticket of presidential electors.

Tappan's new identity as a Jacksonian Democrat reopened his way to political preferment but cost him dearly in personal friendships. One by one his old associates broke with him, including editor James Wilson, lawyer-congressmen John Sloane and Elisha Whittlesey, and finally, most reluctantly, John C. Wright. Politics also complicated Tappan's intimate and affectionate, yet perennially tension-ridden relations with his family back East. Tappan's parents and siblings had never ceased urging him to read his Bible, trust in prayer, keep the Sabbath, and welcome Christian missionaries, whom Benjamin had indelicately termed "vile incendiary rascals." His mother's strictures were particularly overbearing. Thinking that worldly adversity might shake his complacency, Sarah at one point voiced the hope that Benjamin would not prosper without faith. Years later Benjamin still smoldered at the memory of this "mother's curse."[13]

For one ten-year stretch Benjamin did not return home. Finally, in 1821, he and Nancy, who was suffering from breast cancer, came East seeking medical treatment. They visited Benjamin's aged parents in Northampton and also brothers Arthur and Lewis, now merchants in New York and Boston. Arthur, a pious Christian, "dreaded" seeing Benjamin again, yet when they met fraternal devotion overcame religious differences: "Your visit at our house has left an impression on our minds and an interest in our hearts that time cannot efface." Lewis too "bade them adieu with no little emotion." But Nancy's surgery was unavailing. In 1822 she died in Steubenville, leaving Benjamin and a son, also Benjamin, born in 1812.[14]

Benjamin's relatives saw in his bereavement another opening to turn him toward Christianity. "I trust you are now stript of your idols," wrote Sarah. She and Benjamin's father and brothers all offered the consolations of faith. Benjamin spurned them. Within a year, he married again, to Betsey Lord Frazer, a widow with two children. In 1824 they had a son, Eli Todd Tappan. Tappan's love for all his family—parents, brothers, sisters, wives, and especially his two sons—was deep and genuine. Yet he would not compromise his principles to pretend a belief in doctrines he considered superstitious nonsense, including the idea of a Christian afterlife. His own rationalist outlook—what he called his "calm & philosophic view of things"—schooled him to regard death as a normal process, neither to be feared nor unduly mourned. When Betsey fell fatally ill in 1840, Tappan, who was then in Washington in the Senate, did not rush home but stayed at his post of duty. His preparations for his own demise were determinedly routine. His brothers' entreaties to prepare his soul for judgment continued throughout his life and fell to the last upon wholly deaf ears.[15]

Although Benjamin never found (or looked for) faith, around the time of Nancy's death he did find a pastime that suited his outlook and came to occupy much of his energy: the study of natural history, especially in its branches of mineralogy and conchology. In rocks and shells, Tappan found endless fascination. In the 1820s scientific practice, at least in this field, required no elaborate apparatus or formal training—merely a keen eye, an inquiring mind, a smattering of book knowledge, and a network of acquaintances with whom to exchange specimens and information. By 1823, Benjamin was assembling a mineral cabinet. Five years later his first article appeared in Benjamin Silliman's *American Journal of Science and Arts*, the country's premier scientific venue. In 1832 the Historical and Philosophical Society of Ohio organized at Columbus, with Tappan as its president. His inaugural discourse put forth a broad program of research in Ohio's pioneer and political history, Indian ethnology, geology, botany, zoology, and mineralogy.

He also stressed education—real practical education, not the useless study of dead languages, dialectical subtleties, or theoretical abstractions but mastery of "the truths of science" and the "laws and phenomena of physical being." "This," declared Tappan, "is emphatically a matter of fact age." Tappan's scientific activities threw him in with the leading thinkers of his day, some of whom were coming to espouse a radical overhaul of the conventional school curriculum. They wanted to replace memorization and strict discipline with experiential, hands-on learning in an open and encouraging environment.[16]

In 1825 and 1826 a corps of Philadelphia scientists and educators followed their patron, the geologist-philanthropist William Maclure, to join Robert Owen's visionary new community at New Harmony, Indiana. Tappan backed the controversial New Harmony venture wholeheartedly, befriending its members—especially teacher Joseph Neef and naturalists Thomas and Lucy Say—and helping to publicize its innovative schools and scientific publications. He enrolled his two stepchildren there and also contemplated sending his son Benjamin.

Wanting for Benjamin "as good an education as can be obtained in America," Tappan had already sent him east to prepare for Harvard under brother Lewis's supervision. Lewis enrolled the boy in George Bancroft and Joseph Cogswell's famed Round Hill academy in the Tappan hometown of Northampton. There he became the object of a three-way battle for influence between the religious orthodoxy of his grandparents, Lewis's more easygoing Unitarianism, and the irreligion young Benjamin had already imbibed from his father. The boy broke under the strain, became ungovernable, and had to be sent home. The episode ended with Benjamin and Lewis charging each other with intolerance and bigotry: Lewis for requiring exposure to Christianity as part of an education and Benjamin for excluding it. Too old for the New Harmony schools, young Benjamin idled at home awhile, then left for Philadelphia in 1830 to seek a medical education under the guidance of his father's scientific friends. He eventually resettled in Steubenville as a doctor and chemist, but the scars of his youth never healed. He grew up moody and quarrelsome. In 1838, he married the sister of Edwin Stanton, his father's junior law partner and political protégé. The marriage was stormy and ended in divorce.[17]

In politics as well as religion, the senior Benjamin found himself at antipodes with his eastern relations. His staunchly Federalist father and brothers had opposed Jefferson's embargo, the War of 1812, and the move for postwar tarrif protection—all supported by Benjamin—and they viewed his new political and scientific interests with skepticism. "I shall not value your attainments in the physical sciences, if they lead you from the Creator of all things," wrote Lewis (who had himself returned to orthodoxy) in 1829. Religion counted more than "law, de-ism, politics, mineralogy, & conchology." Benjamin's news of his chances for the Senate in 1832 brought only an admonition to "give up politics & read the bible, my brother."[18]

Tappan did not yet get to the Senate, losing to fellow Democrat Thomas Morris. But a year later President Jackson rewarded Tappan's party services by naming him federal district judge for Ohio. This nomination had to pass through a hostile Senate in the highly partisan session of 1833–34. Here all of Tappan's enemies joined to defeat him. Their most potent weapon was his outspoken hostility to slavery. Tappan had, on several occasions, applauded Nat Turner's 1831 bloody slave revolt and vowed his support for other slaves who would rise and slit their masters' throats. This stance, along with his irreligion, extreme partisanship, and injudicious temperament, was enough to sink Tappan's nomination in the Senate by a vote of 28 to 11.

As it turned out, Tappan's rejection for judge actually worked to his advantage. It clothed him with political martyrdom and thus paved his way to the Senate itself. When Thomas Morris's six-year term expired, majority Democrats in the Ohio legislature fixed on Tappan to replace him. In December 1839, at the age of sixty-six, Benjamin Tappan "affirmed" the oath of office and took a seat in the U.S. Senate.

Ironically, it was Morris's tilt toward abolitionism that had angered Ohio Democrats and cost him reelection. His replacement by Tappan astonished those—including brother Lewis, now a leading abolitionist himself—who knew how deeply Tappan also hated slavery. But as Tappan explained to Lewis, though opposed to slavery he was no abolitionist, as he had assured the Ohio legislators who elected him. Abolitionism was a Christian crusade, and evangelical Christianity—like the new Whig Party—was but an old foe in new dress. It was aristocracy, the ancient alliance of kingcraft and priestcraft, the enemy of every democratic and progressive aspiration. As Tappan had written in the 1836 Ohio state Democratic platform, the history of American parties "is a war between aristocracy (under whatever name it may appear, toryism, federalism or modern whigism) and democracy." Only one true route led to freedom and that was through the Democratic Party, which abolitionism threatened to disrupt.[19]

In his first Senate speech in 1840, Tappan accordingly blasted abolitionist petitioners (especially women, who he said had no business in politics) as intermeddlers and religious busybodies, whose ostensible dogoodism masked a deeper design. "Political abolitionism is but ancient

Federalism, under a new guise, and . . . the political action of anti-slavery societies is only a device for the overthrow of Democracy." Throughout his Senate term and to the end of his life, Benjamin and Lewis debated which of their approaches to antislavery was correct—Lewis's, rooted in Christian faith, or Benjamin's, grounded in politics.[20]

Even as they argued, they cooperated on practical matters. Benjamin acted as Lewis's backstairs channel of communication to the Van Buren administration in the *Amistad* affair, and together the two arranged for a black artist, Patrick H. Reason, to engrave a portrait of Benjamin for a biographical article in the *Democratic Review*. Their most important collaboration came in 1844, when President John Tyler submitted to the Senate a treaty annexing slaveholding Texas to the United States. Accompanying the treaty, and communicated in secret, was a paper from Secretary of State John C. Calhoun justifying annexation as necessary to protect and perpetuate the benign institution of slavery.

Benjamin believed that Texas annexation on proslavery grounds would "disgrace the nation," and that public exposure would surely kill the treaty. Privately he sent copies to Lewis in New York, urging their publication in William Cullen Bryant's *Evening Post*. The *Post* did publish, and a furor erupted. As Tappan calculated, the Senate rejected the treaty—after first censuring Tappan himself for his "flagrant violation" of Senate rules. Tappan waved off the rebuke.[21]

Tappan was perfectly willing to acquire Texas if it could be done without overtly sanctioning slavery, and he voted for the congressional joint resolution of 1845 that provided for either direct annexation or reopening the treaty negotiations. Tyler, on his way out of office, acted under the first option. When the new president, Democrat James K. Polk, followed through on his initiative, Tappan and some other prominent Democrats believed they had been double-crossed.

On matters unrelated to slavery, Tappan in the Senate endorsed the ultra-Democratic line, espousing doctrines of popular supremacy, economy in government, and strict laissez-faire. Denouncing bank and corporate charters as engines of monopoly, he proposed in their stead to promote "equal privileges and equal competition" by divorcing all connections between business and government and introducing "the principle of free trade into the banking business of the country." He also touted a constitutional amendment to limit federal judicial terms to seven years. His two closest Senate companions were Thomas Hart Benton and Silas Wright, pillars of radical Democracy.[22]

Tappan's most distinctive service in the Senate was his promotion of science. Like many others of his party, he believed that a free people could reach new heights of intellectual and scientific achievement and that a government under genuine popular control had the right and duty to help them do so. In 1842 the United States Exploring Expedition, commanded by navy lieutenant Charles Wilkes, returned from its four-year voyage through the South Seas, bringing a huge hoard of scientific specimens. The question of who should have custody of the expedition's collections and authority to prepare its scientific and technical reports became immediately intertwined with another controversy, that over the Smithsonian fund. In 1836, Congress had accepted a bequest from Englishman James Smithson "to found at Washington, under the name of the Smithsonian Institution, an Establishment for the increase & diffusion of knowledge among men." But no agreement had been reached on how to apply the money.[23]

In 1840 some well-connected army officers and politicians founded the National Institution for the Promotion of Science (known as the National Institute), in hopes of getting their hands on both the expedition collections and the Smithsonian fund. Tappan, allied with Wilkes, fought them off. Tappan got the authority to supervise the expedition publications directed to his own congressional Joint Committee on the Library. Meanwhile, working with Indiana congressman Robert Dale Owen, he drafted a plan for a Smithsonian Institution entirely separate from the existing National Institute. Somewhat amended, Tappan's bill passed Congress in 1846, a year after his Senate term ended.

After leaving the Senate in 1845, Tappan remained in Washington to supervise the expedition publications as agent of the library committee. He resigned in May 1846, a week after the United States declared war on Mexico. War and territorial conquest soon gave new life to the slavery question. Tappan supported the war, but the dumping of Martin Van Buren for James K. Polk at the 1844 Democratic convention and the subsequent conduct of Polk's administration had shaken his faith in southern Democrats. In 1846, Tappan set up his son Eli as editor of the *Ohio Press* in Columbus and supplied him with editorials favoring restrictions on the spread of slavery.

In company with Salmon P. Chase, Tappan in 1848 helped organize the Ohio "Free Democrats" who bolted the party to espouse the Wilmot Proviso and the Free Soil presidential candidacy of Martin Van Buren. Filled with enthusiasm, Tappan predicted an imminent reorganization of parties around the issue of slavery. But the Free Soil movement dwindled after the Compromise of 1850, and Tappan returned uneasily to the Democrats as the party "most favorable to universal freedom."

Now nearing eighty, Tappan began to slow down. After 1850, he remained mainly at home, reading, tending to his collections and his scientific and political correspondence, and enjoying the company of family and visitors. He also continued good-naturedly to dispute politics and religion with brother Lewis, to whom he drew still closer despite what Benjamin called "our totally different modes of thinking." "I think slavery on this continent is surely drawing to its close," he wrote in 1853, "but no thanks to the Priests" who "as a class & of all religions are the enemies of progress, of freedom." Overall, though, he saw the world improving. Drunkenness, crime, and severe punishments had declined since his youth, while the suffrage had expanded and democratic principles had advanced.[24]

Writing to Lewis, Tappan denounced the fugitive slave law of 1850 and "the Nebrasky swindle" of 1854. In September 1856 his "lamp of life . . . nearly burned out," he roused his strength to pen a farewell to the brother he had loved and argued with for half a century. Benjamin urged Lewis not to mourn his death—and to join the new Republican Party, which would rally the free states, break the South's political power, and thus put slavery on "her march to utter annihilation." It was Benjamin's last letter. Seven months later he died, his faith in science and democracy and his contempt for Christianity undiminished to the end.[25]

Notes

1. Lewis Tappan journal, April 21, 1857, Lewis Tappan Papers, Library of Congress, Washington, DC (hereafter cited as Lewis Tappan Papers).

2. William Edwards to Benjamin Tappan, December 26, 1833, Benjamin Tappan Papers, Library of Congress, Washington, DC (hereafter cited as Benjamin Tappan Papers).

3. The best source on Tappan's youth and early career is "The Autobiography of Benjamin Tappan," ed. Donald J. Ratcliffe, *Ohio History* 85 (1976): 109–57.

4. Lewis Tappan to Benjamin Tappan, June 9, 1818, Benjamin Tappan Papers; Walter B. Beebe to Thomas Ewing, April 10, 1834, Ewing Family Papers, Library of Congress, Washington, DC.

5. Benjamin Tappan to Benjamin Tappan Sr., February 2, 1798, Benjamin Tappan Papers.

6. Tappan oration, July 4, 1801, ibid; *A Memoir of Rev. Joseph Badger* (Hudson, OH, 1851), 26–27.

7. Edward Tiffin to Thomas Worthington, December 29, 1803, Worthington Papers, Ohio Historical Society, Columbus, OH; Benjamin Tappan to Nancy Tappan, January 16, 1804, Benjamin Tappan Papers.

8. *Ohio State Journal* (Columbus), December 26, 1838. On Tappan's political career in the 1820s and 1830s, see Daniel Feller, "Benjamin Tappan: The Making of a Democrat," in *The Pursuit of Public Power: Political Culture in Ohio, 1787–1861*, ed. Jeffrey P. Brown and Andrew R. L. Cayton (Kent, OH, 1994), 69–82.

9. John Milton Goodenow, *Historical Sketches of the Principles and Maxims of American Jurisprudence* (Steubenville, OH, 1819); *Journal of the House of Representatives of the State of Ohio*, December 1817 session, 180; John Crafts Wright to Benjamin Tappan, January 6, 1818, Benjamin Tappan Papers; *Minutes of the Proceedings and Trial in the Case of John Milton Goodenow vs. Benjamin Tappan, for Defamation* (Steubenville, OH, 1822).

10. *Western Herald* (Steubenville), July 8, 1820.

11. Benjamin Tappan to Elisha Whittlesey, December 18, 1823, Elisha Whittlesey Papers, Western Reserve Historical Society, Cleveland, OH.

12. *Republican Ledger* (Steubenville), January 30, 1828.

13. Benjamin Tappan Sr. to Benjamin Tappan, March 5, 1805, and Sarah Tappan to Benjamin Tappan, April 13, 1819, Benjamin Tappan Papers.

14. Arthur Tappan to Benjamin Tappan, December 12, 1821, ibid; Lewis Tappan journal, October 24, 1821, Lewis Tappan Papers.

15. Sarah Tappan to Benjamin Tappan, March 29, 1823, Benjamin Tappan Papers; Benjamin Tappan to Lewis Tappan, June 4, 1843, Benjamin Tappan Papers, Ohio Historical Society.

16. *A Discourse Delivered Before the Historical & Philosophical Society of Ohio, at the Annual Meeting of Said Society, in Columbus, December 22, 1832. By Benjamin Tappan, President of Said Society, and President of the Board of Canal Commissioners* (Columbus, OH, 1833), 14–15.

17. Benjamin Tappan to Benjamin Tappan Jr., February 14, 1826, Benjamin Tappan Papers.

18. Lewis Tappan to Benjamin Tappan, September 26, 1829, August 21, 1830, January 8, 1833, ibid.

19. *Proceedings of the Democratic State Convention, Held in Columbus on the Eighth of January, 1836; With an Address to the People of Ohio* (Columbus, OH, 1836), 19–20, in Benjamin Tappan Papers.

20. *Remarks of Mr. Tappan, of Ohio, on Abolition Petitions, Delivered in Senate, February 4, 1840*, ibid.

21. Benjamin Tappan to Lewis Tappan, April 22, 1844, Benjamin Tappan Papers, Ohio Historical Society; *Journal of the Executive Proceedings of the Senate of the United States of America* (Washington, DC, 1887), 6:268–74.

22. *Speech of Mr. Tappan of Ohio, on the Bill to Incorporate the Banks of the District of Columbia, Delivered in Senate, February 23, 1841*, in Benjamin Tappan Papers.

23. William Jones Rhees, *The Smithsonian Institution: Documents Relative to Its Origins and History*, 2 vols. (Washington, DC, 1901), 1:6.

24. Benjamin Tappan to Lewis Tappan, February 3, 1851, June 6, 1840, November 13, 1853, Benjamin Tappan Papers, Ohio Historical Society.

25. Benjamin Tappan to Lewis Tappan, January 1, 1855, September 19, 1856, ibid.

Suggested Readings

Conlin, Mary Lou. *Simon Perkins of the Western Reserve.* Cleveland, OH, 1968.

Daniels, George H. *American Science in the Age of Jackson.* Tuscaloosa, AL, 1968.

Elliott, Josephine Mirabella, ed. *Partnership for Posterity: The Correspondence of William Maclure and Marie Duclos Fretageot, 1820–1833.* Indianapolis, IN, 1994.

Feller, Daniel. "Benjamin Tappan: The Making of a Democrat." In *The Pursuit of Public Power: Political Culture in Ohio, 1787–1861*, edited by Jeffrey P. Brown and Andrew R. L. Cayton, 69–82. Kent, OH, 1994.

———. *The Jacksonian Promise: America, 1815–1840.* Baltimore, MD, 1995.

Hafertepe, Kenneth. *America's Castle: The Evolution of the Smithsonian Building and Its Institution, 1840–1878.* Washington, DC, 1984.

Holt, Edgar Allan. *Party Politics in Ohio, 1840–1850.* Columbus, OH, 1931.

Maizlish, Stephen E. *The Triumph of Sectionalism: The Transformation of Ohio Politics, 1844–1856.* Kent, OH, 1983.

Miller, Perry. *The Life of the Mind in America from the Revolution to the Civil War.* New York, 1965.

Ratcliffe, Donald J. *Party Spirit in a Frontier Republic: Democratic Politics in Ohio, 1793–1821.* Columbus, OH, 1998.

———, ed. "The Autobiography of Benjamin Tappan." *Ohio History* 85 (1976): 109–57.

Rhees, William Jones, ed. *The Smithsonian Institution: Documents Relative to Its Origin and History, 1835–1899.* 2 vols. Washington, DC, 1901.

Stanton, William. *The Great United States Exploring Expedition.* Berkeley, CA, 1975.

Stroud, Patricia Tyson. *Thomas Say: New World Naturalist.* Philadelphia, 1992.

Wyatt-Brown, Bertram. *Lewis Tappan and the Evangelical War against Slavery.* Cleveland, OH, 1969.

15

George Washington Harris
The Fool from the Hills

John Mayfield

Restless ambition, so typical of this period in American history, characterized the life and work of George Washington Harris. Born in Pennsylvania, he moved to Knoxville, Tennessee, at the age of five and lived there most of his life. Harris was a jack-of-all-trades (metalworker, steamboat captain, journalist, railroader, farmer, and politician), but the master of none. Harris raised a family, held a pew in a Presbyterian church, worked hard, but always remained among the middling sort. He also strongly upheld states' rights, supported the South's secession from the Union, and backed the Confederacy throughout the Civil War. He was viscerally anti-Lincoln, anti-Grant, anti-Republican, and anti-Reconstruction. To say that he was a racist is to understate the truth. Yet this ordinary man created one of the most extraordinary figures in all nineteenth-century literature: Sut Lovingood, a self-proclaimed "nat'ral born durn'd fool." A product of the culture of the Old South, Sut was also a keen critic of its pretensions. Anarchic, irreverent, he challenged the self-importance and posturing of the slaveholding class. His tales, delivered in dialect so obscure that one editor actually "translated" it, concern violence, religion, politics, patriarchy, and sex with a candor and frankness not seen in other writings of his time. Sut is the ultimate subversive, a character who delights in his own imperfections and who shrewdly and pitilessly observed the society around him. Through him we gain a fresh perspective on the Old South.

John Mayfield is professor of history and department chair at Samford University in Birmingham, Alabama. He is a former member of the editorial board of the *Journal of the Early Republic*. Professor Mayfield is the author of *Rehearsal for Republicanism: Free Soil and the Politics of Antislavery* (1980); and *The New Nation: 1800–1845* (1982). He is writing a book about Southern humor.

Let us consider Fools and their uses. Fools hold a special place in every culture's history, and they come in all kinds of guises. In the medieval and Renaissance eras, Fools, court jesters, served an official function. They were virtually the only persons allowed to lampoon a king to his face. Kings kept them around, in fact, to keep a grip on reality. Fools pop up at carnivals, at Mardi Gras, and at circuses. Since the age of print, they have become fixtures in literature, and now they have moved into film. A Fool laughs at society, and, importantly, he laughs at the laugher, so that no one walks away feeling superior or unchanged. Fools keep us from taking ourselves too seriously, and that helps us keep going. They live in the borderlands between life and art; they break down the barriers between what is proper and what is absurd.

Americans, however, are often uncomfortable with Fools. Perhaps it is a manifestation of our business culture or our inclination to take ourselves too seriously. We were, after all, the "city on the hill" all the way back to the colonial era—out to show the world how it is done right—and we are incorrigible reformers. The British are much better at accepting things as they are than Americans, who still hope to improve everything. For that reason, English humor tends to farce while Americans excel at irony. Only occasionally do we let a true Fool take the stage.

Then there is Sut Lovingood, a southerner of no fixed address or occupation. He is virtually unknown outside a few circles, yet he may be the original and best American Fool of all. An east Tennessee businessman, George Washington Harris, created Sut in a series of yarns written chiefly during the 1850s and 1860s.[1] Sut describes himself as a "nat'ral born durn'd fool," without "nara a soul, nuffin but a whisky proof gizzard," with "the longes' par ove laigs ever hung tu eny cackus." His sole purpose in life is getting drunk, getting girls, and getting "intu more durn'd misfortnit skeery scrapes, than enybody, an' then run outen them faster, by golly, nor enybody" (172). When challenged to justify himself, his answer is direct and simple: "Yu go tu *hell*, mistofer; yu bothers me" (232).

Sut Lovingood exists for the practical joke. Anything—rich, poor, male, female, animal, human, old, young—is fair game. So, we have Sut slipping two live lizards up a circuit preacher's pants leg just to watch him scream. "Brethren, brethren . . . the Hell-sarpints *hes got me!*" he hollers, and strips and runs naked through the mostly female crowd (56). Or we have Sut breaking up Mrs. Yardley's quilting bee, for no reason beyond sheer maliciousness, by tying a clothesline row of quilts to a horse's saddlehorn, then splintering a fence rail over the poor animal " 'bout nine inches ahead ove the root ove his tail' " (143). The horse manages to knock down just about everything in sight, including Mrs. Yardley, who dies either from being run over or from the shock of losing a nine-diamond quilt, depending on who tells the story. Sometimes we find Sut at the receiving end, as when he lusts a little too openly after Sicily Burns ("Sich a buzzim! Jis' think ove two snow balls wif a strawberry stuck but-ainded intu bof on em" [75]). Sicily, no virgin she, slips him raw baking soda as a "love potion." As the gas comes frothing out of Sut's "mouf, eyes, noes, an' years" he thinks, "*Kotch agin, by the great golly!* . . . same famerly dispersishun to make a durn'd fool ove myse'f . . . ef thar's half a chance. Durn dad evermore, amen!" (81).

How do we explain a creature such as this? Sut Lovingood is not from the business culture; he is outside modern sensibilities. He comes from a world of physical—not psychological—pain and deprivation, and he responds accordingly with violent and uncompromising energy. Maybe, we hope, he is the voice of the forgotten poor. In the preface to his yarns, for example, Harris lets Sut explain that he will be happy if he can give a laugh to "eny poor misfortinit devil hu's heart is onder a millstone, hu's ragged children are hungry, an' no bread in the dresser, hu is down in the mud, an' the lucky ones a'trippin him every time he struggils tu his all fours, hu has fed the famishin an' is now hungry hisself, hu misfortins foller fas' an' foller faster, hu is so foot-sore an' weak that he wishes he were at the ferry" (ix). Ultimately, though, this explanation does not work, at least not in any traditional way. Poor people come in for his pranks just as surely as rich ones. There is no irony to his life, no expectations. He knows he's worthless and so lives entirely for the moment. He was born a Fool from a Fool. He will die that way, probably from a clean shot to the heart from some young woman's husband.

Still, Sut is not alone in American humor. He has his peers among the bear-eaters and ripsnorters of Davy Crockett's time and in the rough humor of the frontier West, where physical cruelty and practical joking were the norm. A Fool exactly like Sut, however, could only come from the South—the prosperous and poor, proud and humiliated antebellum South that has been the genesis of so many of our national dreams and nightmares. He could not have originated in the North or Midwest. The dry business culture there simply could not sustain a creation such as Sut. Moreover, he could only have been created by a particular type of southerner, one who was fiercely devoted to his region—even to the point of supporting secession without stint or reservation—and who knew the South's customs, proprieties, and expectations to the letter. Only one who knows what is not foolish can create a perfect Fool.

George Washington Harris created the Lovingood stories in a series of newspaper and magazine sketches that began in the 1840s and culminated in a book, *Sut Lovingood's Yarns*, published in 1867. Were it not for the yarns, history would have passed him by, and it almost did. He was born in western Pennsylvania in 1814. Little is known of his parents, except that George was named after his father and that his mother had been married once before and had a son, Samuel Bell, who was Harris's half-brother. Samuel Bell moved to the small town of Knoxville, Tennessee, a few years after Harris was born and brought the young boy with him shortly thereafter. No one knows what happened to George's parents; they may have gone to Tennessee or they may have died.[2]

Harris spent his early years learning skills and developing ambition. Samuel Bell was a trained metalworker who specialized in first-rate small arms, such as pistols, knives, and swords. He taught Harris the trade in a shop in Knoxville, and Harris kept one hand in the profession for most of his life. But George Washington Harris seems to have been a mobile, restless youth who was not entirely happy with the limitations of his half-brother's style of life. He was a small man, reputedly quick and agile, who briefly rode jockey in local quarter races. Like most young men, he was eager to set out on his own. The opportunity came when he was only nineteen. A company took him on as captain of a steamboat making the run from the port of Knoxville along the Tennessee River to the Ohio, and Harris stayed in the job for five years. In 1838, he helped transport Cherokees out of the Tennessee Valley and on to the Trail of Tears to their new homes in Oklahoma. He was apparently good at his job, maintained discipline, and took care of his equipment.

What would have been a lifetime dream for many young men was, for Harris, the first of many jobs. In 1835 he married the daughter of the inspector of the Port of Knoxville (who also owned the local racetrack) and began a family. Whether he grew tired of life on the river or whether his family and father-in-law pressured him to settle down is not known. Whatever the motive, in 1839, he took out a loan, bought a substantial farm near the Great Smoky Mountains, and settled into apparent respectability. He listed his occupation as "manufacturer and trader"—which meant that he probably farmed some, traded some, and made or fixed things. He had a nice house, carpets, books, china, a bay mare, and three slaves, plus a wife and three children. By any measure he had moved, young, into what would later be called the Victorian middle class. He had also contracted that most middle-class of burdens, a large debt. He could not maintain it. By 1843 the farm and house and carpets and at least one of the slaves were gone, and Harris took his family back to Knoxville.

There he opened a metal shop, like his half-brother, and began to settle down in earnest. The shop was large and could handle both delicate jobs and heavy machinework, but the venture did not last. By the end of the decade, Harris had signed on as superintendent of a glass factory (more likely a large shop), while he continued to do some silversmithing on the side. He apparently needed to work two jobs, for Harris still tried to maintain a large household, including two slaves and a washerwoman. If there was any consistency to his career thus far, it seems to be in his capacity for hard work and constant debt in the pursuit of the image of prosperity. During the 1850s, Harris went through an astonishing number of job changes for someone of his age and respectability. He was a steamboat captain again in 1854 and a mine surveyor the next year. The year after that he borrowed money to start a sawmill, which failed, then became for a short time a postmaster, then a railroad conductor. During the Civil War, he moved around, living for a while in northern Alabama and then Georgia. After the war he went back to Tennessee to work for the railroads again. He was still in that line when he died in 1869.

Sometime in the 1840s this fairly unremarkable man, who had had only a year-and-a-half of schooling in his life, began to write. He may have done some newspaper work for the Democratic *Knoxville Argus* in the mid-1840s, but his first attributable stories were for a national magazine, the *Spirit of the Times*, published out of New York by William T. Porter. Porter catered to sporting men from the northern and southern gentry, and his magazine recorded horse racing, fox hunting, and other pursuits of the leisure class. It also fielded some of the best and most original humor of the times, with a preference for southern tales about coon hunts, wrasslin' matches, quaint folkways, and generally weird backwoods characters. Most of the major humorists of the Old Southwest published stories in the *Spirit* at one time or the other, and most followed the formula of having a genteel narrator introduce a colorful character who then entertained the company with a story in dialect. The *Spirit* was a natural place for Harris to start, and his first stories read pretty much like the rest of the magazine's submissions: folksy characters out making fools of themselves for the rich folk to snort at.

Except even these stories suggest something different, something really anarchic, at work. His first story of any worth, "The Knob Hill Dance," is in most respects an ordinary tale of a hillbilly hoedown. For sexual references and sheer irreverence, however, it pushed the limits for its time. Girls come to the dance "pourin out of the woods like pissants out of an old log when tother end's afire" wearing everything from homespun to calico—but not silk. Any girl who wore silk would "go home in her petticote-tale *sartin*, for the homespun would tare it off of hir quicker nor winkin, and if the sunflowers dident help the homespuns, they woudn't do the silk eny good." Translation: What the dancing did not wear out, the bushes would. Everybody drinks, dances, eats, rolls on the bed, and the whole thing ends in a glorious brawl. The narrator describes walking home with his girl, and a "rite peart *four-leged* nag she is. She was *weak* in *two* of hir legs, but t'other two—oh, my stars and possum dogs! they make a man swaller tobacker jist to look at 'em, and feel sorter like a June bug was crawlin up his trowses and the waistband too tite for it to get out."[3] He wants to marry her, or so he says. Porter's magazine was one of the few, perhaps the only, outlet for innuendos such as these, but on at least one occasion during these early years even Porter had to reject one of Harris's stories as too salty.

Harris's output was erratic until 1854, when he discovered Sut Lovingood. The original was probably Sut Miller, a local from somewhere around Ducktown, Tennessee (Harris was working there as a mine inspector). Harris added "Lovingood"—sexual reference no doubt intentional—and put him in the saloon of Pat Nash (also a real person), talking to a gentlemanly narrator named, wouldn't you know, "George." The first story, published in the *Spirit* and revised later for Sut Lovingood's *Yarns*, was a knockout: "Sut Lovingood's Daddy, Acting Horse."

It is unlike any other story of its time. Sut rides up to Pat Nash's saloon on the spindliest horse ever born and begins right away to explain that this nag is "next to the best hoss what ever shelled nubbins or toted jugs," his lamented Tickytail, who is now dead. "Yu see, he froze stiff; no, not that adzactly, but starv'd fust, an' froze arterards" (20). From that unlikely introduction, Sut jumps cleanly into an explanation of how Tickytail's death prompted Dad to act hoss. The whole family—sixteen kids plus a "prospect"—has lazed through the winter, "hopin sum stray hoss mout cum along." It never happened, so Dad lies awake one night "a-snortin, an' rollin, an' blowin, an' shufflin, an' scratchin' hisself, an' a-whisperin at Mam a heap—an' at breckfus' I foun' out what hit ment" (22). Dad will pull the plow himself, act hoss.

He is pretty good at it, maybe too good. Dad gets Sut and Mam to fashion him a harness from pawpaw bark and a bridle from an umbrella brace, and he runs around on all fours practicing snorting and kicking up his heels and trying to bite someone. Mam "step'd back a littil an' were standin wif her arms cross'd a-restin' 'em on her stumick, an' his heel taps cum wifin a inch ove her nose. Sez she: 'Yu plays hoss better nur yu dus husban'.' He jes run backards on all fours an' kick'd at her agin, an'—an' pawd the groun wif his fis" (23). So Sut leads him off to the field, and they do get into it nicely. Dad snorts and pulls, Sut begins dreaming of the corn crop they will get in (and the whiskey it will produce), and then Dad charges straight into "a ball ho'nets nes' ni ontu es big es a hoss's hed, an' the hole tribe kiver'd 'im es quick es yu culd kiver a sick pup wif a saddil blanket" (24). Dad tears off like, well, a scared horse through bushes and then seven panels of fence. He loses the harness, his clothes, everything except the bridle and "ni ontu a yard ove plow line sailin behine, wif a tir'd-out ho'net ridin on the pint ove hit" (25). When he gets to the bluff overlooking the river, he jumps in. While he bobs up and down trying to get free of the hornets, Sut begins mocking him. "Switch 'em wif yure tail, dad. . . . I'll hev yer feed in the troft, redy; yu won't need eny curyin tu-nite will yu?" (26, 27). Dad cusses him back so bad that Sut leaves for the mines for a few days. "Yere's luck tu the durned old fool," he toasts, "an' to the ho'nets too" (28).

That broke the mold. Never mind that Harris's comic imagery and use of language was far ahead of anyone else writing in the field; those are subjects in themselves. He had created a comic masterpiece from a most un-southern, un-Victorian, un-middle-class subject—a father's total humiliation. If he could do that, he could savage every other sacred cow (or horse) in the culture, and he did. The rest of the yarns, published in bits and pieces over the next dozen years and then carefully, painstakingly revised into a book, went after preachers, virgins, marriage, sentimentality, the home and hearth, anything that came within Sut's reach.

Therein lies the incongruity. How could tales this anarchic, this crude, this foolish, come from the pen of an ordinary, debt-ridden small-businessman and devoted family man from what should have been one of the most socially conservative parts of the country? One would expect him to come up with the kind of overblown heroics and sticky romantic goo that made for quick contracts and high-volume sales. Instead, he created a Fool. It all seems incongruous, but perhaps only such a man could have written such tales.

Despite the constant debt and the frequent career moves, Harris was firmly rooted in the culture and politics of a particular place—east Tennessee. It was a place where several of the South's subcultures came together. There were mountain folk and river folk, and Harris had met them on his travels. There were townsmen and businessmen passing through, and Harris had dealt with those, too. There were slaveholders, not the cotton snobs from south Alabama or Mississippi, but slaveholders nonetheless with a claim to all that implied in the complex social relations of the South. There were the rich and the frightfully poor, and Harris saw them. His whole environment, in fact, was a mosaic of often contradictory ideals.

So was Harris. Consider, for example, his religious convictions. Harris was a solid, traditional Presbyterian. For years the First Presbyterian Church of Knoxville had a Harris family pew, and one of Harris's sons was named for the pastor there. Harris's devotion to his church was no mere social formality. Friends called him a "blue Presbyterian," which meant simply that he took his church seriously, did not work on Sunday, and raised a strict household. The religious culture around him was a good deal more diverse. East Tennesseans worshipped through established churches, circuit preachers, evangelical and holiness groups, revivals, tent meetings, and virtually anything else that prayed or sang. Some parts of the church-going population stayed strictly to themselves; others moved in and out of these religious expressions as the spirit—and opportunity—moved them. Still other parts preferred to have nothing to do with the whole scene, considered preachers frauds and hymn-singing noise, and saved Sunday mornings for the hangover. Harris pretty certainly was familiar with all these practices and shades of opinion; as a riverboat captain and railroad man, he must have seen it all. At the core, however, he was a proper man.

He was also a southern fire-eater. Harris began and ended life a staunch southern Democrat. He supported James Buchanan in 1856, wrote a rather bad political satire about the Republican and Know Nothing candidates, and got rewarded with the postmaster job. That same year, Harris was elected a city alderman. More important, in 1856, Harris went to Savannah for the Southern Commercial Convention—a loose cover for the crazier secessionists of the time. In 1859 he went to Nashville for the Democratic state convention and got appointed to the state central committee. His politics became more and more extreme. After Lincoln's election the following year, Harris wrote three vicious parodies of the new president, comparing him to a dried-out frog nailed to a board. This sort of thing was more popular in west Tennessee, where secessionists held a majority, than in unionist east Tennessee, so Harris left Knoxville. After the war, Harris wrote more nasty satires—this time on Grant, abolitionists, and radical Republicans. These satires were not his best work.

The convergence of Harris's middle-class propriety and his rabid, arrogant sectionalism is suggestive. In real life, Harris was a fairly ordinary, proper townsman with a business to run, a family to raise, and a house to maintain. His record of successes, failures, ventures, and losses was not radically different from his peers in towns all over the country, South and North, or indeed over western Europe and England. Like it or not, Harris was a member of the urban middle class and partook of its Protestant ethics.

What Harris fancied himself to be may have been something different. His failed attempt at living the life of a country squire during the late 1830s and 1840s is intriguing, because it is at that point in his careers where he acquired both debt and slaves. Given the cost of slaves, even young ones, the two were intimately connected. Moreover, he kept slaves—as many as he could—even after his move to the city made servants a luxury he could not afford. The possession of slaves more than anything else defined status in the antebellum South. It was the entry card to the elite, the connecting link to the planter class. Like members of this planter class, Harris dabbled in horse racing, delighted in telling stories and generally being sociable, and fancied himself a rising politician. With a twist of luck here or there, Harris might have moved in the same circles as the great slave-owning class. With or without that twist of luck, he certainly knew what that class expected of its members. At the same time, he knew from daily experience what was expected of a Presbyterian businessman in a small southern town.

Harris, then, lived in the borderland between two worlds, two sets of values, two elaborate codes of behavior. On the one hand was the work ethic of the urban middle class, driven by respectability, self-discipline, commercial diversification, and success. On the other was the southern beau ideal—the leisured world of the gentleman planter with his slaves, horses, great and usually costly generosity, and touchy sense of honor. At points, these worlds crossed over, to be sure. The southerner's racism cut across occupations and class lines, and both the townsman and the planter were businessmen living off the profits of their enterprises. Moreover, it is arguable that the planter's real life was not leisured and hardly ideal. But as ideals, as something to strive for, the two styles were powerful—and essentially antagonistic. They could not coexist indefinitely. The Civil War destroyed the planter's hegemony, and in that sense the townsman won and created the New South. Before that happened, however, life was a good deal complicated for someone like Harris. Who should he be?

Alone among the great southern humorists, Harris rose up from nothingness, worked for a living at whatever came his way, and suffered the consequences of his mistakes directly, with no family safety net to cushion the blow. He also wrote when time was running out. The Lovingood yarns first appeared as newspaper and magazine articles during the 1850s, and Harris probably revised his material during the war years. These were precisely the years when the planters' dependence on slavery ripened into secession, when their sense of personal honor became translated into a sense of regional honor, when their cocky indifference to death and their penchant for violence got field-tested in humiliation and war. Harris, with his fire-eating secessionism and rabid hatred of Republicans and reformers, was right there with them, in spirit if not status.

Harris was a small businessman, however, and he came from a unionist part of this South, where the dominance of the planter and his style was just weak enough to let reality creep in. This was the area that produced Andrew Johnson. The slaveholding "aristocracy" was not popular among these nonslaveholders, who during the war refused to fight in the Confederacy and sometimes sent draft agents home across a horse. Still, slaveholders, even here, wielded great power. Harris was neither a fully independent townsman nor a slaveholder; he tried to be both, and he tried to do it in a particular place where the tensions between progressive South and planter South were acute, even deadly.

The range of pretensions and hypocrisies open to Sut's/Harris's mocking rage was sizable. Consider the properly Protestant side of Harris's South, the one that would surge through the New South like a collective atonement after the Civil War and turn Baptists into businessmen and Methodists into rich businessmen and crowd the whisky-drinking Episcopalians onto the golf courses and leave them there. Here Sut's favorite target was the self-sanctifying, meddlesome, predatory preacher. It is not that Parson Bullins, who gets the lizards up his pants leg, is a bad man. He is just an irritating windbag with an eye for women who has humiliated Sut by catching him in the bushes with a girl and then tattling to the girl's mother. So Sut goes to the service, full of repentance and lizards, to hear the parson work the women into a fever with the fear of Hell-serpents. "Tole 'em how they'd quile [coil] intu thar buzzims, an' how they *wud* crawl down onder thar frock-strings . . . up thar laigs, an' travil *onder* thar garters, no odds how tight they tied 'em, an' when the two armys ove Hell-sarpents met, then—That las' remark *fotch 'em.*" (53).

At this point the women are screaming, the preacher is waving his hands, and the lizards start their own travels up *his* garters. It is particularly satisfying to Sut that this preacher, who has seduced half the girls in the county, literally gets exposed. "Passuns ginerly hev a pow'ful strong holt on wimen"; says Sut, "but, hoss, I tell yu thar airn't meny ove em kin run start nakid over an' thru a crowd ove three hundred wimen an' not injure thar karacters *sum*" (58). In other tales, Sut extended the same treatment to lawyers and sheriffs—anyone who pretended to be a pillar of the community.

The pretensions of the slaveholding class presented more of a challenge, yet Sut was up to the job. It may be difficult for modern readers to understand just how ingrained the idea of honor was to southerners. One's honor was a subtle, powerful combination of family name and social class, all expressed through an elaborate code of etiquette that made language, gesture, and appearance matters of life and death. To call someone a name, tweak his nose, or leer at his lady would bring instant and violent response. Above all, honor was about being manly. A gentleman had manners and poise; a common man was rough and plain. Each defended his honor among those of his social status. Gentlemen dueled and gave gifts; common men fought and bought each other drinks. Slaves were literally not men in this strutting culture, because they had no way to defend their honor and no gifts to give. A manly man did not fear death and would rather die—in a fight, in a duel, in a war—than be humiliated. Humiliation, in fact, separated men from notmen. Those who endured humiliation (and that included failed businessmen and people who work the retail trade, which is a daily exercise in fielding insults and snubs) may have qualified as Christian saints. They would not have made it as men in the Old South.[4]

Humiliation is central to the Lovingood tales. Sut does not just violate every rule; more to the point, he takes himself outside the rules. He humiliates himself but makes himself the central, most energetic and important part of the story. In that sense he negated the whole code of southern manhood. "I'm no count, no how. Jis' look at me! Did yu ever see sich a sampil ove a human afore? I feels like I' be glad *tu be* dead, only I'se feard of the dyin. I don't keer for herearter, for hits onpossibil for me to hev ara soul. Who ever seed a soul in jis' sich a rack heap ove bones an' rags as this? I'se nuffin' but sum newfangil'd sort ove beas'. . . . a sorter cross atween a crazy ole monkey an' a durn'd, wore-out hominy mill. I is one ove dad's explites at makin cussed fool invenshuns. . . . I blames him fur all ove hit, allers a-tryin tu be king fool" (106–

107). In that one paragraph, Sut rejected most of what was essential to a southerner's manhood. He admits to being ugly, poor, afraid of dying, of dubious lineage and parenthood, indifferent to God and duty, and vengeful of his father. What is worse, he is actually proud of it.

The list goes on. Where true southern men were generous and off-hand about taking on a friend's debts, Sut simply steals. Where no man would stand for being called a liar, Sut announces to the world that he is a great liar, one of the best in creation. Where bearing and deport-ment were concerned, and no man could stand to be "unmasked" as fearful or even human, Sut unmasks himself, literally and physically (in one sketch he tries on a starched shirt, can't stand it, and ends up jump-ing buck naked from a sleeping loft). His kind of "duel" is to kick a dandified stranger in the rump and then run 119 yards between shots when the fop unexpectedly pulls a two-barrel derringer on him. Noth-ing in the code of southern honor fits Sut.

When it came to women, Sut violated every rule and mocked every ideal set forward by both Presbyterians *and* planters. The whole culture had made ice queens of women and put them on pedestals. Sut looked up the skirt. In "Rare Ripe Garden Seed" a man marries, then leaves for Atlanta after helping his young bride put in a garden of "rare," fast-growing seeds bought off a Yankee peddler. When he comes back, four and a half months after the wedding, she presents him with a newborn baby girl. He can count at least to nine on his fingers and is beginning to express some doubts, but his mother-in-law takes him in hand. It was eating the produce of the rare garden seed that made Mary develop so fast, she explains. "This is what cums of hit, an' four months an' a half am rar ripe time fur babys, adzackly," she says. "Tu be sure, hit lacks a day ur two, but Margarit Jane wer allers a pow'ful interprizin' gal, an' a yearly [early] rizer" (236). The real father, incidentally, is the local sheriff, whom Sut and the husband humiliate in a later tale.

More explicitly, Sut rated unwed women like horses. Young girls were fine, and old maids could be tamed, but widows were best. "Hits widders, by golly, what am the rale sensibil, steady-goin, never-skeerin, never-kickin, willin, sperrited, smoof pacers. They cum clost up tu the hoss-block, standin still wif thar purty silky years playin, an' the naik-veins a-throbbin, and waits fur the word, which ove course yu gives, arter yu finds yer feet well in the stirrup, an' away they moves like a cradil on cushioned rockers, ur a spring buggy runnin in damp san'. A tetch of the bridil an' they knows yu wants em to turn, an' they does hit es willin es ef the idea wer thar own" (141).

It is misogynist cant, but at least it is sincere cant. It utterly lacks the patronizing tone nineteenth-century men used to describe women, and one has to choose which attitude is worse. Sut's at least has a certain simple directness. "Men," he announces, "wer made a-purpus jis' tu eat, drink, an' fur stayin awake in the yearly part ove the nites: an' wimen wer made tu cook the vittils, mix the sperits, an' help the men du the stayin awake" (88). A woman who stepped outside that role, who wanted to take command and not simply cater to men, was greatly to be feared. "They aint human; theyse an ekal mixtry ove stud hoss, black snake, goose, peacock britches—and d——d raskil. They wants tu be a man; an ef they cant, they fixes up thar case by bein devils."[5] This comes from a writer who was devotedly married to one woman for thirty-two years, until her death, and whose second wife was reputedly every bit as bright, intelligent, and assertive as he was. Harris was ever the devoted family man.

And that brings us back to Dad. Dad, of course, is the fool's Fool, the creator of Fools, the original of Fools. He is the antithesis of a Southern patriarch and the whole manly social order built thereon. Lineage—breeding, if you will—was so vital to the South's social order that marriages were made on it, unlikely names came from it (for example, St. George Tucker), and whole genealogies were constructed around it. It is said that one never asks a true Southerner who someone is when all you want is the name. Who you are goes back generations and out to fifth cousins. But Sut's dad is just Hoss, and when he dies, Sut and his Mam borrow a shingle cart for a hearse, ride the body around the field a few times, then drop it into a convenient crack in the ground, rather like dumping waste. Later that night, Mam says " 'oughtent we to a scratch'd in a littel dirt on him, say?' 'No need, mam,' sed Sall [Sut's sister], 'hits loose yeath, an' will soon cave in enuff.' 'But, I want to plant a 'simmon sprout at his head,' sed mam, 'on account ove the puckery taste he has left in my mouth.' "[6]

Harris wrote that particular story after the Civil War, and arguably it is his final comment on the collapse of the Old South. Probably not. The story is entirely appropriate to the Fool that Harris had constructed before the war intervened and exploded the myth of southern superiority. Nothing that Sut Lovingood ever did was intended to support or even to reform the established order of the American South. He was anarchic, chaotic, irreverent, and true to his sense of self. He was a Fool. This may be what Faulkner meant when asked why he liked Sut. "He had no illusions about himself, did the best he could; at certain times he was a coward and knew it and wasn't ashamed; he never blamed his misfortunes on anyone and never cursed God for them."[7] It was probably George Washington Harris's best epitaph.

Notes

1. George Washington Harris, *Sut Lovingood: Yarns Spun by a "Nat'ral Born Durn'd Fool," Warped and Wove for Public Wear* (New York, 1867). Except where noted, all quotes from the tales are taken from this original edition.

2. The best biography of Harris is Milton Rickels's fine book (which also explores the notion of Sut as Fool, although from a different perspective). Milton Rickels, *George Washington Harris* (New York, 1965).

3. George Washington Harris, *High Times and Hard Times*, ed. M. Thomas Inge (Nashville, TN, 1967), 47, 52.

4. The literature on Southern honor is large and growing. Two places to start are Bertram Wyatt-Brown, *Southern Honor: Ethics and Behavior in the Old South* (New York, 1982); and Kenneth S. Greenberg, *Honor & Slavery: Lies, Duels, Noses, Masks, Dressing as a Woman, Gifts, Strangers, Humanitarianism, Death, Slave Rebellions, The Pro-Slavery Argument, Baseball, Hunting, and Gambling in the Old South* (Princeton, NJ, 1996).

5. "Sut Lovingood's Chest Story," in Inge, *High Times and Hard Times*, 120.

6. "Well, Dad's Dead," ibid., 211.

7. Quoted in Rickels, *Harris*, 95.

Suggested Readings

Blair, Walter. *Native American Humor*. 1937. Reprint, San Francisco, 1960.

Cohen, Hennig, and William B. Dillingham, eds. *Humor of the Old Southwest*. 1964. Reprint, Athens, GA, 1994.

Day, Donald. "The Life of George Washington Harris." *Tennessee Historical Quarterly* 6 (1947): 3–38.

Greenberg, Kenneth S. *Honor & Slavery: Lies, Duels, Noses, Masks, Dressing as a Woman, Gifts, Strangers, Humanitarianism, Death, Slave Rebellions, The Pro-Slavery Argument, Baseball, Hunting, and Gambling in the Old South*. Princeton, NJ, 1996.

Harris, George Washington. *Sut Lovingood: Yarns Spun by a "Nat'ral Born Durn'd Fool," Warped and Wove for Public Wear*. New York, 1867.

———. *High Times and Hard Times, Sketches and Tales*. Edited by M. Thomas Inge. Nashville, TN, 1967.

———. *Sut Lovingood's Yarns*. Edited by M. Thomas Inge. New Haven, CT, 1966.

Kuhlmann, Susan. *Knave, Fool, and Genius: The Confidence Man as He Appears in Nineteenth-Century American Fiction*. Chapel Hill, NC, 1973.

Lynn, Kenneth S. *Mark Twain and Southwestern Humor*. 1959. Reprint, Westport, CT, 1972.

Mayfield, John. "The Theater of Public Esteem: Ethics and Values in Longstreet's *Georgia Scenes.*" *Georgia Historical Quarterly* 75 (1991): 566–86.

McClary, Ben Harris, ed. *The Lovingood Papers.* Knoxville, TN, 1962.

Meine, Franklin J., ed. *Tall Tales of the Southwest: An Anthology of Southern and Southwestern Humor, 1830–1860.* New York, 1930.

Rickels, Milton. *George Washington Harris.* New York, 1965.

Shields, Johanna Nicol. "A Sadder Simon Suggs: Freedom and Slavery in the Humor of Johnson Hooper." *Journal of Southern History* 56 (1990): 641–64.

Wyatt-Brown, Bertram. *Southern Honor: Ethics and Behavior in the Old South.* New York, 1982.

Yates, Norris W. *William T. Porter and the Spirit of the Times: A Study of the Big Bear School of Humor.* 1957. Reprint, New York, 1977.

Index

Jesup, Thomas Sidney: commissioned
in U.S. army, 101; dispute with
Ripley, 104–5; interest in territorial
expansion, 103–4; observer at
Hartford Convention, 103; personal
life, 107–8; and presidential politics,
110–12; professional values, 104–5,
112–13; as quartermaster general,
105–7, 110; reassigned to Eighth
Military Department (Baton Rouge),
103; service in Seminole War, 108–
10; in War of 1812, 101–3
Jocelyn, Simeon, 150
Johnson, Richard M., 206
Jones, Evan, 119, 127

Kentucky: business operations in, 39–
40, 42–43, 44–46; economic
development of, 38–39, 42; land
distribution, 36; settlement, 36–38
King, John, 23
Knights of the Golden Circle, 127
Know Nothing movement, 182, 236

Lafitte, Jean, 88, 92, 96, 104
Lallemand, Charles François Antoine,
87, 97
Land speculation, 9, 215–16
Latour, Arsène Lacarrière: as agent for
Spain, 95–96; apprenticeship as
architect, 86; career as architect, 89–
90, 97; drafts city plan for Baton
Rouge, 88–89; emigrates to Louisi-
ana, 88; as engineer in New Orleans
campaign, 90–93, 94–95; explores
Southwest, 96; *Historical Memoir*, 95;
as intelligence scout for General
Jackson, 93–94; maps Louisiana, 88;
and Saint Domingue rebellion, 87
Law and Order Party (Rhode Island),
59, 60
Lewis, Meriwether, 74
Liberator (Boston), 149
Lighthorse force, 134–35
Livingston, Edward, 89, 90
Lord, Robert H., 182
Louisiana Purchase, 43, 75, 88
Lovingood, Sut (fictional character),
230, 234–35, 238–39, 239–41

Maclure, William, 222
Madison, James, 100

Manifest Destiny, 113
Manual Labor College for Young Men
of Colour, 150, 151
Market revolution: effect on traditional
values, 40–41, 43, 46, 61–63, 70,
79, 202; on frontier, 35–36, 38–39,
44–45, 46–47, 68, 70–71, 79; and
politics, 73, 79
Marriage and marital relations: Eaton
affair, 200–201; in Kentucky, 107; in
Louisiana, 79; mixed-blood, 121,
127; in New England, 8, 9, 57, 216;
in Ohio, 69, 221; in Virginia, 22,
169, 171, 172, 175–78
Matrilineal clans, 116, 117
McKean, Thomas, 3
McMinn, William, 121
Meigs, Return J., 121
Methodist Church, 11; and African
Americans, 27; in British North
America, 21–22; and Cherokees,
119; and circuit riding, 26–27; and
democratization of American society,
21; in England, 20–21; in
postrevolutionary America, 28, 31; as
separate community, 27–28; and
slavery, 29
Mexican War (1846–1848), 100, 107,
112, 225
Michaux, François André, 42
Moffatt, Mary Anne Ursula: *An Answer
to Six Months in a Convent*, 182
Monk, Maria, 182
Monroe, James, 103, 104, 111, 168,
207
Morgan, David B., 94–95
Morris, Thomas, 223
Mushalatubbee, Mingo, 134, 137

National Convention of Free People of
Color, 149–50, 158
National Institution for the Promotion
of Science, 225
Nativism, 182, 185, 188, 192
Neef, Joseph, 222
Nell, William C., 158, 159
New Harmony (Indiana), 222
New Orleans campaign (War of 1812),
83–84

O'Flaherty, Reverend Thomas J., 188
O'Neale, William, 201